Portals

Reflections on the Spirit in Matter

Genese Grill

SPLICE

Table of Contents

I feel that there is much to be said for the Celtic belief that the souls of those whom we have lost are held captive in some inferior being, in an animal, in a plant, in some inanimate object, and so effectively lost to us until the day (which to many never comes) when we happen to pass by the tree or to obtain possession of the object which forms their prison. Then they start and tremble, they call us by our name, and as soon as we have recognized their voice the spell is broken. We have delivered them: they have overcome death and return to share our life.

And so it is with our own past. It is a labour in vain to attempt to recapture it: all the efforts of our intellect must prove futile. The past is hidden somewhere outside the realm, beyond the reach of intellect, in some material object (in the sensation which that material object will give us) which we do not suspect. And as for that object, it depends on chance whether we come upon it or not before we ourselves must die.

Marcel Proust
trans. C.K. Scott Moncrieff

Threshold

This book is a conversation with many people, alive and dead, some of whom may strongly object to some of the ideas of others presented within its pages, some who harbor ideas with which I, too, may disagree. I bid the reader consider—contrary to contemporary fashion—that we may learn important things even from people we don't particularly like or approve of and that truth is something best approached provisionally by many different and often crooked paths. I am grateful to those friends and also to those fiendish provocateurs who have discoursed with me over the years or who have left stirring words behind them, giving me the gift of their thoughts. Some have provided ballast for my own presentiments, while others have provided stimulating opposition. For one of the most thrilling aspects of nature is that nothing at all can exist without some tension. Without some resistance, there would, of course, have been no firm substance from which to cut and carve my own thinking; no shape without shadow; no self without other; no light without dark; without friction, no spark.

Apologia: Why Do We Write?

When so many others have written before us, illuminated, explained, shown, arranged, described the world and human existence, when so many others more eloquent, more learned, more witty, more poetic have polemicized and preached about what is important, about how we must live, about what is wrong with society, with our lives, with our thinking, when the world is arguably in countless ways even worse now despite all the words, when it is even less humanistic, more materialistic, less poetic, more utilitarian, when humans seem even less connected, more isolated, even after generations of writers have toiled to share their insights and inspire us to a better existence—we persist in writing, in feeling that writing might be a meaningful way to save the world, save our souls, right the wrongs, make up for disappointments, overcome alienation and despair.

We continue to write despite the fulminations of those contemporary theorists who believe that reading and writing belong to a hopelessly corrupt past, that they are the tainted remains of a paternalistic Enlightenment attempt to control people's thoughts by an élite whose members, the theory goes, misguidedly or even treacherously posed as reformers, teachers, fellow human beings. Such theorists, in the spurious interest of freeing mankind from the discipline, authority, and standards of the old world, have contributed greatly to the denigration of so much which makes life worth living. They have aimed—when they aimed at culture—at the wrong enemy; and if today's citizens are more free than they were two hundred years ago, we need only ask, as Nietzsche did: free for what? To go to the mall whenever they please? To never challenge themselves at all? To live lives where natural and artistic beauty, reflection, relative silence, awe and wonder are present in only the scantiest proportion compared to the fragmented techno-cratic busyness and consumerism that have become the norm? Is there no other way to be free?

Are great books really something to defend against, to ridicule, to knock off a pedestal? Or have they not always, mainly, been a powerful force of liberation, often a critique, often a means toward humanizing, toward inspiring tenderness and compassion? Ironically, the great books of the past seem to have increasingly induced a sort of revolutionary fervor which has itself taught people to doubt, to deconstruct, to denigrate books themselves. The educated professor snarls at the great works of the past like an ungrateful cur who has forgotten who first taught him the word freedom. Like Caliban, who complains that Prospero taught him language, the ingrate only knows how to curse the magic of culture. But poor Caliban, the reader may object, is Prospero's colonialist slave, so he may well begrudge his master's "kindness." Quite right, my skeptical postmodern reader, quite rightly read. Yet who but Shakespeare taught us this?

Now that people read so little, it is even more difficult than ever to measure the "use" or benefit of writing (leaving aside for just a moment its all-important non-utilitarian aspects). We might even ask why, if writing is efficacious, it has not succeeded in ensuring a practicable love of reading in our society, where, according to one dire calculation, the average person reads but one book a year—at most. If we really want to change the world, if we really want—indeed, even in a maligned Enlightenment tradition—to inspire reform, reach people, impart urgency, does writing a book make sense? Who will read it? What will it *do*? Won't it just be ignored?

Do words and ideas impact the world at all, or are we raising our voices like that passionate orator Mynheer Peeperkorn in *The Magic Mountain*, howling at the edge of a riotously loud waterfall, our words hopelessly drowned out by the spray and sensation of a force—in our case of media, convenience, technological sensationalism, consumerism, novelty and speed—a force far stronger than all our dusty-fusty intellectual intensity and our airy ideations? Why do we persist in writing when writing seems sometimes to make so little palpable difference? Do we continue out of a self-indulgent personal love of a way of life that has now become solipsistic or stubbornly antiquarian? Because it is what we like to do or because it is *the only thing* we know how to do? Or can it be that the act of writing itself—yes, real writing, inscribing, on paper, with ink, for printing in books that one can hold in one's hands—is now something of a revolutionary act in itself, an act that is more than just an empty fatalistic last gesture in honor of some lost world?

I wager that, yes, to write books, to read and treasure books and ideas and intellectual discourse, *is* a revolutionary act. We might even venture that one of the reasons reading is so out of fashion is not that it is boring and ineffectual but because it has the power to function as a sort of flaming conscience illuminating the "bad faith" of a general state of denial and a neglect of higher ethics and spiritual aesthetic values. When Kafka wrote that a really great book is like an axe that breaks the frozen sea within us, a metaphorical axe still had the sort of sharp edge that could cut deep and make a reader experience the real confusion that feeling and thinking instantiate, a personal cataclysm far messier than any anodyne new-age "transformation." Do today's humans care to be thus destroyed, broken down, burnt up, challenged? Whether they do or no, it is imperative that we strain and strive to rouse to wakefulness whoever remains the least bit conscious, even if it means pouring a bucket of cold water upon our fellow humans and, yes, even upon ourselves in our most comfortable and ethically lazy hiding places. To write is to challenge the negligent, disinterested, *laissez-faire status quo*. Culture, in the coinage of my friend Stephen Callahan, is the new counterculture. We may not win the war, but we have no choice but to fight, or write, as the case may be.

But let us return to the aforementioned non-utilitarian aspects of writing and reading. These aspects are inextricably bound up in everything which is to be gained or lost along the way. Outside of the content and import of what there is to be said and argued and persuasively insisted, the *experience* of writing (reflective, committed, difficult, grappling, ruminative, essayistic, careful, aesthetic, emotional) and the *experience* of reading (in relative quiet, with respect to the considered ideas of another human being, critically, with margins, with emotion and intersubjectivity, with devotion) bears its own weight and its own significance in today's fragmented and casual society. In other words, the way in which we read and write is directly commensurate to the way in which we construct meaning and measure value in our lives, our world, our history, our future, our fellow beings. Reading and writing are two very representative practices that demonstrate the essential dynamic relationship between spirit and matter. Ideas and words, living and breathing in books and sentences, synthesizing, dissecting, and reanimating realities, influence and engender our physical world. By altering these practices, or by marginalizing them, we are, in essence, altering the very way we conceptualize, share, proffer, process, and manifest ideas. Thus, I begin with an underlying assumption about the ability of spirit to matter in questions of matter and with hopes of breaking internal frozen seas on an individual and universal level, one reader, one tiny fissure, one tiny idea at a time.

Writers all *sometimes* believe they have something new and important to say that has not been said in quite the same way and quite the same context as before. Other times they fear they have absolutely nothing at all of value to add. Even our own "freshest" ideas are but reanimations and reworkings of mostly the same things that have fascinated us since the beginning of our personal consciousness. We think we have come upon something new only to find it in much the same words in a notebook from a decade ago. Yet the slight variations of syntax, and of the context into which we place our ideas, may make a world of difference, may be the small strand of hay that breaks the proverbial camel's back. A small idea may be waiting, hidden in a large book, for the right reader, just as a despairing romantic in a country house deep in the woods, with naught but a candle in the window, is waiting for a surprise visitor.

Something another writer has said may make us furious, or egg us on to verbally spar; we may be exhausted by received ideas, by questions which seem to leave only two equally unsatisfactory possibilities as answers. We may think we know how to pose a new question altogether or provide a third or fourth answer which, as Cummings hoped, asks its own new question, and so on and so on. I am reminded of the utopian visionary Charles Fourier who, in the preface to his opus *The Four Movements*, claims that he alone, finally, after so many centuries, has discovered the single most important secret to human happiness that no-one, not one person ever, has even begun to imagine before him. An outrageous, majestic, beautiful, absurd claim! Nevertheless, it is true that each new voice may add something invaluable to the conversation. Imagine how bereft the ensuing centuries would have been had Fourier not had the courage of his crowing and kept his revolutionary ideas to himself! This French visionary is an exemplum of the way in which spirit works on matter, because his ideas were, in fact, directly influential on actions. The words that he committed to paper in a tiny room in Paris formed a good part of the basis of American utopian communities like the late Brook Farm, even if their puritan-tinged interpretation of his phalansteries and phalanxes left out some of his wilder and more improbable imaginings: the sea that would turn to lemonade, the evolutionary development of human tails, the benefits of unhindered passional attractions.

Once, on the train to Concord, Massachusetts, to attend a transcendentalist conference, I met a fellow scholar with whom I fell quickly into a surprisingly heated argument about whether or not the intellections of the abolitionist movement had had anything significant to do with the ending of slavery. This fellow maintained that all the ideas, all the writing, all the speechifying, all the newspapers and broadsheets of the period had really had no significant influence on the success of abolitionism in comparison to that effected by the Northern soldiers' experiences of going into Southern states and seeing the horrors of slavery with their own eyes. While it certainly makes sense that this real-life experience was revolutionary, it seemed rather odd to me to deny that ideas and words had contributed to changing things. The eyewitness experiences of these soldiers were, in fact, written down in letters home or in essays for Northern journals; and other firsthand accounts, by escaped slaves and penitent slaveholders, or in fictional accounts, such as *Uncle Tom's Cabin,* surely crystalized vivid experiences into words, ideas, and theories.

Why, then, did my fellow traveler want so much for it to be the case that words did not do anything, that ideas were ineffectual in history? I knew why I wanted the opposite to be true. I need, with every fiber of my being, to believe that ideas changed the world, for better or for worse; whereas he, whose dislike of Emerson turned out to be no accident, needed to believe the opposite. He wanted to take the power out of the hands of the educated classes, and away from the individual, self-reliant, supposedly elitist genius, and place it in the *many* hands of the illiterate soldiers, or into the slippery hands of fate, as Tolstoy tries to do in *War and Peace,* where he argues, in the plot as much as via essayism, that history is not made by individual choices or heroes but by the random forces of accident.

But this dualistic split between the élite educated classes and the illiterate masses is, to my mind, a dangerous and largely unexamined construct that demands unpacking and revisioning. Is it really necessary to throw out culture and intellect because one portion of humanity has traditionally enjoyed exclusive access to it? Would it not be better to work toward providing more members of society with the skills and agency to critically consider philosophical, social, and aesthetic ideas, and to participate in a meaningful and reality-relevant conversation about how we are best to live and function as a society? Anti-intellectualism seems to be a persistent American trait which somehow is inextricably bound up with the mythology of democracy. But is the vilifying of culture really a helpful response to our current problems?

My desire to believe in the efficacy of ideas and writing combines a commitment to the preservation of high culture and dedicated scholarship with a conviction that the realm of ideas and words should never be something to which only one class of people has access. I am also certain that such culture is best, most lively, most meaningful, when kept in the closest possible contact with our real lives and experiences, not separated into abstractions or decontextualized from social practices or the lives of others. I believe that almost anyone can learn to read, write, and think, and that the insights and depth of consideration to be gained through the process of wrangling with the written word are richer and fundamentally different than those acquired through the more casual and relatively non-committal process of conversation (though speech might also meaningfully aspire to more careful and sacred consideration). I also maintain that almost anyone has the power to change the way the whole world sees and acts and lives, with little more than curiosity, some learning, and a passionate discipline, and that the words and ideas of any one individual can and do and will move others immeasurably.

In my years as a community college instructor, I have seen with my own eyes how even those students with little to no academic preparation, students who are struggling to hold two jobs, go to school, and raise children on their own, can and do become immediately engaged in the philosophical, social, and aesthetic questions which need to be considered before beginning to live a considered, ethical, and socially responsible life. While it is of course easier *by far* to engage in philosophical and poetic activity when one is not under the constant strain of putting bread on the table or buying a new pair of shoes for one's children, to thus conclude that only those who have easy access to leisure can participate in reflection, critical thinking, and spiritual and aesthetic experience is really the worst form of cynicism—one which hides a treacherous snobbery under its supposedly compassionate condemnation of the alleged elitism of culture. For to deny anyone the right or responsibility to participate in the communal reflection on and creation of the world is to me a crime: it is to deny that person his or her humanity. Instead of silencing further those whose concerns and ideas have all too often been traditionally undervalued, this is a call to innovative and positive inter-action rather than continual complaint about the restrictive and technocratic structures and systems that do, it is true, tend too often to confine and define us; a call to utilize the language and the raw material given to us instead of stubbornly calling foul and refusing to participate in a system, history, and culture that are, indeed, deeply flawed and haunted by ghosts of all kinds. This communally-created labyrinth of oscillating desires, repressions, rebellions, resistances, and generativity remains, despite or even by virtue of its darker shadows, also a culture rich in beauty, humanism, tenderness, striving, inquiry, imagination, and myriad evidences of the most ecstatic forms of life and love.

The conflict between intellectual culture and popular action had of course been rehearsed before we twenty-first century people repeated it on the suburban train out of Boston—by former now-famous Concordians. The transcendentalist movement notoriously split off into two factions comprised, on the one hand, of individualist thinkers and writers, and, on the other, of engaged activists and communal utopians. But this narrative of a clean split is quite misrepresentative of the movement's true complexities and overlappings. Bronson Alcott, possibly the least grounded of all the Concordians, felt impelled to actually experiment with his ideals in the real world, and founded the Fruitlands community, which eventually foundered on an unworkable proportion between the physical and the spiritual realms. George Ripley founded Brook Farm, which made a formidable attempt at bridging the gap between ideal and reality. Both utopian communities featured excellent progressive schools and were fundamentally attempts to give working people access to higher learning and to give the all-too dainty middle- and upper-class intellectuals the chance to get their hands dirty. Hawthorne quickly learned that he could not get any literary work done after a day's toiling in the fields; but others found the combination of matter and spirit salutary if not precisely conducive to the creation of great works of literature. Finding the right balance of body, mind, and soul is never easy.

Hyper-educated "bluestockings" like Elizabeth Peabody and Margaret Fuller (who claimed she had the headaches of a genius) suffered myriad physical pains in their striving for intellectual transcendence. Margaret, at least, finally ran off to fight a real revolution in Italy and take on her first lover, supposedly an Adonis with limited intellectual talents. Elizabeth educated herself prodigiously, wrote, edited, taught, and ran the most intellectually exciting bookstore in Boston, while simultaneously supporting and caring for a large and unruly family of siblings and various unstable and sick relatives. Her two sisters, Mary and Sophia, won away from her the only possible suitors she entertained: Horace Mann and Nathaniel Hawthorne. It may be difficult to measure the real-world effects of her genius (despite her share of headaches) but after all is said and done, although largely unappreciated, I think they were not minor.

The abolitionists (spearheaded by fiery women strategists) kept spreading the word, with and without the intellectual authority of rousing speeches by Emerson and Thoreau; Thoreau built a real house in the woods, instead of just writing about an imaginary one, but scorned the jailers who tried to imprison his soul within the walls of Concord jail (because his soul, his conscience, his mind was free); committees and clubs were founded; gardens were planted; journals begun, printed, proliferated, and abandoned; walks were taken; hands were grasped; love was and was not consummated; letters were written and sometimes not sent; and, as Emily Dickinson cryptically noted from nearby Amherst, "people must have puddings."

Bronson Alcott's inability to take the physical world into consideration, exemplified by his comical attempt to move his family home without putting a foundation under it, was counteracted by his daughter Louisa's intense focus on ensuring material security. And indeed, with *Little Women*, she earned more money from her pen than any other writer of the period, with the exception of Harriet Beecher Stowe. But her traumatic experiences with an inept spiritualist for a father may have kept Louisa from ever daring to enter into conjugal relations with a man. When a visitor asked if there were any animals laboring on the farm at Fruitlands, Louisa's mother famously answered, "Only one woman," but of course her daughters helped out, too. Ironically, Louisa's practical innovations were all in the interest of avoiding more physical labor by providing herself and her family with the financial support necessary to dream and imagine. In a similar, though more philosophically complex, strain, Thoreau began his paean to transcendence with a chapter entitled 'Economy'—an economy calculated to afford its readers with a model most conducive to musing, intellectual activity, aesthetic experience, walking and communing with Nature, the World All, and the timeless reverberations of morning moods.

The painted trays, quilts, and pies made by abolitionist women supported the more ineffable traveling lectures given by escaped slaves as well as the writing and publication of propaganda journals and the lobbying and advocacy that influenced the legislative process. The theories and words of social intellectuals were answered by the actions of smugglers on the underground railroad and even more violent physical acts of daring such as the raid on Harper's Ferry. Or perhaps the actions inspired the words—quilts and pies and gunpowder and risked lives worked in tandem with ideas, words, and ideals. Either way, the idea craves and creates action and manifestation; the experience and the action are object lessons, rituals, or manifestations that inspire ideas and fresh conceptualization. The experimental enactment is spurred on, checked, re-evaluated, and given meaning by the idea, the vision, the transcendental imagination. Material choices are made on the basis of spiritual values and spiritual values must be made on the basis of certain unavoidable material realities. Of course, there are times in history or in one's personal life when actions may be taken that fly in the face of physical practicality and prudence, when a person literally sacrifices his or her bodily comfort, convenience, or even existence for an idea or ideal. For ideas and values that are not lived, or have not touched and changed or colored our lives and perceptions, may as well not have been thought or written down at all.

We write in the hope that our words could mean something to someone, somewhere, across time and space. Has *Walden* made a difference in the world? Have Thoreau's words been heeded? On the one hand, when we see the mass of men and women in quiet desperation who prefer to go on with their accumulating and wage slavery rather than consider living in a different way, his words certainly do not seem to have mattered much. When we see the persistent and total destruction of the ecosystem, we may wonder about the power of his statement: "Thank God they cannot cut down the clouds." For, as if in refutation of a cryptic oracle, they (or is it we?) really have managed this seemingly impossible feat, as clouds are visually cut down by skyscrapers, airplanes, and countless towers of technology. On the other hand, we know how much a book can "mark an epic in a man's life," as Thoreau himself noted in his chapter on reading. We all know how much certain books have meant to us, how they have changed our lives both materially, in terms of conduct of life, and spiritually, in terms of directing how we see the world.

Like the awkward anti-heroes of a fairy tale, like Dumb Hans or the Goose Girl, we write as if we were attempting to complete some impossible task against all odds. We are climbing the mountain of glass, separating the millions of lentils from the millions of stones, weaving gold from straw before dawn, trying to guess the magic word in three days, and scooping the ocean out with a leaky thimble, day after day, decade after decade, on the chance possibility that some drop, some word or phrase we write, will get through to someone and make a possible reader feel less alone, confirm our own suspicions, solicit a response, an echo, a challenge, across the watery abyss. And if it sometimes seems as if writing has made no impact at all on the rushing, raving world, let us at least consider that it might have been an even uglier, colder, more callous world still, without the absurdly Sisyphean labors of writers and thinkers who have constantly brought all their small weight to bear against the weighty downward slide, who might, in fact, be the ones responsible for keeping total chaos, destruction, and utter indifference at bay—just until now.

If we were to let up at long last, give up, resign ourselves to silence—I dare not even suggest what might happen, what horrific indifference and simulated emptiness might ooze into every last crack and bury us alive, unable to remember the slightest thing, unable to form sentences or consider our actions, unable to value, denounce, celebrate, or dream. We may never know what nasty nightmare our often thankless little efforts keep at bay. But let us, at the very least, write in thanks and tribute to those who have persisted in the past, against such odds, in believing that writing, that ideas, that visions and images *do* matter. One thimble-full of salvaged words, one pearl of sweat or salt tear, one drop of ink, made of belief and commitment, made of love of humanity, of history, of culture, and of nature, no matter how humble, no matter how seemingly quiet, inarticulate, or out of tune, no matter how seemingly unheeded, may be precisely the enlivening, moistening alchemical liquid needful to keep the well of inspiration from running dry once and for all. Was it in despair or in hope that Robert Burton, in his *Anatomy of Melancholy*, counseled thusly: "Writers! Open the vein!" Did he mean we had better end it all? I like to think, rather, that he meant we ought to write as if our own lifeblood, our experiences, our thoughts and feelings, were flowing onto the page, that we might die even in the midst of writing—of making visible and hopefully intelligible—whatever it is we have within us.

I.

Matter and Spirit in Conversation

> And this is the reward: that the ideal shall be real to thee and the impressions of the actual world shall feel like summer rain, copious, but not troublesome, to thy invulnerable essence. Thou shalt have the whole land for thy park and manor, the sea for thy bath and navigation, without tax and without envy; the woods and rivers thou shalt own; and thou shalt possess that wherein others are only tenants and boarders. Thou true Land-lord! Sea-lord! Air-lord!
>
> Ralph Waldo Emerson
> 'The Poet'

I AM A GIFT to the finders; I lose everything, as if I had holes in all my pockets or the most slippery skin in the world. Perhaps this is so because, as much as I adore things, there is some unexamined impulse in me which suspects, like the much-maligned Descartes, that none of this is real: *mundus est fabula*—the world is a fable. From a more reasonable standpoint—and I imagine that this is probably a prime reason for the traditional prejudice against matter—I can see that the physical world, while real, certainly isn't permanent. Everything beneath the moon will fade and rot and pass away, a reality which must have induced those who could not bear such alteration to create an elaborate defense of that which supposedly lasts, *i.e.*, spirit or soul. If body and spirit were separate, the special pleading went, then the death of the body might not mean the death of the soul. Yet it seems more likely nowadays, considering that all of us are carrying the material of ancient stars in our bodies, that it is the physical which survives our fleeting mortal particularities—in the form of cells, particles, stardust—rather than some numinous individual soul or self. But as long as we are alive, we each cling to our particular collection of matter and call it self, individuality, agency; this clinging takes the form of concern, creative energy, and love, and the continual challenge of attempting to make sense of impermanence, loss and change.

Without being inclined, then, to reject the reality of the physical world, feeling still the reverberating tingling of certain real knocks, burns, and falls as well as the lingering pleasure of a caress, a taste, a visual and aural harmony, let us say that, in my perceived cosmos, the physical has weight, sensation, texture, temperature, and quality—and that this physicality is something to be celebrated and enjoyed as much as suffered. At the same time these physical sensations and characteristics are telling us, imparting to us, *something*, something about life, about how to make meaning, about something I will call spirit—a term expanded for me by a consciousness of the German word *Geist*, which encompasses definitions including mind, feeling, culture, and the intellectual, as well as that more metaphysical realm usually associated with our English word "spirit." The physical world impresses upon or influences the mind as sensory apparatus; but the particular mind, colored by its particular cast and propensities, by its physical (genetic, biological) and its possibly less explainable characteristics—*i.e.*, temperament, will, imagination, desire—filters and chooses the way in which the given world is seen, read, understood. To admit to having a soft spot for this thing called spirit seems to suggest a disparagement of matter, but I would not want to associate myself with a society of anti-sensualist prudes, nor would I willingly affiliate myself with any ideology that sought to escape the mortal, beautiful, and awesome reality of the natural world, its reason-defying beauties and its sorrow-inducing fading, its horrors and its delights. And yet I often find myself tempted, as I imagine you do too, to drift away into an imaginary dream amid the mind-numbing reality of the everyday. And I also find myself asking the question of what it is that makes all of this materiality so meaningful.

I know from experience that there is great liberation to be gained by throwing off the shackles of what often amount to imaginary material needs. By giving up certain things that many people see as necessary for survival, one reaps a harvest of hours, a bounty of time that might otherwise have been spent working for money. As Thoreau so powerfully formulated it, "The cost of a thing is the amount of what I call life that is expended for it now or in the long run." It seems worthwhile to me to relinquish certain physical conveniences or even creature comforts in exchange for the incalculable luxury of reflection, of sufficient margins wherein aesthetic experience, philosophizing, poeticizing can reverberate. While many may feel that they have to work five or seven days a week to insure their material security, or may choose consciously to trade their days and nights for an uninhibited flow of cash, a larger lodging, an expensive telecommunications device, a bottle of fine bourbon, I can play a queenly pauper blessed with an open day. An uninhibited flow of moments and sensations and a synthesis of physical and spiritual beauties: these are the infinite riches of nature and culture which belong, by right, to anyone who loves them, makes of them a priority, and makes room for them. While it is well argued that one's primary physical needs must be satisfied before one can indulge in higher spiritual reveries ("First comes the feeding, then comes morality"—Brecht), I am not the first to suggest that our current assessment of how much one really "needs" to consume, or stuff one's face or garage with, is exceedingly out of proportion with the development of our moral, ethical, intellectual, and aesthetic sensibilities and inner resources. The choice to value time, reflection, and culture over consumerism may not necessarily preclude prioritizing materiality, since the free experience of nature, for example, is—strictly speaking—no less material than a new coat (nature is matter); and yet there is a way in which the experience of nature or art or love (physical love included), or of anything that ought not be quantified, used, or bought and sold, is thought of, correctly or not, as spirit's part.

While Thoreau argued that it might be better to sleep in a railroad box and thereby keep his days and nights free to dream, Théophile Gautier asserted in his preface to that great aesthetic novel, *Mademoiselle de Maupin*, that while a coffin would, indeed, be enough space for a man to "literally live," to observe nothing but the strictest economy in such things would be to turn all of Paris into a virtual Père Lachaise, *i.e.*, a cemetery, where the supposedly living were doing little more than literally existing. Thoreau conversely saw a liberation in a coffin-sized box, noting that many of his countrymen living in larger more comfortable houses buried the better part of themselves long before death (presumably under obligations, possessions, work). But Gautier, who complicated the equation by asserting that he would rather go without shoes than without poems and that he would sell his breeches for jam, if necessary, was far from really having to consider the possibility that a railroad box might be the best means to afford the opportunity to make and experience poems—an experience unattainable by one of the more over-stuffed and prohibitively comfortable bourgeois persons he mocks for their utilitarian economies.

And the complexification is instructive, for the logic has far too often been reduced to a dualism pitting material things against spiritual experiences. Here, instead, we see that there are material things that are more or less "spiritual," *i.e.*, more or less utilitarian and prosaic than other material things. Material things that make us dream, that inspire and stimulate the mind, in other words, are to be preferred over those that drag us into the gutter or into the stock exchange. Wilde, who wished that he—a human being presumably made of a mixture of spiritual and physical stuff—might live up to his blue and white china, suggested as much. The work of art, albeit in this case made of a refined species of mud, is deemed the loftier substance, perhaps even because it has no needs at all. The aesthetes, had they paid Thoreau a visit in his little cabin (he did not, after all, ever really try living in that railroad box), would probably have found it quite charming. In short, together,

Thoreau and the Wildean aesthetes all ask us to consider what it is we need to feed our souls as well as our bodies. And we may conclude that the things some call luxuries are necessities to others, and vice-versa. Each of us must discover what we most need and what we are most willing to sacrifice in order to attain and sustain it, while simultaneously sacrificing as little as possible of other things that feed us, in all ways.

I would, then, rather than disparage matter in favor of spirit, or spirit in favor of matter, embrace physicality while celebrating the imagination, and stress that, at best, the most freely non-compromised spirit may play with the structures and arrangements of the physical world, proving the immediate creative potential of the human mind to act upon and alter the "real" and already-established world with its utopian imaginings.

The mind, of course, is part of the physical world, and yet some of its functions seem unexplainable from a purely mechanistic perspective. Seeing, for example, is, strictly speaking, a physical activity; but our perception and understanding of what we see seems to be dependent upon preconceptions and learned ideas about space and extension. Further, when we take in something seen through the eyes and it enters our minds, its physicality is transformed into non-physical ideas and images which we seem to carry with us, and possess, without owning or holding the seen things. The beauty of the physical world is material. And the sense organs we use to behold it and process it are physical. But when we move what we see from the world into our minds (both physical), what is seen becomes somehow spiritual, *i.e.*, imaginary, remembered, thought. This is all impossibly dizzying, which is one of the reasons we usually do not even bother to think about it. At the same time, it is exciting that mere ideas can induce physical vertigo. And we should think about it, even at the risk of swooning, for our conclusions about the relationship between matter and spirit are deeply relevant to our relationship with meaning-making and, as such, to our sense of our roles and responsibilities in the world.

The brain scientist Terrence Deacon, in his book *Incomplete Nature,* writes that "consciousness doesn't appear to have clear physical correlates even though it is quite ambiguously associated with having an awake, functioning brain." He argues eloquently that one of the reasons why consciousness has not been located by scientists is that it is not material, in the sense of "stuff," but rather that consciousness is a process, a dynamics of possibilities, and, what's more baffling, a consciousness of reduction, taking away, selecting out. Each cell, each neuron continually fights against entropy and chaos in order to maintain its own integrity, and this "auto-genesis," intent upon maintaining self-creation on the cellular level and then, exponentially complexified, on the level of personhood, is a sort of agency, will, desire, self. The mind is moved and inspired by this autogenesis to focus on and select out patterns of matter amid myriad possibilities, and in turn the mind chooses and emphasizes what it has seen, loved, feared, noticed, which changes in response to the mind's new ideas and visions of what is really in the world, and then is, again, seen by new minds, and altered, *ad infinitum...* Remarkably, we find a similar description of creative consciousness in Novalis' fragments from the 1780s:

> What an inexhaustible amount of materials for new individual combinations is lying about! Anyone who has once guessed this secret—needs nothing more than to decide to renounce endless variety and the mere enjoyment of it and to start some-where—but this decision is at the expense of the free feeling of an infinite world—and demands restriction to a single appearance of it. Ought we perhaps attribute our earthly existence to a similar decision?

The selecting out necessary for creation by an individual artist (or by any individual perceiving and creating his world) may be similar to the process by which the human brain creates its self or consciousness. And death, as Deacon suggests, would be a return to the original chaos of everything, an infinite world without choices, without selections, without direction. Living, then, is choice-making, delineation, discrimination, blind spots, even a sort of negation of one arrangement in favor of another, which we can call an affirmation if we choose to.

Deacon argues that events or entities which he designates as "ententional phenomena" and "absential features" within consciousness "make a difference in the world. ... [W]e are surrounded by the physical consequences of people's ideas and purposes. ... [E]ntentional causality... assumes the immediate influence of something that is not present... and it seems like 'magic'." Or, more poetically, in the words of Heinrich Heine,

> The thought wants action, the Word wants to become flesh... and amazing! Man, like the God of the Bible, only needs to speak his thought and the world is created. There is light or there is darkness, the waters separate from solid land, or wild beasts appear. The world is the signature of the Word. Note this, you proud men of action. You are nothing but the unconscious extensions of the men of thought, who often, in modest silence, have precisely predetermined all of your doings.

The objects of the physical world have been rendered as signatures of spirit, as very important symbols, metaphors, and dream-images of some other realm transcendentalists from Plato to Emerson have thought of as "the really real." This prejudice against matter *qua* matter has often explained away the physical world as a shallow and airy phantom of a moment's deluded perception: we ought therefore set our eyes and hearts on what is eternal, so runs the argument, and strive not to be distracted and seduced by the pleasures and desires of this prison house, these clayey lodgings, the body. But the spirit, along with will, desire, agency, choice, love, ethics, has been banished entirely by others for almost completely opposite reasons. These would explain the world as fundamentally lacking in meaning or purpose and our human bodies and their urges as the accidental detritus of mechanistic necessities such as the survival of the species. Deacon quotes Richard Dawkins as representative of this view: "no design, no purpose, no evil and no good, nothing but blind, pitiless indifference," and then notes that autonomized explanations of the world dispose of the idea of self altogether: "Your body is a chemical machine," and feelings and thoughts are unreal. There is possibly "no one home." This materialistic worldview paradoxically denigrates the physical just as much as the alternative. It divests matter—and with it human life, love, suffering, and the experience of beauty—of any trace of meaning. But Dawkins' conclusions about the human potential to create viable meaning are not as dire as Deacon's excerpt suggests. In *The Selfish Gene,* Dawkins coined the term "meme," which term itself, as if in evidence of his theory's correctness, has exhibited all of the characteristics Dawkins noted were necessary for a meme's survival: longevity, fecundity, and copying fidelity. A meme, according to Dawkins, takes over where the gene leaves off, initiating the proliferation of "tunes, ideas, catch phrases, clothes, fashions, ways of making pots or of building arches. Just as genes propagate themselves in the gene pool by leaping from body to body via sperms or eggs, so memes propagate themselves in the meme pool by leaping from brain to brain." Contrary to the suggestions of many scientists, Dawkins does not believe that the survival of a particular meme provides an evolutionary advantage. Thus, a meme, propagator of new cultural mores, can actually contradict evolutionary and biological determiners if it finds fertile receptors in a given society, on the basis of which, Dawkins writes, "[w]e have the power to defy the selfish genes of our birth and, if necessary, the selfish memes of our indoctrination." It would even be possible for us to cultivate "a nurturing, pure, disinterested altruism—something that has no place in nature, something that has never existed before in the whole history of the world."

Despite Dawkins' fertile suggestion, science has still not been able to definitively figure out why, if there appears to be no necessary reason for humans to make poems and develop ethics, we still do, thereby leaving those who would insist on a mechanistic explanation really unable to fully explain themselves. This latter view tends to explain things like poetry, tender feelings, ethical scruples, or the history of architecture as nothing more than elaborately evolved mating rituals. Perhaps Deacon's theory of autogenesis brings us closer to a more acceptable understanding of agency, will, self-generation, and self-hood as exponentially complex versions of simple biological processes; the alternative explanation for consciousness, which usually assumes some sort of *a priori* reason or imbedded purpose for all of this, founders on many fronts, but most practically upon the impossibility of absolute justification of particular assessments of good, bad, beautiful, or true, since an action thought to be the highest form of tribute in one culture may be the basest insult in another. In other words, physical actions and objects are, of course, given meanings by individuals and societies (along with names and associations) which are often not inherently necessary or consistently characteristic. This seems to suggest that anything can be anything and mean anything and the only possible recourse we have for assessment is utility and physical pleasure. But even those criteria are hopelessly variable, since something may be useful to one person in one situation and an annoying obstacle to and in another; and, of course, one man's pain is another's pleasure. Which leaves us where?

In simplistic terms, there are those who want to believe that there is meaning and something like a reason or purpose for being here and those who prefer to believe the opposite—and then there is another sort altogether, of which I count myself. This sort of person believes that while there are certain basic facts in the universe—gravity, for example—both the individual and the group mind necessarily do and must and should impart meaning and purpose to what might essentially be meaningless phenomena. If, as seems likely, there is no reason why we are here, it behooves us to create our own reasons, our own desires and goals and necessities, albeit always with a consciousness of our powers to change these as we ourselves, or as the circumstances, change. We are meaning-making and meaning-seeking animals, and this trait (be it biological, evolutionarily useful, or just a random accident) seems to be an unexplainable fact. According to E.O. Wilson, in *The Meaning of Human Existence,* the extreme growth in the human brain over a relatively short period was most likely due to the biological advantage of collaborating in small groups. Such collaboration required that individuals remember faces and experiences, a talent that was facilitated by gossiping and telling stories. One can easily imagine that a meaning-making trait narrating causes and effects might have been helpful in protecting one's tribe from repeatedly succumbing to potential dangers.

For whatever complex of reasons, we cannot help but ascribe meaning and purpose to phenomena, to events, to objects. And while some people have come to call this meaning-making a form of mysticism or social construction and impugn it as a conscious and malignant endeavor to foist the values of the people in power upon others less fortunate than they are, this is itself a social construction—a narrow narrative of the really complicated and chaotic development of mores and beliefs. Such a narrative willfully neglects the possibility and probability of any individual being waking up to a world interpreted by his or her own vision and coloring it in a fashion so irresistible as to reawaken the whole of humanity to see what she sees. Anyone can, and everyone must, change the world at every moment. We are doing it now, for better or for worse. Which is, of course, what art is and does, and why it is so important. The artist takes the shared raw material of the world, its realities and its appearances, its tendency to delude and its momentary revelations of terrible and beautiful truths, and shapes these infinite elements into something new and something necessarily subjective, something that is at once untrue and true. The artist teaches us, at best, that we too can and must do the same.

And while philosophers have often strained to separate the two realms of matter and meaning, some insisting on the "true" reality of one over the other, I am interested not in further polarizing body and mind, matter and idea, reality and art, but rather in exploring the ways in which they have occupied different positions in our ethical and aesthetic consciousness depending on the context. I am concerned that our conceptions of their separateness or synthesis are at the basis of an often-unexamined conduct of life, and are embedded in our language, resulting in the pervasive conflicting beliefs that there is something the matter with matter and simultaneously that materiality is the only thing capable of bringing us happiness.

Of course, this investigation already presupposes that the way we arrange matter in our minds determines what we see, seemingly privileging mind over matter; but minds—human brains—are matter too, and the objects and elements that the brain arranges are also mostly (if not entirely) from the physical world, as we imagine combinations of things and places and people we have already seen with our eyes or felt or experienced with our bodies. We may also be capable of conceiving of fresh abstractions based not on the external world, but on some interior structures (called at one time innate ideas; now, perhaps more accurately termed subjective constructions). We see, apparently, only what we believe is possible, and this requires a certain creative observer whose provenance and process may or may not be traceable by modern science. Whether or not there is anything new under the sun may come down to the brain's ability to conceive of something never before imagined, something that is not just a combination of perceived, seen, felt elements. And if this is possible, we can look for it in the realm of art, a process of creation which, as my friend Alexandra Gaydos once pointed out to me, is not strictly in service to matter, or to the needs of the moment, but which enables us to transcend whatever temporal reality we are in, which enables us to be somewhere, someone, somehow else. Art—usually a physical object or sensuous experience created out of images or sounds and their arrangements—is inspired at least in part by the realm of matter, even if only as a rejection or deviation from natural laws (consider a sculpture that seems to hang suspended on air), and is simultaneously something that is born of spirit, *i.e.*, feeling and mind, into the physical world. While certain works of art do sometimes reinforce or justify imbedded cultural mores, by ensuring that, say, a person behaving in a socially unacceptable way is punished and a socially-conforming character rewarded, or by mindlessly romanticizing particular power structures or moral strictures, such conformist, didactic tropes are the lesser part, the *inartistic* part of art—always challenged and often exploded by the unique vision of a true artist. Art, then, is never disengaged from reality or the concerns of social life, but is always inherently and radically participating in guiding and challenging us to see and thus to live in new ways.

This aesthetic experience is inherently related to ethical possibility, as the choices we make to see this and not that, to narrate differing causes and effects for shared experiences, to judge an event, a person, an action, or a society's mores from radically deviating perspectives, seem to suggest that the mind has more say in the matter than a monopoly of matter allows. George Berkeley, who famously questioned whether matter existed at all outside of our senses, outside of the mind, notes in *The Principles of Human Knowledge* that the spirit, as agent, is able to excite "ideas in my mind at pleasure and vary and shift the scenes as often as I think fit. It is no more than willing, and straightaway this or that idea arises in my fancy: and by the same power it is obliterated, and makes way for another. This making and unmaking of ideas doth very properly denominate the mind active." But a skepticism about the nature of physical reality, entailing a skepticism about the mind's ability to read reality, no matter how paradoxically empowering it is to mind's free imagination, need not devolve into a skepticism about the very existence of the physical. Berkeley is quite sound in suggesting that we have no way of ever testing whether reality does exist outside of our senses, because our senses remain our only mode of testing. Still, if we accept that there is a reality outside of ourselves and concede that this reality is not absolutely solid, nor completed, this realization should encourage a more engaged process of existential choice-making, not an attitude of carelessness, whether hedonistic or indifferent.

That the physical world and our constructs of time, space, and necessity may be less certain than they sometimes appear to be, that matter is permeable, both waves and particles, and subject to constant change, does not mean that what we do and how we think is irrelevant, but rather the contrary, since our actions and thoughts are largely responsible for the world we continue to inhabit. Whenever we think we are stuck or that the "real" world has us in a corner, we may experience the powerful force of spirit—this time in the form of will or a consciousness of agency—as possible rescue operations, alternatives, or even simply new ways to experience the perceived bad situation occur to our searching minds. Even the very idea of a god, for which there is no possible natural precedent except perhaps childbirth, is evidence not of its truth, but of the mind's ability to imagine something that may not exist. If, in other words, we can imagine and invent something for which there is no *a priori* necessity or precedent, and arrange our lives and choices around this figment, then mind must play a substantial role in the construction and experience of reality. This is all the more reason to be as aware as possible of our role in creating realities and to see to it that, while we should hold fast to our ideals and priorities, we do not allow ourselves as individuals or societies to petrify into any one particular figment or phantom arrangement as if it were absolutely necessarily one way or another. Probably many of you have often been told that you were being "unrealistic" as to your expectations or hopes for a better world. The only possible answer to such a taunt is to change the very reality which has your interlocutor in its deadly grip.

Medieval theologians often called the physical world "God's Book," within which we, who grasp abstractions only with difficulty, might better read the ineffable messages of the Divine. While many people today, conversely, assume that symbols are stand-ins for real things, that they "mean" or "equal" something specific and tangible, we do well to reverse this at least for a moment to regard and experience the supposedly real things as symbols, or rather heralds of something even more real, something lasting and un-measurable, as hieroglyphs approaching some silent explanation of what it means to be alive. Starting from the physical, we may proceed to the imaginary, the conceptual, the as-yet-unconceived. Thus, we can see that reading the "meanings" of the physical world need not mean either a disregard for physical reality or a rigid reading of matter. One important difference between the medieval Christian symbol system and ours was well explained by Emerson in his essay 'The Poet', when he noted that the mystic (meaning the dogmatic mystic) nails every symbol to one meaning, whereas the poet sees multiple meanings in every "sensuous fact." While a medieval theologian would usually read the decay of the body as a simple forewarning against attachment to the flesh, *we* need not interpret it as an admonishment to not enjoy what is fleeting. Although the very fleetingness of physical joys, their tendency to alter, fade, and disappear altogether may be precisely that which we call an object lesson, the story's moral need not be that we should not care for objects at all or that we should denigrate the sensual world. For physical things—skin, colors, tree bark, bread, chocolate, kisses, gold coins, paper money, shoe buckles, filigree, crenellations, gilded books, ponies, eyelashes and fingertips, marbleized frontispieces, photographs, hips and napes of necks, smells and sounds and textures—all simultaneously partake in the spiritual and the physical, are all miraculously self-generating evidence of a teeming life force at play, a universe in love with its own creative energy, with human hands and minds and eyes in its willing service, evidence of a force—we may call it love or simply natural desire—of perpetual making and rejoicing in that making.

I lose things, but not really, never really having had them in the first place, and still being able, in so far as I may recall or imagine them, to recover them again. And then, just as much as I lose things, I find things that have been lost by others, seeing things that others overlook, picking them out, pointing them out, pocketing them for later. Memory, too, is a loser and a finder, a shuffler, a parser, a re-arranger. Deliberately or not, we slip back and forth between physical things and the memories of places and events and persons, real or remembered, that the mementoes recall. A Proustian paving stone, or that famous madeleine given to me by reading a book, equally belong to my collection as much as any weighty bronze sculpture I hold in my hand. But only the choicest pieces may be displayed in the more public cabinet of curiosities which constitutes the conscious mind, while secret drawers are crammed with forgotten, repressed, or tragically neglected keepsakes, broken amulets, stopped pocket watches, and fragments of lost letters, sentences now illegible after that vial of holy water brought back from the Ganges or from Glastonbury broke and spilled, making the ink bleed. I tend to overflow, squander, shuffle, scramble, and hope that when the time comes whatever it is will fall into my hands. And sometimes I am surprised by what can only be a miracle: that this or that tiny object, a key, a slim volume, a scrap of paper on which I had written a word or a number, a quotation lost in a two-thousand-page book, suddenly appears before me, even when it is the last minute before I must run out the door and absolutely need to have found it. But what *has* been lost—moments, names, melodies, facts, details, sensations, intricately wrought hatpins, pressed flowers, locks of hair, lovers' promises, things and events we swore at the time we would hold onto forever—is inconceivable and criminal. People sometimes even burn letters or leave family photos out in the rain. But we would rather not think on that.

Pippy Longstocking was a notorious finder, as is my friend Stephen Callahan; they called him "finder boy" in his youth and he was always called upon to look for something someone had mislaid. This is suspicious, now that I think of it; maybe he was actually a thief, like that seeker after truth Nietzsche writes about, who hides something behind a bush and seems surprised to find it precisely there where he once hid it! But any artist is this sort of magician, an artist of the sleight of hand, swiping what others do not appreciate and setting it so that it becomes suddenly desirable, arranging it so that its original owner comes to miss it. Artists are people who endeavor to notice what was always there *in potentialis*, who are able to make the ordinary suddenly important, to see it new, to make others wish that they had found whatever it was first. And, of course, all philosophical systems and worldviews are a particular kind of arrangement by individual vision, a setting of the raw material of the actual world (what is) into possible other patterns or designs (what could be), rather than resting in a merely habitual rut of received ideas. Really, the arrangements we make may as well be utopian, elegant, joyous, sacred, ecstatic, experimental, serious funhouse mirrors and creative extensions of preexisting "reality," rather than a slavish mimesis of some *status quo*. Let us look at "reality" as a diamond in the rough, raw material, continually reset by ourselves, as creative royal jewelers, in infinitely fantastical tiaras which we can try on both inside and outside of our heads to help us see and act and experience in new ways. If existence precedes essence, as the existentialists have it, then we can and must choose what we are and what the world is and means, how we act, what we value and reject, even if our choices are sometimes limited by a few natural laws and unavoidable circumstances. It shouldn't be a surprise, after all, that finder boy grew up to be an aesthetic utopian who collects and arranges objects with an attention as devoted as that he renders to the design and conception of his ideal Nowhere, striving always to manifest it in the physical world.

Spirit may be understood as the arranger and the meaning-maker, while matter provides the colors and textures and shapes with which it plays. Why some people—even Emerson—conclude that therefore matter is the vulgar part of this union and spirit, *i.e.*, form, the higher part of art, can probably be traced to our inherited prejudice against anything that doesn't last, but it is as difficult to imagine a sculpture without marble or clay as it is to imagine experiencing the world without a body. A clay model of a body, a medieval Golem for example, is a rather pathetic thing without the in-spiration of *ru'ah* (Hebrew: breath; holy spirit) to make it come to life.

Pippy Longstocking knew what was important: the freedom to imagine, adventure, and roam unhindered by obstacles, whether physical or mental. She was, in fact, unconstrainable; she couldn't be socialized; didn't like school; she knew her own strength; she threw gold pieces around with a carelessness unmatched except by the denizens of Moore's *Utopia,* where precious stones were to be found lining the gutters. Speaking of marvelous finders, I shouldn't neglect to mention Phinneus Sonin, our local junk man with his shining eyes and multicolored rickshaws, who is always, always, finding and redispersing the detritus of civilization, as if to show us that all our possessions are like the ribbons and shreds picked up by birds, always able to be transformed into new shapes and new psychic dwellings for fledgling dreamers. He reminds us that nothing is ever useless, even if it has outworn its original purpose. Also not to be forgotten is our wild, mad friend, Robin Simon—may she ramble somewhere safely, despite her neglect of gravity, time, space, and other natural laws—whose gifts of miraculous treasures discovered in the streets unearth themselves even today from under piles of boxes or out of drawers in my room, and hurl themselves onto the floor moments before a letter from her—the first in years—appears in my mailbox, as if the objects were fore-echoes of the words on their way. A little Chinese box with lacquered scenes from fairytales, a porcelain mask and an embroidered sash, a pair of velvet dragon knickers, a miniature teacup with a world inside. Telekinesis? Perhaps; it probably is easier to make physical objects move if one doesn't believe in their actual weight. She was fluid with possessions, as rings she had picked up off our bureaus would just as innocently be slipped onto the fingers of seeming strangers or new friends, or tiny baubles pocketed in silence be left in tree nooks or upon the stairwell of a passing dandy wearing a pretty cape. How, she seemed to say, can any one thing belong to any one person? She allowed the objects their own agency, as if they were animated by attractions and fascinations to find their way into the hands of those who deserved them.

Some people claim that their dead friends and family, their ancestors, send them things as messages from other worlds when they are wandering in rummage sales or antique shops: a teapot, a letter opener, a bearskin cape with a silver leaf-shaped clasp. And there are, indeed, times when an object seems to give us inordinately intense pleasure, either because it seems connected to a person or an idea, or because of its peculiar shape, weight, color, or smell, times when an object seems to be just precisely the thing to fill us with happiness, a sense of meaning, purpose, connection. In such a case, the true bohemian knows that no amount of filthy lucre is too much to spend or expend on the item, and, in fact, the squandering of mere money for something like that is part of the pleasure of the exchange. I enjoy spending money—not just the getting of the thing, but the actual act of giving the bundle of bills away. Some people feel pain when they pay; I feel a sensual pleasure, a sense of freedom and luxury. And it is not because I have unlimited supply—I live at present well below the poverty line—nor because I have overlooked the fact that time is money. It is certainly not because I do not know what the "cost of a thing" is in Thoreau's priceless definition.

Of course, we all know about the common folly of trying to fill spiritual emptiness with material riches, but somehow today's cultural impoverishment has something to do with a misunderstanding of the spirit inhering in various forms of matter, in art, in artifacts, in certain kinds of physicality. In fact, a look at the history of our cultural relationship with matter and spirit reveals that inhering spirit in matter has been one of the greatest taboos, called by the name of idolatry. Taboo, as is well known, has a way of creating more perverse attachments, and the fetishism of objects as well as of human bodies in the form of consumerism and pornography may be a result of this insistence on the separation of spirit and matter. The widespread impoverishment in the face of so much material debauchery and excess impels us to discover a more meaningful connection between matter and spirit, body and mind, a connection that has largely gone missing among the sometimes-extreme polar categorizations of ideal and real, physical and transcendental, carnal and spiritual. In the essays that follow, I look more closely at our unexamined assumptions, our cultural prejudices, and the way we have become at once unabashedly materialistic and piously, moralistically anti-aesthetic. It has turned out to be a worse bargain than was once calculated, for we have not only lost our souls, but have gained no compensatory worlds in return.

Everyone speaks about the problem of Americans being glutted with a base sensuality, but really, as is often the case with overindulgence, we have become grossly insensible to the finer sensations. We cannot listen amid the incessant noise, we cannot see amid the rushing images, we cannot touch because we have become calloused all over. We are obese—but at the same time, we starve ourselves; our garages are filled to the brim with expendable and already broken junk; our landfills are mountains of eternal toxic shame; but few people seem to notice that this over-consumption is related to a numbness, a blind-deaf-and-dumbness to the faint stirrings and whisperings of the spirit that once could be traced in the lineaments of the physical world, in art and in nature, a numbness whose source is a tragic misunderstanding about how little one actually has to pay in order to be as wealthy as Emerson's poet.

When people speak about the loss of spirit, they tend to suggest we cure the malady with a turn inward, a turn away from the physical world which implicitly negates the complex relationship between matter and spirit, between sensory and transcendental realms. This cure comes in many forms: minimalism; piety; asceticism; attacks on beauty and on the aesthetic components of art, music, social experience; an advocacy for pure conceptualism; a disregard of surroundings and environments; an insidious argument for technological consumerism; a leave-no-trace attitude to existence, whereby one is enjoined that the best thing a human could do, after not existing, would be to have as little impact as possible. While the last is a natural and to some extent admirable response to the abuse of natural resources and a very real environmental crisis, it has been adopted as a general platform for existence, suggesting that less is always more, and that there is nothing, literally nothing, that a person can contribute to the cultural or material richness of the world. One's traces of natural affirmative human impressions and expressions are inadvertently erased in the rush to minimize one's "carbon footprint," but, alas, environmental damage is still spreading more quickly than can be counteracted by all the good will in the world, while culture and participatory engagement are disappearing faster than the ozone layer. A return to spirit and culture really requires very little in the way of natural resources since one can walk, bicycle, read, talk to a person nearby, experience nature, listen to what little silence is left, without using fossil fuels and without creating toxic waste, without wasting any electricity at all; but governments and individuals choose instead to spend millions of dollars and use up more and more resources looking for some complicated technological means to continue to live unsustainably amid myriad distractions and annoyances, even though most of us agree that our gadgets, our jobs, our highways, our machines do not actually make us happier or better people. And as we recklessly deplete our natural resources, we are literally running out of the vital matter to make more matter—and the cost, in terms of the horrific physical and anti-aesthetic desecration of the land as well as the ethical and spiritual degradation that comes with selfish greed and a neglect of human and natural consequences is devastating even now.

The spread of technology, with its concomitant defense of the virtual, has contributed greatly to an apparent devaluing of the physical; yet this "revolution" has not translated into a spiritualization of existence or a real reduction of tedious, meaningless work for harried humanity. Instead, the spiritual has been eradicated along with the physical connection. The technological devolution seems to be little more than a ruse for selling the newest device or gadget, without which the supposedly timeless-spaceless modern being feels unable to function. He has given up his memory, his ability to synthesize and understand ideas, his freedom, as well as any simple access to human or neighborly help, knowledge, or warmth. This price is too high to pay for a dubious return in the form of a promise of immediate access to data and information or the ability to buy things without leaving one's home or office (minus the sensual thrill of handling dollars and seeing, smelling, touching the world). He has gained the ability to work and be reached at all times upon any mountaintop, in the middle of any conversation or experience, and the constant anticipation of some small chance of a random surprise salvation from what really can only honestly be characterized as an unbearable and shallow existence—an existence so unsatisfactory that one hopes constantly that it will be interrupted by something better.

The allegedly virtual is fatally bound to a merely materialistic culture lacking in spiritual foundation. It costs much more than it returns, as its incessant buzzing, roaring, and ringing drown out any possibility of enjoying the "free time" theoretically to be gained by the convenience of technology. As it turns out, keeping the infrastructure of virtual reality switched on for twenty-four hours a day requires much more wasted energy than we like to think, thus flagrantly obviating any supposed return in environmental protection. A knapsack filled with free books checked out of the public library (a spiritual institution which is not by accident suffering an immense financial crisis while multinational information technology companies are thriving) is a much better bit of baggage to take to that desert island—or into the post-industrial future—than the newest oil-based and electricity-dependent plastic monstrosity; and one gets physical exercise while carrying it, not to mention the mental exercise, the experience of synthesizing organic, complex knowledge, the real experience of reading, digesting, reflecting in silence on whole books instead of downloading snippets and summaries, or dilutions of data and co-opted cultural capital, into a fact-crammed brain.

There is an immense gulf between information and knowledge, and the way we as a culture seem to have forgotten this may have something to do with the commodification of even spiritual wealth into cultural capital, something to be utilized, manipulated, transferred, bought and sold for some mercenary purpose. Education—one that engages in ethical and aesthetic reflection and questioning, fruitful confusion and uncertainty, dialogue, synthesis, and unaccountable experience—cannot be bought and sold across cyberspace or implanted via a chip in the brain. Speed reading is not reading. The medium is the message, and a book should be heavy, if only to weigh upon the reader and slow her down.

Emerson spoke of every "sensual fact" as a material manifestation within the world, as a symbol for a complex assortment of ideas, not to be reduced to one mathematically or dogmatically predetermined solution or answer. And this interplay between the physical as symbol and its spiritual extension regenerates itself infinitely, at no material, environmental, or ethical cost. Reflection, and its resulting provisional stations of synthesis, is one of the most essential processes for the development of new ideas, fresh insights, original arrangements; and it is something our society has almost entirely neglected, abandoned, forgotten. We can see the results of this neglect around us already, but only if we stop for a moment and reflect.

What I suspect is that an important cause and effect of this neglect is a confusion about matter and its relationship to spirit, and while this or other solutions to our presently unsustainable predicament might occur to any of us were we to sit a moment with the rare discomfort that gushes in if we recuse ourselves temporarily from the rush and rage—the hope and hype—of commodities, data, and progress, we rarely dare to release our hold (although we are really the ones being held) on whatever it is we feel we must do in order to not fall out of step, not lose our jobs, homes, social standing, security. We are so frightened of losing our grip that we do not risk the smallest danger (darkness, loneliness, confusion) to change our lives. We are so busy acquiring things we think we need, and doing things we think we need to do, that we do not even take the time to consider whether we really want the situation or success after which we are striving; nor do we have the leisure or quiet to enjoy or admire all that already belongs to us by right. "Things are in the saddle," warned Emerson, back when it had not gotten nearly so bad as it is today, "and ride mankind." But the poet, he also reminded us, is "Sky-lord, Land-lord, Sea-lord," for everything she sees or even imagines is an enduring possession. But we cannot possess it if we do not have the leisure or senses to enjoy it. There is—in effect—nothing which we can really lose, except perhaps the flexibility and fertility of our minds.

What then is the most fruitful relationship between physical entities and their associated ideas and spirit? We may consider that any individual specific object, mountain, or building is in contact with the idea or even the ideal form of that object, an idea or ideal form of mountain, of building. We might even assume, as many have over the course of the history of ideas, that anyone who is overly attached to a particular temporal physicality is somehow less spiritual, and here we have a philosophy and theology of spirit seemingly born in the service of sparing us the pain of loss and death ahead of time. Non-attachment might appear to be a wise method in the sub-lunar regions, where all is fleeting and time triumphs—but it rather seems like a ruse, or a case of special pleading, considering that we do have bodies, and appetites, and we do suffer the pain of loss and lack, despite all attempts to assuage it. We also, it must not be forgotten, experience pleasure, and it seems an act of bad faith to accept the one and reject the other. Though it hardly appears to be an admirable achievement, some spiritual practitioners may manage to neither suffer nor enjoy anything at all. Rather, I suppose that the individual experience of losing a specific physical thing or person is a meaningful object lesson in the reality of death—it may lead us to enjoy life all the more, to attend more to our whereabouts, to concentrate on our pleasures and on all sensations, even seemingly unpleasant ones, for we will not have the luxury of experiencing them forever. We should pay attention to the fate of matter, to fading, to physical decay and the processes of natural fermentation and regeneration. We should pay more attention.

Pain, delight, pleasure, beauty all come, in any case, in both spiritual and physical forms, and usually, in fact, in a mixture of both. We cannot, or rather should not, try to minimize or limit our experience out of a moralistic or even practical stoic defensiveness. Some bit of pain or trouble may be salutary, even stimulating; some types of burdens are worth carrying, if only to build physical and spiritual muscles, if only to experience the delicious relief of laying them down and doing absolutely nothing afterward or in between. If I seem to be stressing the didactive benefit of the physical, let me add that matter is to be enjoyed for its sensual properties as well, and maybe even in tandem with the sensations of its stings and arrows, as contrast at least. Renoir asked: "Why should beauty be suspect?"—and while we have some ideas as to why, we would do well to consider that pleasure and delight make up at least one part of what real life consists in. While we might even entertain the idea that property is to some extent and in some cases a form of theft, let us not forget that we need not own something to enjoy it, and that the bounty once pillaged from ancient civilizations serves to enrich millions of people every day in public museums, people who are themselves possessed by the beautiful forms, materials, and historic and cultural significance by merely looking. While such loot has often been egregiously ill-gotten, it is not matter's fault that people have abused each other to possess it in the past—indeed, we may hear the cries of the massacred as well as the songs they sang while making their objects if we hold the objects close to our ears. Today we might (though too often we do not) choose more consciously to make and to attain things without such high human, environmental, and cultural costs—thereby hopefully merging spirit more meaningfully with matter. But before we banish materiality in the interest of morality, we would do well to carefully weigh which feeds the human spirit more: beauty or pious censure. It is no simple task to calculate how much pleasure and spiritual profit can be gained with the least amount of pain and inhumanity, especially if we admit that by merely breathing, we kill organisms, and by walking we cannot avoid stepping on the smallest of creatures.

While Thoreau is most famously quoted as saying, "Simplify, simplify, simplify," I read him a bit more closely and find that he is not absolutely vilifying matter—in fact, he learns all about his "higher laws" by pushing up against the bounds of the physical and through a practically hyper-aesthetic attention to physical details and forms. He is asking only that we seriously consider matter's relationship to spirit, and entreating us to refrain from sacrificing spirit—in the form of values, artistic and ethical freedom, our integrity, the sanctity of nature, and the realm of transcendental imagination—to an exterior covering which has been reduced to merely a simulacrum of meaningful humanity. It is not the exterior that is evil, but an exterior out of touch with its interior. He suggests we be worthy of our clothes, our castles, our pomp, and be as noble on the inside as on the outside. Beautiful things should thus be made in beautiful ways, in ways that are not in themselves ugly and in ways that do not cover up a multitude of aesthetic, ethical, or environmental crimes. But we must not get too fastidious about the messiness of making, living, experimenting, for we do not always even know which seemingly good act engenders unseen negative consequences, or which seemingly bad or disengaged one might do worlds of good.

Today's Americans may, indeed, be as vulgar as their exteriors portend; but this is a problem, not a noble unpretentiousness about which to crow. Rather, let us be pretentious first if it is a means of growing into or living up to a premature external glory. Thoreau, in my view, is quite a bit closer to the dandies and bohemians of Europe than to the Puritan utilitarians of Massachusetts. The transcendentalists and the aesthetes together raise the imagination above Mammon, and rail against those who, as Wilde mocked, know "the price of everything and the value of nothing." The dandies and the naturalists have more in common than at first meets the eye, despite Wilde's horrified exclamation: "Enjoy Nature?!"

As Baudelaire notes, in his excursus on the dandy in 'The Painter of Modern Life', the child and the savage, and by association the aesthete and the transcendentalist, share an "adoration of what is brilliant—many-colored feathers, iridescent fabrics, the incomparable majesty of artificial forms—the baby and the savage bear witness to their disgust of the real, and thus give proof, without knowing it, of the immateriality of the soul!" And, in a letter from 1894, Proust writes, echoing Jesus' famous dictum about the kingdom of heaven: "You have happiness within you: that is the safest, if not the only, way of having it. In any case, whatever may be the happiness you dream of (to dream of it is to already have it in the most ideal sense of the word, which as a good idealist I believe to be the only true one) I am sure it is a happiness of the very best quality." A classic bohemian from Mürger's *Vie de Bohême* is indeed a transcendentalist of sorts when, instead of heavy and expensive furniture he moves from garret to garret with a folding screen upon which his beautiful chairs, tables, divans, and bed are painted. In a more neo-Platonic than a strictly Platonic sense—where a "disgust of the real" is not a denigration of art, but of the *status quo*—this painted screen is a manifestation of *the idea* of furniture, a sort of cosmic joke on society's expectations, freeing the artist from what Thoreau called "shriveling one's self up into a nutshell of civility," freeing him from ignoble pleasing, flattering, lying, cosseting, selling, or compromising himself to the non-ideals of the marketplace in exchange for a couple of chairs that are usually not even as beautiful as the ones a poor bohemian might invent. Better to sit on the floor than on a chair purchased with one's dreams and at the expense of one's values. But the higher truth is that we must have beautiful chairs *and* beautiful dreams, or rather, we must see to it that our dreams come true, furnishing even the physical world with our spiritual fancies.

II.

Almandal Grimoire: The Book as Magical Object

In a famous still-popular Jewish dreambook [from around 1513], we find a section devoted to the "higher beings" such as "the planet and stars, thunder, and books."

Joshua Trachtenberg
Jewish Magic and Superstition: A Study in Folk Religion

Almandal is an Arabic word for the wax tablet altar on which the magician engraves divine names and the seals of Solomon with a silver stylus. It was also the title of a "guide to the ritual invocation of angels," Almandal Grimoire.

Owen Davies
Grimoires: A History of Magic Books

When my nephew was a young boy, he got it into his head that I was a witch, and I have never denied it. He earnestly implored me to teach him magic, by which he meant flying and telekinesis. Magic, to him, was necessarily bound up in visible and palpable changes in the physical world. He would not be satisfied unless he could travel to other realms or make heavy furniture hurtle across the room. I wrote him a letter, illuminated with colored inks and closed with a wax seal, gently explaining that real magicians could not be bothered with merely physical tricks such as lifting our lumbering human bodies or bulky old chairs in the air.

Feeling somewhat like a charlatan employing special pleading, I tried to convince him that real magic dealt with numinous ethereal substances, not to be tested by our physical senses or by crude mechanical devices. And that we witches could travel in time and space, but it was more expedient and much more graceful to leave our bodies behind when we did so. Simultaneously, I maintained that real magic does alter the physical world, but not usually immediately, and not in the way he expected. Magic works on the physical world because intentional wishing and imagining motivate us to live differently and to believe in our fantasies enough to actuate them, because living and performing ritual acts like scattering rose blossoms under the bicycle wheels of beloved strangers and making love often produce quite remarkable transformations in our real physical circumstances. And because sending a handwritten letter through space really is a wondrous way to make ideas real.

He may have been too young at that time to understand existentialism, but I think he did grasp what I was trying to say, and I hope I escaped the shame of disappointing a small boy who believed I might teach him to fly. Now, years later, he is an artist and musician whose ideas and dreams become manifest in sounds, words, and actions; I hope he still thinks I am a witch, not least of all because I write books and paint pictures (anagoges, my friend Kathryn Barush calls them) which aim to levitate people, if not objects, from the merely prosaic into some other realm of consciousness, or to inspire us all to see the magic shining in matter. Although I may have seemed to denigrate matter in the letter I wrote to my nephew long ago, claiming that real magic does not deal in bodies, the opposite is just as true, for without a body there can be no imagination. A body, more than any other physical object is a powerful portal to the spirit. Another entity that mediates between matter and spirit in a similar way is a book. Magic books, called grimoires, were from their inception fundamentally physical objects believed to have the power to change physical circumstances.

What, then, is the significance of disembodying books? And what dire consequences may be lurking behind the commonly optimistic celebration of "transcendent" textuality? The age of the disembodied book is upon us, and I fear that a book bereft of its bindings is a dire symbol of the disintegration of the powerful and contested bond between ideas and reality, words and action, imagination and manifestation. The proper confluence of the allegedly dualistic realms of spirit and matter has been contested over the course of thousands of years of theological and philosophical debate. A book, traditionally a product of the marriage of matter and spirit, ideas and formal materiality, is a vivid symbol through which to assess our current relationship to these polarities within the context of historical perspectives. My instinct rages against the idea of disembodying any book, and my research and philosophical reflection have explained why: when we wrest a book from its bindings, we are undermining a magical connection between thought and life, dreams and flesh. We are undermining the human capacity to change physical reality by virtue of imagination.

Books have often been created and studied for the express purpose of effecting magical transformation, either literally or metaphorically, and this impulse on the part of book makers and book readers is a perfect object lesson in the confluence of spirit and matter. As books begin to lose their physical objecthood, we must ask whether the spiritual part that remains still holds on to its potency. Changes have occurred in the form and the process of making books over millennia, dramatically exemplified by the invention of the printing press, but today we are faced with an incalculably more extreme transformation, one that wrests the soul of a book from its physical body while telling us we have everything to gain and nothing to lose in the process. As Roger Chartier, one of the leading scholars in the field of book science, explains in *Forms and Meanings: Texts, Performances, and Audiences from Codex to Computer*, our current revolution "modifies not only the technology for reproduction of the text, but even the materiality of the object that communicates the text to readers." The electronic text revolutionizes the "text's status," he continues, because "for the materiality of the book, it substitutes the immateriality of texts without a unique location." In contrast to the former arrangement of text, margins, and pages, allowing for "the immediate apprehension of the whole work," this new form substitutes "the free composition of infinitely manipulable fragments... textual archipelagos that have neither shores nor borders."

Anyone who thinks we will be able, in the future, to have both real and virtual books in any significantly equal proportion is ignoring the history of new media supplanting old, from orality to writing, from hand-illuminated to letterpress printing, from letterpress to offset, and beyond. Braids and knots are thought to hold spells and wishes and potencies. If spirit and matter were strands of silk twisted around each other, holding magical powers in the crux of their twining, whereto would these powers disperse were they unbound? What is a book without its binding?

There have always been those who would deny the book its materiality and champion the spiritual ideas within its pages at the expense of its physical bindings, weight, typography, end papers, margins, and ornament. Such people insist that a book is best when it makes us forget the world around us—when, absorbed in its pages, we forget we are reading, forget we are sitting in a room, forget what city or country we are in, forget the season, the century, and even gravity itself. And they do have a point, for to be transported into the freezing Arctic on a sweltering August day, or to a sultry island while shivering in one's unheated garret, or to be temporarily rapt by the sufferings of others instead of one's own, or to be in the company of charming and erudite (albeit cold and dead) thinkers and poets rather than among one's own dull and vulgar fellows is no small magic. Abstract ideas alone have warmed me with eternal-seeming fires on nights when I was forced to wear fingerless gloves to bed, daring only to let my hands out from under the covers to turn a page. And on many occasions, I have found closer companions between the pages of a novel than in the waking world.

Leah Price, in *How to Do Things with Books in Victorian Britain,* calls people who "conflate the practice of disinterested, linear sustained attention with the object that is the printed book" "nostalgists," noting that "secular novelists such as Dickens, Eliot, Brönte, and Trollope assumed that absorption in the text required forgetting its medium." She suggests, therefore, that the best reading is "platform independent... binding blind and edition deaf," a claim I find disturbing on at least two counts. First, if we were to accept fully that disinterested reading is the highest form, we could certainly argue that a bound book allows for absorption and forgetting—forgetting even the volume one holds in one's hand—where an electronic medium, with its infinite possibilities for distraction and digression, does not. Second, this disinterestedness—like any attempts to radically separate aesthetic experience from our lives—is itself somewhat suspect. Paradoxically, I am one of the first to celebrate the paramount importance of "art for art's sake" and its incomparable opportunity for free play of the mind in non-conscripted, open-ended experimentation and pleasure, but such an experience—if it is to have meaning in our real lives—cannot be fully separated from the sensuous. Is forgetting or ignoring the material world really the point of reading?

Imagination functions freely. Ideas cannot be burned or destroyed by even the wildest of bonfires, nor can they be blotted out by the most insidious inquisitions or boards of censorship. But the idea of championing the spirit over materiality is itself one of those eternal ideas—and, for all its beautiful liberation, it also has been associated throughout time with some less-than-beautiful concepts and consequences. Consider Hans Christian Andersen's little match girl, lighting match after match to keep warm on Christmas night while seeing visions of turkey supper, Jesus, and warm fires—and in the end blissfully going up to heaven to meet her dear grandmother. Is the girl not freezing to death in an alley with only the consolation of Christianity to warm and feed her? Is this something to celebrate, or is it a suspicious morality tale designed to soothe those who would in truth do better to change their material circumstances, by self-actualization or by revolution, as the case may be? We can rejoice to imagine her physical suffering possibly being transcended by spiritual succor, but we might also deem a moral fable such as this—dependent as it remains upon physical eyes, physical comfort, and the physical book it is preserved in—a sort of pious fraud.

Here it is meet to ask whether the relationship between spirit and matter may be facilely reduced to an equation where physical equals utilitarian scaffold and spiritual equals all that we really value. When I say utilitarian, I am referring to a general favoring of utility over other human values, not directly to Jeremy Bentham's idea; but his "greatest good for the greatest number" does immediately raise the question of what sorts of things are considered to be good for human beings. His is a valuation that raises utility, convenience, and reduced economic expense over other forms of "good."

And this is where we see how complicated the answer has to be: although I agree with Thoreau that not only the body bleeds, and I question Brecht's "erst kommt das Fressen, dann kommt die Moral" (first comes feeding, then comes morality), it is certainly true that without a body one cannot harbor moral thoughts nor bleed either spiritually or physically. Why, then, is physicality so often relegated to the realm of base use when it encompasses and allows so much more? Moreover, the mass-produced electronic texts that are replacing books are—and here the ruse is exposed—still read on something physical, albeit something we hypocritically pretend is transcendent. We are simply trading one type of physicality for another—a physicality lacking in spirit, beauty, or human touch replacing one that has for centuries been a symbol for, and carrier of, the most sacred devotion of human artistry and love. Science may well avail itself of new technologies, and insofar as scholarship is a science, we may use digitized texts to great benefit; but even here we run the risk of losing touch with the magic that drew us to books and images in the first place. We must continually refresh our senses at the stream of the real, and we must remember the great scholars of the past who conducted encyclopedic and profound feats of research without any of the technologies we have come to see as necessary today.

The proponents of new forms of reading often appeal to an ideal of greater accessibility and wider reach—advancing a probably quixotic hope that if texts were more readily available than they currently are, more people would read and more would become informed, active citizens. There are public libraries throughout America, and even though they are underfunded and underappreciated, they are still used by many. Sadly, the great majority of these visitors may be people purchasing on free computers things they don't need rather than borrowing free books filled with immaterial ideas. I fear that the really desperate state of literacy in our modern democratic society today has had something to do with the same forces that were up in arms at the birth of print—forces which had then and have now an interest in repressing the belief that the ideas inhering in the material object of a book have the power to alter and transform the material and spiritual reality of those who read, share, write, and otherwise interact with works held in hand. Ideas can change reality, but only if we believe that they do; and most people, I am afraid, were you to ask them, would say their ideas, thoughts, words, and actions have no effect whatsoever on the physical world around them. What then is the existential significance of disembodying a book? Is this gradual process of dematerialization not similar in intent and ideology to some other attempts over the history of civilization to deny spirit the ballast of its physicality?

In the beginning, all books were grimoires, unapologetically physical objects, consciously created from carefully prepared and selected materials with the express intention of altering and affecting physical reality. For a long time, since many people who owned books could not read them, the physical nature of the books was more important than their linear or literal content. Magic books often contained different languages and "gibberish" mixtures of Hebrew, Chaldean, and hieroglyphics with spirit names, circles, stars, symbols, numeric equations, and magic squares.

Enoch is said to have invented books in the age before the Great Flood; the 'Books of Enoch' filled with astronomical, astrological, and angelic lore were, according to Owen Davies, circulating at the time of Jesus. The legend tells that Enoch's grandson Noah was in possession of astrological tracts like Enoch's, and through these books he communicated with the Angel Raziel. Raziel's transmitted knowledge was "then written on a sapphire that Noah kept in a golden chest that he brought with him in the ark." Inherited by one or both of Noah's sons, Ham and Shem, these books "preserved the arts of magic and idolatry." In the Mesopotamian region, Davies also tells us, cuneiform tablets of clay with magic rituals and incantations have been found dating from the fifth and fourth centuries BCE. Spirit is literally embodied when desires, wishes, and sacred words are inscribed upon clods of clay with the intention of altering the physical world.

The way a book was made from the early Middle Ages and into the Renaissance affirmed the broader essential marriage of matter and spirit. Some thought it a good idea to sew the bindings of a book from something called "Virgin parchment," made from an immature animal, or even "Unborn parchment," made from the amniotic sac of aborted animal fetuses, "to ensure the purity of grimoire or charm." Papyrus was made from the pith of the wetland plants of the Nile Delta. Ink was consecrated by a priest or mixed with particular ingredients such as myrrh, "and blood was sometimes intermingled, as in a dream spell that required the blood of a baboon, the sacred animal of Thoth-Hermes..."

The origin of the book as grimoire has something essential to do with the inversion by which a book today is so often considered a purely spiritual entity whose objecthood is seen as secondary at best, and something to be denied or obviated at worst. Priests and other religious authorities practiced ritual activities—with and without books—involving mixing, manipulating, symbolically arranging, and transforming matter. These activities were intended to ensure physical comfort and safety, earthly gain and bounty, even the physical discomfort and death of enemies. When religious practitioners implored God to hear their pleas and grant a salvation here on earth from the pains and terrors of matter, it was called religion and sanctioned as something holy. When laypeople (peasants, warlocks and witches, healers, mystics, alchemists, and free thinkers) attempted to affect reality by any means other than those strictly prescribed by priests, such actions were called magic and were condemned as devilish and were often, as we know, punishable by death. A particular taboo obtained for any unsupervised action that seemed to combine spiritual with physical things: to worship an object, an image, or even a book in place of a god was called idolatry; to attempt to gain a physical boon was seen as a vulgar use of prayer which, at least in principle, ought rather to have been directed at some less tangible good (such as spiritual peace or humility). Further, to supplicate the gods to provide safety in disasters, to kill one's enemies, to deliver desired bodies into one's bed, or for earthly riches was tantamount to an attempt to usurp the power of God and, by association, the power of God's intercessors.

Magic books often instructed people to carry out ritual actions, which were symbolic and, as such, were themselves forms of image making, or an imitative-metaphor magic, wherein one physical thing or word or image stands for, represents, or relates to another. This mixing of physical and spiritual, while frowned upon for lay practice, runs through formal religious practices. One particularly flagrant instance is the Eucharist, wherein the wafer and the wine are, depending on differing doctrine, either really the body and blood of Christ or merely symbols. Jesus is God made flesh and the world, again, is God's book; Nature is imbued with divine essence. Curiously, a prayer that one's soul might attain heaven was at least in some minds a prayer for physical peace, as the terrors of hell were conceived of as physical and the soul was thought by many to be accompanied in heaven by its own body in its most perfected state—before the onset of old age, before scars, before illness.

Calling the names of the angels inscribed in magical books and asking them for material boons is not as taboo in Judaism as it is in Christianity, yet there seems always to have been some wariness in the Judeo-Christian heritage about using physical objects as mediums of intercession between people and angels or gods in the interest of physical gain. It is probably also no accident that the original sin is eating the fruit of the tree of knowledge of good and evil and that, since the fall, books have most often been made of trees. (What will it mean if they come to be most often made of something else?!) The Genesis story signals an early warning in the long, complex, and passionate history of conflict around the search for knowledge that is now embodied in books. And indeed, the intense history of book-burning and confiscation of books throughout the old world is evidence enough that the book was once thought to be a very powerful and dangerous object. Davies tells us that the early Church burnt Papyrii-magic books, seeing them as threatening the clergy's mission to convert the pagans. Those found with such books were often condemned, imprisoned, burned...

In contemporary times, up until recently, books have generally been believed to be more or less harmless and negligible, hardly capable of inciting or inspiring someone to interact in a revolutionary way with the physical world. They have generally been thought to have as much power as magic is now admitted to have. Instead of seeking them out, burning them, or punishing those who read and possess them, our society had seemed to have learned over centuries that when things, ideas, and people are martyred, they gain more (not less) power, so we had discovered a more subtle method: ignoring, belittling, and trivializing powerful magical forces and diverting attention from them toward things that really are trivial, belittling, and negligible.

The idea that spirit cannot help but change reality is indeed terrifying for some people: those interested in maintaining a *status quo* and a fatalistic sense that there are no alternatives to remaining stuck would, of course, have an interest in suppressing the vital relationship between the book's body, the ideas encased within it, and the world outside. By disingenuously pretending that a book is somehow separate from the physical world, the culture industry had suggested that a book and the ideas in it have no effect on reality or on our lives beyond mere fantasy, frivolity, or escape. Ignoring books may have been much worse than making them the martyred objects of witch hunts and book-burnings. Books are left rotting in damp basements or by the side of the road, and barely a soul has "room" for them in today's crowded life.

Should we be glad, then, that today books are once again considered dangerous enough to attract the attention of a new moral brigade, intent on expunging words, ideas, and images from books and "disrupting texts" in school curricula and removing them from libraries? Today books and words are imparted an almost preternatural agency and are believed by some to be the direct cause of immediate physical harm. While this may seem like a victory for a belief in spirit as an energizing mover of matter, in fact today's censorious prohibitors are descendants of the medieval or Renaissance Church or the censors of ensuing centuries, who had a vested interest in undermining the possibility that the regular folk might harness the occult forces of books and knowledge *to think for themselves*.

Whether society ignores or censors books, we can see a dual process whereby a sense of individual agency and free thinking is undermined by a power intent on conformity and sleepy obedience, a process which marginalizes books and their potential to provide individuals with a means to interact and participate in the creation of their own physical and spiritual (political, social, aesthetic) environment without oversight by the keepers of moral or political correctness. While, in the recent past, people might not have read difficult books because they were too busy being entertained by the bells and whistles of popular sensationalism, or too tired from working, because they were fatally out of touch with the cultural referents or vocabulary, or because they lacked the attention span—excuses which still carry a certain taint of shame—today *not reading* a wider and wider selection of authors is practically a moral imperative, as contemporary citizens "unlearn the evil" and protect themselves from any idea or image or feeling that does not fit with the current program. Reading today—especially if one reads books written in the past—is more likely to be considered counter-revolutionary than a danger to the *status quo.*

Consider our contemporary distrust of reading in comparison with the *Lesewut* of Goethe's time. Roger Chartier writes that this "rage for reading" was considered to be "a danger to the political order... as a narcotic... or as a disordering of the imagination and the senses," and adds: "There is no doubt that it played an essential role in the critical distancing that alienated subjects from their monarchs and Christians from their church throughout Europe and especially in France." Printing was described as a black art in the fifteenth, sixteenth, and seventeenth centuries, and books as "silent heretics," and many people thought that the devil of reformation was behind printing. Indeed, as Davies stresses, the success of the Reformation depended on printing, with Luther as the most published author of the era. Rowland Philips, an English Catholic clergyman, said, "We must root out printing or printing will root out us." Itinerant travelers and foreigners carried "viral texts." A man named Robert Barker was put on trial in England in 1466 for having "a book, and a roll of the black art containing characters, circles, exorcisms, and conjurations; a hexagonal sheet with strange figures; six metal plates with diverse characters, and a golden wand." Typically, these magical items were used for physical gain, to conjure a spirit to direct the possessor to gold and silver; Barker was "sentenced to public penance, walking around the market places of Ely and Cambridge in bare feet and carrying his books and magic paraphernalia, which were subsequently burned in the Cambridge market place." The Pope gave a license to the University of Cologne in 1475 to censor books, printing, and publishers. Lists of prohibited books were on the rise thereafter, to limit "the influence of non-Christian religions." The Spanish Inquisition has a reputation as the "most ruthless persecutor and censor of books," and "[s]ome early historians have depicted it as being so influential that it retarded Spanish intellectual life until the 19th century." But, Davies argues, it was not as successful as historians maintain. Books survived: Jewish texts were hidden in wells and buried in gardens by "conversos" who secretly kept practicing in Spain; Jewish texts were smuggled in from Italy and the Netherlands; and the role of colporteurs or peddlers was crucial to the spread of grimoires because "[i]n their packs they carried knowledge from other places, other worlds." Illiterate people also owned grimoires, because, as Davies writes, "the mere possession of non-diabolical grimoires was thought by some to have a protective function." Eamon Duffey, in *The Stripping of the Altars,* explains that wildly popular reformation primers were often conceived as "channels of secret power independent of the texts they accompanied. The fifteenth century had seen the circulation of devotional woodcuts which the faithful were encouraged to meditate on, to kneel before, to kiss."

Centuries later, colonialist missionaries tried in vain to repress bibliolatry, and to direct the natives' attention to the spirit of the Bible rather than its physical bulk. In *How to Do Things with Books in Victorian Britain,* Price explains that since most natives could not read the Word to begin with, it made a certain sense to them to cut the Bible up into small pieces to be shared among the populace. There were, in effect, two crimes against spirit in regard to books (especially Bibles): Reducing them to matter entirely—as waste paper, toilet tissue, fish-wrappers, pulp—or, at the other extreme, raising them to the level of idols (bibliolatry). And more than Bibles have been worshipped or blasphemed. In 2009, Price notes, a British newspaper reported that elderly parishioners were buying up secondhand books from charity shops because they were cheaper to burn than coal. And Dibdin, whose "bibliomania" went to the extreme of placing ecstatic emphasis on a book's exterior, might indeed be rightly accused of a certain materialist objectification of his possessions. He was known to search out uncut copies of books, whose pages he would not dream of defiling by way of cutting or reading.

From the too too sublime to the too too earthly, we should not be surprised that the natives did not grasp the missionaries' all too subtle and hardly reasonable conceptualization of a physical thing that was intended to inspire only spiritual musings. This dualism reiterates our cultural split and our perverse relationship with matter. Matter is either seen as base because it is bereft of all spirit, concept, and idea, or else somehow base via misplaced idolatry, *i.e.*, fetishism. James Kearney, quoted by Price, notes that Christianity is "a religion of the book that was always made uneasy by the materiality of the text. ... The book became an emblem of the desire to transcend the merely material and irredeemably fallen world of objects." Despite this desire, "[t]o evince a belief in the power of the object was to engage in a fundamental category mistake that separated superstitious and credulous others... from the rational European man."

Where there are taboos, there are powerful forces to repress. The marriage of the physical and the spiritual is just such a dangerous powerful force, and the attempt to dematerialize the book is one of many aimed at suppressing this power. Because magic books were mostly used as means to negotiate an often-terrifying relationship between a soul and a world—a world of wars, plagues, death in childbirth, unexplainable natural forces, and random, often brutal attacks by powerful and unpredictable rulers or marauding invaders—they were from the outset important magical objects in an ongoing attempt to attain some small agency, some small chance at self-actualization amid myriad mysterious powers. Knowledge is power. And the attempt to destroy books is a brutal but clever process of mocking the transcendental materiality of the books, a move to imperil or blot out the individual's right and ability to change his or her reality, to alter the world, to have agency outside of the already restricted policies and methods of the Church and State. The book is inherently anarchistic, but also paradoxically centralizing and essential to a shared cultural conversation.

Really, the first people who would argue that a book's body is not essential to its soul are those who do not want us to believe there is a direct and dynamic relationship between a book and the world, those who would have us prize a book as harmless or even frivolous. Another contingent is comprised of those who rail against authors and their authority and would replace individual expression with a many-voiced throng. A third group of people is made up of those who find themselves in a desperate situation wherein books are threatened by oppressive totalitarian forces (perhaps we are now in such a situation, though of our own making). Such persons will feel the need to exercise a certain bravado in declaring that the most important thing about a book cannot be destroyed, that the spirit of a book lives on even if it is incinerated, banned, or hidden away. It is some comfort to tell ourselves that we might memorize the contents of many books and carry them secretly from country to country and over generations if need were to arise, but it is probably more to the point to note as Heine did most presciently in 1821: "When they have burned books, they will end in burning beings."

Changes in the form of the book and of the technique of writing have moved over centuries in the direction of dematerialization. Books have become smaller and easier to transport and now, finally, virtually without body. The decrease in bulk and in the importance of the physical nature of the book has led to an expanded access, making books more readily available. This change has not occurred, however, without accompanying consequences or powerful ideological causes. In *Book Illumination on the Middle Ages*, Otto Pächt explains that the change from antiquity roll to medieval codex "coincided with a shift in intellectual outlook, in the values attached to experience of the physical world," leading, in extreme cases, to iconoclasm in the Eastern Mediterranean, and "a positive hostility to figurative art in the West," where there "was a growing inclination to regard external reality as a transient metaphor for the true, primary, and invisible transcendental world. A distinction began to be made between outward and inward looking."

When I first started studying art history, I was confounded by the way medieval artists seemed to have never seen the naturalistic works of the Greeks and Romans. Depictions of human bodies were suddenly flat, crude, and un-sensuous, but how had this transformation occurred? Surely not because of a decline in ability, but rather because of a radical shift in ideology. The medieval artist, as Pächt explains, looked at the physical world—if he did not look at it as a dangerous illusion—mainly as a symbol of some higher idea: thus it was not only no longer necessary, but more or less frowned upon, to paint a body in all its glory. And yet the works of medieval art (especially in the realm of book illumination) are teeming with beauty, with vines and flowers and insects rendered joyously from nature, wound about and buzzing about symbolic patterns colored by inks and paints ground from pigments found in plants and minerals. The beauty of the natural world could not be repressed. It grew from the cracks left around the margins, irrepressibly erupting.

William Blake—perhaps the consummate artist of the book—later consciously combined the abstract with the physical, celebrating the nakedness of woman and the imagination which can move from two-fold to four-fold vision, transcending from the physical to the spiritual and back on a line of ink. As Kathryn Barush explains in *Every Age is a Canterbury Pilgrimage,*[1] Blake did not try to "outdo God's creation by undertaking mimetic expression." He "felt no need to over-articulate his images—an outline here, a wash of color there to indicate water,

[1] Barush's 2011 dissertation at Oxford University has been published by Ashgate Press as *Art and the Sacred Journey in Britain,* 1790-1850.

or The Vine of Life, or a tombstone was enough to leave the images open for interpretation." Barush, whose study of pilgrimage traces the anagogic relationship between real pilgrimage and visual depictions of the spiritual journey, notes that Reformation critics of pilgrimage often saw it "as an essentially earthly journey to a material shrine (or, at worst, idol)." Blake, who did not see the distinction between earthly and divine in the same way, saw his books, writes Barush, as sites of pilgrimage wherein "an immediate dialogue was created between the outward form and what was contained within." To trace the edges of his lines was "akin to a pilgrimage through the networks and streets and architectures of the imagination." To journey from physical to spiritual, the viewer requires a line etched by hand in metal and one drawn in the imagination.

But not all artists and thinkers were as adept as Blake in tracing the liminal space between spirit and matter. A common morality, already powerfully present in Blake's time, came to distinguish censoriously between those who cared for a book's spiritual qualities (its content) and those more concerned with its physicality (its binding), as if it were in all cases possible to delineate a dualist split between lovers of the surface and lovers of the depths, as if the surface did not correspond to the depths. As Price writes: "Cover and content, authenticity and experience: the language of insides and outsides makes any consciousness of the book's material qualities signify moral shallowness. ... Not content to ignore the outsides of books, a good reader actively scorns them." To judge "by the cover of a book" has even proverbially come to be something wise people are supposed to avoid; we are instructed to be concerned with higher things, with inner beauty, with morality, with anything but the sensory experience of people, of our environment, of books and other objects, as if we were still living in a world where the pleasures of the flesh were thought of as dangerous and sinful delusions muddying our vision and inhibiting us from seeing an immaterial higher beauty. A contemporary morality has taken over where Platonism and Christianity left off, leaving us still suspicious of the physical when it comes to the realm of humanistic activity (love, reading, art), but somehow, we are still (or even more) earthbound. And art, reading, and love (all activities that are both material and spiritual) may be endangered species in a world where material possession and accumulation vie with virtual pleasures for our attention and devotion. Here as elsewhere, the separation of spirit and matter spells hollowness.

Heirs to a centuries-old taboo against inhering spirit in matter (idolatry, fetishism, or the scandal of uniting romantic and sexual love), we carry unexamined fixed ideas along with us—ideas which, while simulating freedom from the burden of the physical and promising infinite choice and immediate access to everything we could want, instead work to undermine the magical and necessary intercourse between world and word, body and soul, individual and social system, book and binding. I challenge the idea that books are merely transmitters of ideas or non-physical abstractions (or, more damaging still, information, data) and that they thus could be replaced by machines which can process or hold an infinite number of words without altering their effects—as if paper, skin, hides, parchment, bark, leaves, ink, pigment, blood, hands, oils, mortars and pestles, inscribing, carving, and burning were not in themselves essential processes of transmission, vivification, regeneration of the Word and its in-spired Breath. The spirit of an idea is like a match that is only lit when the hand inscribes it into material substance, willing it to alter physical as well as spiritual reality—believing in it, in other words, and manifesting its reality by literally going through the ritual motions of writing, engraving, embedding, making. The little match girl's flame, alas, had nothing to catch on but itself, and went out far too soon.

The machine—its plasticity, its anonymity, its practical purpose as proliferator of consumable reproductions or simulations—in contrast to the papery substance of a book, destroys the magical aura of the ritual object (a work of art and a work of mind) that is the book. The machine reduces the alchemical transmission of ideas, poetry, essence, atmosphere, voice, artistry, individuality, time, space, margin, attention, and concentration to a material and economic exchange of data commodity.

The printing press was, indeed, a form of mechanical reproduction, and one decried by some. A.W. Schlegel's lecture, 'Critique of Enlightenment' (ca.1801), counts printing as one of the crimes of the Reformation, though not for the same reasons expostulated by the Catholic church. Oral rhapsodization, he writes, "arouses an entirely different suspense and attention than lonely unsocial reading. But the printing of books itself has stolen to a great extent the magic of writing. Because of the difficulty of attaining books, a single one was already a precious possession that was passed down from generation to generation: it was a romantic poverty." In brackets, Schlegel here has inserted a reminder to himself to discuss the "custom of keeping books chained," another evidence of the way books were once esteemed as precious and even worthy of stealing. "Now," Schlegel continues,

> due to the ease of ownership people have become so casual about owning the most excellent book, that they mostly read it without any devotion, but rather for thoughtless distraction. In contrast, the desire for a book in those days had grown so great that one could barely stand to be bereft of one, and one had to attain one through a transcription, and princes would send messengers to this end back and forth.

Further, Schlegel laments the general influence of the Enlightenment on Poesie, an influence that can be felt today in arguments for the practicality of virtual transmission: "The exclusive orientation toward the useful, when taken to its conclusion, must really mean a farewell to Poesie."

The cheapening of the book trade and the subsequent slippage from physical to virtual books would certainly have disturbed Schlegel even more. The printing press is a machine which has taken us further away from oral transmission and the community that such rhapsodizing encouraged, and then again away from the idiosyncratic beauty and uniqueness of hand-illuminated manuscripts, but the increasing commodification and homogenization of texts has taken us far further than he could have imagined. As we move toward increasing the utility, convenience, and immediate accessibility of books, we lose a great deal of what makes them magical.

The printing press is a machine, yet one that creates weighty objects that can be held and carried—objects featuring gilded and embossed bindings, decorative endpapers, and fans of curling textured paper made from natural materials. When printed on a letterpress, the text on those pages is literally pressed into the paper with an imprint that can be felt with one's fingertips. Some people compare those who regret the shift from hand-illuminated books to printed books with those who decry today's dematerialization of books, poo-pooing the latter's concerns as nostalgia and resistance to change—but to pretend that the transformation occurring today is strictly analogous would be facile. Printing also diminishes the personal and sensuous nature of the book, rendering the letters uniform and the pages more and more smooth and devoid of texture, but today's technological reproduction is even more dematerialized, still colder, merely virtual. Such transmission of ideas may empty even the most revolutionary gesture of its magic in three important ways: by removing the essential physical element of the experience; by turning it into a soundbite, a simulation, a momentary fragment; and by diminishing through technology's pervasive presence in our lives the ability of the viewer, observer, or reader to concentrate, appreciate, and experience whatever is being shared. The reception of these reduced and reassembled reproductions makes them something different than what they were, while providing the illusion that one is really experiencing the work or the image. People think they know or understand a painting viewed or a poem read on a machine amid myriad interruptions and distractions; but such experiences may be worse than nothing, like a fake rose without a scent. No wonder young people turn away from literature and art to other pleasures; the subtle aroma, the rose's very essence, is no longer present, and a rose is no longer a rose at all.

After my grandparents died, I was surprised to discover two elaborately decorated tallit bags (pouches used to hold the ritual items of orthodox practice), embroidered with the initials of my grandfather and his father, tucked away behind rows of papers and photo albums in their house. My grandfather was a completely secular Jew who, outliving the Holocaust, arrived in the United States with little more than a small suitcase, his wife, and their little daughter—my mother. He must have packed and preserved those tallit bags throughout their hiding, their numerous moves, while so many other objects had gone missing, things which might have been, on the surface, more useful to his life as a doctor, a lover of music, and a new immigrant struggling to learn English and support his family in New York City. Why did a man as practical as he, a man who had little time or sympathy for dreaming or mysticism, keep these physical symbols of his Jewishness even when they might have been the cause of discovery and death for himself and his family? Why were mere ideas not enough to preserve some sense of a heritage to which he was still connected and a religion he had largely rejected? Perhaps these bags were for him like the Ark of the Covenant for the wandering Jews, a physical embodiment of home where there was no central stable place.

Régis Debray, in his essay 'The Book as Symbolic Object', explains that Greek culture had sacred places, if not books; Jewish culture had only its sacred book, "always kept under the mantle, as the substitute for an absent place." The Ark of the Covenant was a "portable covered conveyance often represented as a miniature temple of Solomon. The book is... the mobile center of the exile's or nomad's existence. ... Our hearth and home, we who have none, is the book of books, the codex-ical Gospel, patria of expatriates. ... It is stable, tangible, indubitable." The original codex, large, architectonic, hand-bound, with clasps, served as "a pledge of legitimacy and permanence, a shelter against the flight of time, degeneration, death...."

Today, when fluidity and decentralization are the catchwords of utopia, the bodiless, placeless book may be a perfect test case in the problems inherent in a total embrace of a decentralized, rhizomatic, fragmented, multivocal, infinite network. Chartier writes of the dream of a universal library and notes that the burned library of Alexandria was "an exemplary and mythic figure of this nostalgia for lost exhaustiveness." Referring to our current capabilities, Chartier notes that a library without walls creates "immeasurable possibilities," but also does "violence to the texts by separating them from the original physical forms in which they appeared and which helped to constitute their historical significance." The dream of democratization of knowledge has been pursued in parallel to that of a library without walls, and we can trace the technological means by which this open access has been approached over centuries. The first stage of democratization, as noted by Vico, may have been the invention of an alphabet. A hundred and twenty thousand hieroglyphic characters, difficult to master, were replaced by a few letters, as Chartier notes. Vico denigrates the Greek alphabet as "vulgar letters," because those letters "break the priestly and aristocratic monopoly over images and signs," emancipating "knowledge from the all-powerful hold of divine reason or an absolute state authority." Much later, Martin Luther expanded the readership of the Bible by translating it into the vulgate (which then was repeated in other languages as well), and Gutenberg expanded readership still further through the popularization of printing. In America, the public education system continues to be an open experiment in expanded cultural literacy and informed citizenry; advocates of new technologies hawk their programs to schools as cure-alls for the troubled student whose primary problem may well be the pervasive presence of technology in our society.

The history of writing and the book (from orality to writing, from hieroglyph to alphabet, from roll to codex, from handwritten manuscript to printed book, from authored work to anonymous text, from anonymous text to multi-authored screen) seems to have been in the interest of a gradual and steady democratization of knowledge and voice, yet there are many questions still to be answered about the extent to which these new methods of communication have really worked to liberate humanity or to increase the agency of individuals. One important question is about the value of universal access to an infinite amount of information. Might not such easy access be fundamentally at odds with an actual deep engagement in selected and specific knowledge? Both the printing press and the virtual book involve a wide proliferation of texts, and thus seem to serve the cause of the democratization of knowledge—but, significantly, these developments have garnered different enemies. The people up in arms about the printing press were explicitly concerned with stopping the spread of the word and the implied decentralization of power; critics today who lament the demise of the physical book have nothing against spreading culture or knowledge, but are concerned about how the loss will work toward destroying whatever culture we have left. We fear that, instead of spreading knowledge, the virtual text spreads information and data as commodities while divorcing a work from its context and its place in history and space. And, though it may be true that some proponents of new media are in favor of authorless or multi-authored texts, and that those protecting the sanctity of the physical book have a vested interest in defending the role of the author, any attempt to attribute anti-populist tendencies to the defenders of authorship is a gross simplification of the problem. The real question is, are we more or less empowered or disempowered by fragmentation and dispersal? Electronic media can provide the illusion of an infinite number of choices; in reality, there is no need to make a choice at all as the possibilities proliferate, unbounded. We must (to make art, to act ethically) choose, reject, favor, select out, discriminate, say yes to one thought and no to another—for at some point (which we have probably already reached), to welcome all is to welcome nothing, and to have all is to have nothing at all.

We now have access to almost any piece of writing or any image at a moment's notice, but the "work" has been reduced to "text," just as Roland Barthes had hopefully predicted in his famous essay 'From Work to Text', in what now looks like an excess of revolutionary zeal; the reverberating image has become an often all-too-shabby reproduction. A two-pronged and antithetical force is driving technological reproduction: on the one hand, the corporate technocratic progress-mongers who are always ready to sell us some new "necessary" commodity; on the extreme other, the radical theorists—such as Derrida, Foucault, de Certeau, Benjamin, or Barthes—have, in an attempt to revolutionize society, worked in the past century to divest art and culture of their position as magical experiences. How is it that two such antithetical motives arrive at the same end? Perhaps certain strains of contemporary thought harbor an inherent nihilism that aims to overturn the language and culture of the Enlightenment "oppressors," even if that means dispensing with cultural discourse altogether. As Carlo Ginzburg writes in his introduction to *The Cheese and the Worms*, while discussing Foucault's "archeology of silence," this strain of thought may be more interested in the "act and criteria of the exclusion" by rational scientific discourse of the non-literate, than in giving the excluded a voice or in empowering the excluded to be author of their own story. Rather than embolden new authors, the deconstructionists would de-author. The author, who uses the language of an oppressive heritage, himself becomes an author-ity figure to be overthrown. Thus, we should not be surprised that rebellious thinkers have often rallied to replace the individual authority with a multi-voiced throng of ever-changing authors. The fallacy here is the idea that writers of what Roland Barthes calls "Works," as opposed to those who now write "Texts," have presented a homogenous party line that asserts absolute and eternal truths.

In 'From Work to Text', Barthes makes a glaringly simplistic differentiation between what he sees as the mono-voiced authority of the static Work of the past and the multi-voiced *jouissance* of the Text of the near future (now upon us), forgetting that a mob can just as easily speak in one oppressive voice as can an individual. Anyone who loves and knows literature will have trouble recognizing beloved books in Barthes's description of a "work" as static, monistic, Newtonian. Ignoring Shakespeare's celebrated irreducibility, what Keats termed "negative capability," Barthes writes, "[t]he work has nothing disturbing for any monistic philosophy. ... [F]or such a philosophy, plural is Evil. ... The plural of demoniacal texture which opposes text to work can bring with it fundamental changes in reading... diffraction of meanings..." Barely hidden in Barthes' critique of the text is a suspicion of the material: "the work can be seen (in bookshops, in catalogues, in exam syllabuses)... the work can be held in the hand, the text is held in language, only exists in the movement of discourse."

Vilifying the process of making worlds through writing not only calls into question the power of Enlightenment élites, but simultaneously robs any individual dreamer, utopian, reformer, or renegade of the possibility of creating alternative worlds, thereby disempowering personal agency and existential action and leaving so-called reality a stubborn and static master. Let she who can seize power, seize pen, seize voice, and speak for the liberation of us all. The repression of voice comes from two sides, one which wants people to be passive and the other which laments our powerlessness but does not want to use the tools of the "oppressors" and so languishes in victimhood. People do express themselves every day via electronic platforms, yet the medium—favoring as it does the fluid, authorless infinity of voices—reduces such expression to a fatally compromised and muffled message. Although some platforms are certainly more bounded than others, the "user" (compare "user" with "reader" and worlds of difference are revealed), can always easily abandon any site for another with casual ease.

To cry out at every change (innovation, revolution, devolution) in social practices would indeed be reactionary, but we must recognize that these changes proceed in tandem with ideological principles (either as impetus or result) which fundamentally alter our relationship with, in this case, knowledge, culture, agency, and authorship. Many today would like to insist that new forms of reading do not significantly alter the essence or content of what is read or threaten the existence of traditional forms. Benjamin, in his paradoxical essay celebrating the revolutionary changes in what a work of art was in the "age of mechanical reproduction," exposes the fallacy of this assurance. Instead of pretending that the medium does not alter the message, his entire essay is a celebration of the way in which the new abilities of technological reproduction *will* destroy—in violent cataclysm—the ritual and cult value of art. "Every day," he writes,

> the urge grows stronger to get hold of an object at very close range by way of its likeness, its reproduction. ... To pry an object from its shell, to destroy its aura, is the mark of a perception whose 'sense of the universal equality of things' has increased to such a degree that it extracts it even from a unique object by means of reproduction.

The dematerialization of the art object in its original state is a function of equalizing and ultimately destroying what made it valuable in the first place. Benjamin made a devil's bargain in a moment of extreme historical crisis, giving up what he knew to be essential to art in the fight against totalitarianism. What is especially tragic about this deal is that the overcoming of distance, the destruction of the ability to concentrate, and the lure of the simulacrum were all already being used at the time of his writing by totalitarian regimes to increase surveillance, create a sense of being everywhere at once, to proliferate treacherous mythic images, to simulate meaning, and to dazzle (shock and awe). The bargain presupposed that the destruction of the aura would really bring liberation. Instead, where there had been sacredness, ritual, and the humanistic communication of values, the technocracy has all too often replaced real meaning with its simulacrum, not improving art with an engaged politics, but vitiating it with advertising and, even more treacherously, with totalitarian or at least tendentiously ideological propaganda. In most ways, the destruction of the aura has brought superficial simulated consumerism, a void of values and meaning where any ad man can slip in and provide a sense of meaning.

My defense of the book as sacred object is connected to a defense of author—questioning the *idée reçu* that associates the literate individualized voice with the stuffy oppressors and forces of the *status quo*, and the robust collective voice of the relatively illiterate with all sorts of good things like freedom, collaboration, and an end to hierarchical thinking. The voice of the individual author has, in countless examples to the contrary, been raised on the side of liberation and humanism, and one might even dare to state that all good writing, all great "works" of literature, are, contrary to Barthes' critique, open-ended, participatory, dialogic, alive. And this living voice can be best proliferated by the continual making of books.

While I would not go so far as to advocate returning to the days before printing, I do see some salutary benefit in a renaissance of alternative individual book production. As a response to the current glut of technology, people may be returning to the physical, even handmade book for a radically individual and non-mediated means of communication. The proliferation of the physical handmade book is unhindered by secular or religious dogma, free of publishers' marketing concerns, free of the need to please the public or society. Anyone may make a handmade book and give it away right now, without using any electronic technology at all—or may make a small edition on a hand-powered letterpress. Of course, without the help of printing of some kind, one would have to transcribe the book by hand to give out more than one—or the recipient would have to—but the act of inscribing and re-inscribing only multiplies the magical potential of the offering. Blake, as is well known, hand-etched all of his plates (backwards!)

and then hand-colored the prints. He might have made more copies by resorting to a different method, but they would have been entirely different books. Now we must actively work to re-connect, re-animate, re-inspire the magical relation between matter and spirit through processes that will seem merely superstitious to those unable to see their significance. We must consciously enact rituals that consummate imaginary desires with real manifestations, with paper, folding, pressing; we must embody performances that bind words to pages, we must burn and carve inscriptions into wood and leather, stitch prayers and incantations into silk and skin, weave enchantments out of hair, willow branches, spun wool. We must build guerrilla libraries in the streets, re-purpose telephone booths as public book stalls, proliferate broadsides, burn spells into fallen leaves, and scatter them in the porticos of office buildings. We must laboriously trace the lineaments of Celtic knots and Arabian mosaics, illuminating impossibly large pages with the smallest of quills. We must believe in the magic of books.

What is a book? A record, a new thing, a reflection, its own shining, a synthesis of all that there already was or is into something never before in existence? A book, as a novel arrangement of ideas and images in new proportions, needs to exist in space and to take its place next to all the already existent objects of the world—not erased or deleted, but firmly present in weight and dimension, density, thickness, and height. In-scription, in-spiration. What is spiritual in a book must interact with the physical, with carving, with breath; it must push up against what already is, against a resistance of the real. Lacking weight, a book lacks substance, lacks power, heft, lacks reality. If imagination is to gain credence, have purchase over *status quo,* it must be given body in art, in the author-ity of the book bound with intention and care. A book exists in the in-between liminal realm between that which already is and that which is mere fancy or thought. It is not frozen or fixed like reality as a given event, choice, object, or mode of life, but is still freely intermediary as possibility, as embodied experiment, as offering... as one book among many, next to other books, a midrash, conversation, over ages, timelessly present.

What is a book? A considered arrangement of words and ideas and images, a statement or explanation of passionate concerns, it is bound on both sides, necessitating some choice, closure, provisional decision and selecting out. It is not the whole world, though it may offer itself as microcosm, as metaphor or metonym for the whole. It is a contribution to the larger cosmos, one voice in a choir. It is observer and witness and also evidence and artifact; it is a record of what happened and of what did not, of what is and what could be, a polemic, an elegy, a wish and a regret. What is a book? A moment and a time traveler, a reflection of the present and a conversation reaching backward over time and forward into the future, speaking with the long dead and booming forth so that the now living can speak with those who have not yet been born.

There are particular volumes we love, the *Vie de Bohême,* passed around and signed; as each person reads it, he or she becomes a member of the Bohemian club: the favorite foxed Keats, the Hafiz with the golden marbleized silk, the crimson leather *Looking Glass,* purchased in Bath. And together they make up a rainbow, their variegated spines lining the walls, the cocoons of our studies that are like another layer of mind around our skulls, where the ideas and fancies can circulate, where we might even open up a volume to refresh our memories as we reach into the repositories of the mind itself when grasping after a word, a passage, a line that haunts us. We may find a pressed flower, a lover's beribboned lock, a note slipped in by former readers or by unknown friends who stopped some afternoon, like us, upon a special passage in the same book, and reflected on its import as the rain poured down outside, or sun, or hail, or cannon fire. A book may have travelled far in time and space, and seen many things it does not tell straight out, though tell it might were we to read between its lines and trace the signs on spine and endpapers, in foxings, spills, folds, inset slips of paper or leaves, annotations and marginalia, and other tokens of lives once lived. Conversations with the ages, and curious bookmarks from bookstores long gone under...

The smell of a book, said my friend Stephen Callahan, is like the smell of a woman; one loves it if one loves the woman. And, I add, whosoever does not love the smell of women and men and books, well... for them there is no help.

There are the books put away in annexes because they were for special tastes only, yet when the exotic seeker finds them he feels himself as lucky as any treasure hunter, though decades had gone by before anyone dreamed of wanting them. There are books tied up with string, brittle leather covers crumbling, pages falling out like loose teeth and the thin white hair of sages, still whispering wisdom, but so low we must lean in close to hear, before they turn entirely to dust and the secrets are lost forever.

To see the collected libraries of beloved long-dead authors, the books they read and gazed at from their chairs, thumbed and pored over, perused and fell asleep beside, read from to a lover or a daughter, fervently sighed or fulminated over... to touch the passages where they were first discovered, in original margins and on the page—atop, below, betwixt one page and the next—can mean so much... what word is underlined, what drop of sweat atop what page, what well-worn even dog-eared much returned-to creased passage? Will there even be libraries like these in the future, or will the writers and readers of tomorrow leave no trace at all of their obsessions, their particular passions, their guilty pleasures, of the concatenation of strange taste next to more catholic, of ancient next to contemporary, of scientific next to fantastical, of poetical alongside logical treatise... no trace at all of what, if anything, they cared about enough to own, to arrange, to carry, to move in heavy boxes from house to house, nor what of all the wit and wisdom of the world was granted a place in the limited space of their mortal bookshelves?

A book will show its age and the age of what was written in it. Its binding faded and pages foxed and worn, its weathered pages tell a history—whether, say, it survived a fire, or was salvaged, water-logged, from a flood, swollen and heroic, its pages like the waves themselves, no virgin parchments more, but experienced travelers, a testament to salty, briny life, and death and grit. It carries more than just its content, its body itself is encrusted with life, with barnacles and breath, signs of contact with the past and signs to carry into the future, as messages of what we loved and of what we thought and dreamed.

A book has a place of origin, a home and history, bound in the materials of its birthplace, of Spanish leather or Chinese silk, in Irish linen or American flax, in Japanese rice paper, or Indian hemp, its type and design teeming with tell-tale signs, its orthography shifting from decade to decade, with emphasis in black letter or in sans-serif, hand-colored or with gilded spine, embossed and crammed with delicate serigraph portraits and etched maps and charts that fold out and expand the very world.

It has a place and time of death; when the spine is so cracked it falls away from itself and reveals the interior organs of the book, what sort of old papers were used to glue on the spine, and what type of string used to stitch. When the book begins to die we see how it was born, and marvel at the sturdy but delicate art that bound the separate fascicles, and married the cover boards to the rest, with marbleized or silken end papers. We see its hopeful beginning, as it was christened with colophon and edition, and sent out into the world; and though its title might be barely visible, rubbed off by many loving fingers, and its leaves are close to crumbling, perused over centuries by our fellows, we can take it one more time up to our noses and inhale its smell of life and moldering decay, and in this bouquet we recognize our own fate, and listen carefully to the whisperings of this old sage, as the pages crumble in our hands. There is always that last moment when we know that to turn the page may be to consign it to oblivion; yet we hope that it may speak to us one last time, so we dare, and touch, and hasten thereby the inevitable force of time. But, oh, my mortal friends, this is life. And a well-made book, although it comes to crumble and fall to dust, lasts much longer than most of us.

III.

Re-Materialization, Remoteness, and Reverence

ON JANUARY 2, 1967, in the city of love, beauty, art, and sensuality, four provocateurs, named Buron, Masset, Parmentier, and Toroni, declared that "[i]nasmuch as to paint is a function of aestheticism, flowers, women, eroticism, the daily environment, art, dada, psychoanalysis, the war in Vietnam, WE ARE NOT PAINTERS." The next day, they withdrew from the Paris Salon because, among other reasons, "[p]ainting is by nature objectively reactionary."

Surely everyone has heard by now, fifty years later, that "painting is dead." Even a curator in a small gallery in the largest city in rural Vermont was in the know enough in 2010 to inform a group of visiting college students that "a paintbrush is just a stick with dead hairs on it," saving them just in time from imminent embarrassment; a few slipped out to their studios during lunch and discarded the evidence of their naiveté, and became—ta da!—up-to-date, sophisticated, and post-postmodern, no longer weighed down by the physical trappings of artistry, nor its technical travails—but possibly also not bothering to stop to ask questions about the origins of this rejection of aestheticism, flowers, women, environment, art, &c., or the uncategorical embrace of the abstract disembodied conceptualism that took its place.

Running the risk, therefore, of being accused of provincialism, conservatism, or—worse still—some lack of hipness, I suggest we ask some questions about the dangers and delights of de-materialization, and trace some historical parallels to its ideological trappings. While I find myself arguing for a creative union between concepts and materiality in art, I am also aware that another less tangible criterion lies beneath my call for re-materialization, one that looks for a sense of ritual in art, a reverence and a sense of wonder in response to the beauty and the horror of the material and spiritual world. This would be an art, conceptual or material, that engages in an earnest exploration of meaning and is an attempt at translation, transmission, communication from one human being to another, an art that is activated by—to use an old-fashioned and certainly sentimental word—love. While on the surface, the presence or absence of love in a work of art might seem wholly unrelated to the proportion of corporeality and conceptuality contained in it, I imagine that materiality matters just as much to art as it matters in romantic relationships; that is, it matters quite a bit, although it is not everything. And while it is best not to put the love object up on a pedestal—better, usually, to see the beloved as an active subject rather than an object—when it comes to the art object, a pedestal might actually serve a functionally significant purpose: as margin, as separation from the world of chaotic everything, as ritual entry point or magic portal into another kind of experience.

An artist friend of mine, who weaves and paints and sews and creates embodied performance pieces—but who is also a fine analytical and conceptual thinker and writer—has a reminder pinned up on the wall of her art studio announcing "The Failure of the Object." While I think I understand her desire to curb or hone her aesthetic practice with the edge of thought, it makes me wonder what the object's failed mission allegedly was. Having read postmodern critiques of Modernism's belief in "aesthetic redemption," I assume the object was being accused of naively attempting—and failing—to redeem the world, right the wrongs, educate and challenge suffering and blind humanity, which may also be a veiled accusation against the art object's more serious crime: attempting to be beautiful. Since all of the great art of the preceding centuries had not managed to definitively remove misery from the world or make us unerringly compassionate or equally beautiful, a new art movement was born, and blossomed for about six years in the late 1960s, aiming to succeed where the pathetic useless object (the painting, the sculpture, the tapestry) had not. If not aesthetic redemption, it might, at best, have been aiming at moral or social reform—or else, at worst, a cynical and ironic hopelessness. Lucy Lippard, in her epoch-making collocation, *6 Years: The Dematerialization of the Art Object, &c...*, explained that this new movement aimed to both "de-materialize and de-mythologize" art, and that its works often consisted of little more than documentary evidence of ephemeral happenings, lists of words, instructions for the viewer or participant, or, as in the case of one artist by the name of Keith Arnatt, a musing on the question: "Is it Possible for Me to Do Nothing as My Contribution to This Exhibition?"

In a quoted excerpt by Lippard and John Chandler from 'The Dematerialization of Art', originally published in *Art International* in 1968, we read: "During the 1960s the anti-intellectual emotional intuitive processes of art-making characteristic of the last two decades have begun to give way to an ultra-conceptual art that emphasizes the thinking process almost exclusively... a number of artists are losing interest in the physical evolution of the work of art... provoking a profound dematerialization of art, especially of art as object, and if it continues to prevail, it may result in the object's becoming wholly obsolete." In a letter to Lippard and Chandler in response to this article, the Art Language Group of Coventry concurred, saying that in the art of the period, "the idea is 'read about' rather than 'looked at'," and suggesting that "art should produce a material entity only as a necessary by-product of the need to record the idea." While we might view all works of art as records of the artist's thinking and feeling process, traceable through the marks or the imprints of the hands or tools used, or—in the case of a manuscript—through the palimpsest of marginalia, erasure, and crossing-out, I suspect that the Art Language group meant this in a less physical way, allowing only the intellectual "by-products" (a term not by accident taken from the realm of industry) to remain as the detritus of the art event. This was a radical change of aspect for art, but one in a line of evolution from the Platonic rationalist fear of art's pharmacological powers, to the Hegelian attempt to turn art into philosophy or the Benjaminian prophecy that art would become politics. De-materialization was a distant echo of these earlier incursions on the aesthetic, and in many ways its aims and problems are similar.

Certainly, there are benighted people who still paint, and commercial galleries that serve them, but the truly sophisticated scoff or snigger up their sleeves at such reactionary sentimentalism, at such unscrupulous pandering to the bourgeois market. The sophisticates can wryly sniff at those uneducated hicks who claim that they "don't get conceptual art"—but there are some legitimate, pressing, and not wholly naïve questions raised by the rejection of—or alleged failure of—the art object. Of course—let me just get this out of the way—all art is at least in some measure conceptual, and even so-called conceptual art cannot escape from some materiality or aesthetic character, even if that character is emphatically anti-aesthetic in nature. Let us not forget that all words were once names for objects, or metaphors. The more we remember this, the more our words will bear weight and carry us through space. (My colleague Eric Berlin reminds me that the word for metaphor in Latin means "to move," "to transfer," and that there are moving vans in Italy with "metafora" written on their sides.) So, words too are born of our relationship with the material world and, however they may lift us up into the realms of imagination, they also—at best—bring us back down to earth. Thus, it is not helpful to pit conceptual against aesthetic, or abstract against mimetic, spiritual against material, though we may make general assessments on where a work's or an epoch's tendencies lie.

As discussed in relation to the question of the materiality of the book, anyone who has looked at Medieval art after looking a long time at Greek or Roman art will wonder what happened to the naturalistic facility of the sculptors and painters. Did the Medieval world wake up one morning with a concussion and forget how to depict curves in space and detailed individuality in portraiture? Of course, the flattening of the medieval picture and sculpture is not a result of a loss of skill, but a result of an historical and ideological change of emphasis from the externally beautiful and naturalistic to the internal and symbolic, or conceptual, image. That being said, Medieval art never utterly abandoned the sinful pleasures of the sensory world, and corporeality and objecthood were very much at the heart of Christian worship. Art created in an era ruled by Catholicism was aesthetic, but in a different way than that of a humanistic (though still largely religious) era like the Renaissance, while Protestantism's iconoclasm was clearly veering toward the intellectual and the anesthetic. Blake's eighteenth-century rejection of positivist realism and "Newton's curse" in favor of "fourfold vision" is more easily aligned with the conceptual powers of imagination, yet Blake was one of the first heretics to note and to celebrate the fact that the nakedness of woman is the creation of God. Abstract expressionism may be a return to a disinterested art for art's sake, but de-materialization is a cycling back to a certain kind of iconoclastic protest against matter (and author-ity?).

Though people may argue that conceptual de-materialism often avails itself of physicality, especially, say, in performance art or the contemporary movement sometimes called "social practices," there is an important distinction to be made. With the refreshing exception of a certain craft-based, often feminist, conceptual formalism whose very existence is evidence that conceptuality need not engage in a rejection of the body or its hand-made products, the physicality of many conceptual works is often indistinguishable from the objects or movements and arrangements of everyday life. What it looks like is usually less important than what it imparts; or its appearance is consciously casual or inartistic. Further, certain types of conceptual art do feature objects, but often (though not always) this objecthood is consciously ironic, made of plastic or other impermeable materials. Plastic effectively seals itself off from any possible in-spiration of matter by breath, limits the traces left on its surface, the marks of human hands, sweat, scratches, and accidents, diverting participation or interaction by the human maker, and resisting the markings made upon more permeable materials by time or other natural elements. Conceptual art often references popular culture icons and generally is either simply a joke or a critique of materiality. Whether this deconstructing tendency to make everything a joke is inherent in conceptuality, or whether we are dealing with a case of two separate elements keeping common cause, is not entirely clear to me: some conceptual art is serious and reverential in nature. But I do suspect that a rejection of materiality is sometimes intrinsic to a general tendency toward irony, or a tendency to look away from the abyss of reality in all its fearsome beauty, danger, disorderliness, and delight. Body-based performance art might be an important exception, as it often deals directly with the challenges and pleasures of embodiment. But it is as ephemeral as the duration of the performance itself, and usually only leaves disembodied traces of its presence.

Conceptual de-materialization and contemporary social practices (both more idealistic movements than plastic pop-art deconstruction), often favor creation by a group over that of an individual artist, or, better yet, accidents of randomness (acts of nature, social repercussions) over deliberate choice or artistry. Sometimes the work is a kind of social experiment, with some minor controls established wherein life can play its irrepressible part. Lippard's book itself is an object lesson in collaborative creation, as it is mostly a collection or collage of fragments written by many voices, wherefrom echoes, contradictions, and themes emerge naturally.

These dematerializing practices are born of a democratic impulse, to be sure, and one in harmony with the tendency of conceptual art to overcome the traditional distance between the viewer and the work of art, and the reverence toward the work of art that went along with that remoteness. This tendency aimed to dissolve the separation between art and reality, choice and randomness, individual artistry and communal cacophony or accidental harmony. While many contemporary artists—

taking off from Benjamin's celebration of the death of the aura and the subsequent destruction of distance and concentration—seem to feel that this confluence of art and life is a positive development, an end to the elite specialization of art, and a democratization of the art experience, I wonder how much the removal of ritual and remoteness has instead contributed to a general debasement of both art and life.

For the experience of encountering objects consciously, with respect to their formal characteristics as well as their complex provenance and their relative role in social life, is not an experience of escapism to be overcome or corrected by moral strictures. Indeed, the sacralized experience of art teaches us about *ethics* in a supremely special way, as the separated realm of shapes, sounds, contrasts, and dynamics, themselves reverberations or abstractions of the very real nature of the world, can perhaps only begin to be comprehended from a distance, as an aesthetic experience. To denude this artistic experience of complexity, distance, sacredness—making it more like dull, pedestrian, habitually unconscious life—is to reduce the world to a black-and-white didacticism. Art, at its best, is a relief from such tired, reductive simplification—and it functions from a distance that enables us to see the larger outlines, the eldritch shape of things as both particular and universal. Art paradoxically allows us to gaze upon the flaming, frightening, thrilling abysm of the real, without being blinded. And its special relationship with materiality, the fact that artworks are so often made of perishable substances, helps us to bear what is otherwise unbearable—inevitable decay, certain tragedy and mortality.

A more meaningful task than polarizing and categorizing types of art, thus, would be to trace some fruitful point of contact between embodiment and de-materialization. This is a call for the re-materialization of the art object, without reductive recourse to rigidly dualistic categories of spirit and matter. Art has forever oscillated between its urge to please and its urge to inform—or reform; between its reliance on ideas and its resistance to them, its uses and abuses as didactic or merely suggestive. Perhaps it is precisely in the friction that obtains between these poles that art's value for life lies. But, if objects—like that dead paintbrush—mean nothing but their functional definition, a human being might well be nothing more than a machine for destroying nature; love, a purely mechanical function.

While I enjoy a good thought experiment as much as the next person, and in no way would want to discourage conceptual provocateurs from prodding, puzzling, or scandalizing the art audience, or the unsuspecting public, with ideas that engage us in the problems posed by conceptual dualities—real and ideal, physical and spiritual, materialistic and material, truth and illusion, political justice and corruption, conformity and capitalism—even so, these sorts of experiments seem to me to serve a very different purpose than sense-based and formalist object art. Such activity can beneficially supplement what sense-based art does, or, indeed, mark out for itself an activity with an entirely different name: activism, criticism, politics, social media. But when it threatens to entirely displace the aesthetic characteristics and powers of the object, as it does today, it is time that we asked questions about what is going on and why.

Is the need to "get away from the object" not to some degree a nihilistic rejection of the teeming beauties of the world, its colors, textures, shapes, and dynamic juxtapositions? A desire to avoid the messiness and irreducibility of sensuality and its uncontrollable effects on emotions? An art that plays with forms and rhythms, with expanses of space and sudden lyrical gestures, with deeply grooved or emphatically etched markings; an art that images forth the ineffable and irrational processes of the mind, heart and body, is an art, that, as Dickinson had it in reference to poetry, makes us feel as if the top of our head were coming off (she also said that it made her body so cold no fire could warm it); it makes our breath stop, our heart beat faster; it is an art that we feel in the body, not just in the mind, an art that does what analytical philosophy, theory, rationality, discourse cannot do. Such an art arranges words or images or sounds or silences in such a way that parts of us we did not yet know existed are awakened, and when we encounter such breath-taking formal choreographies, new cells in our bodies are generated, and what was, one moment before, dear old dreary normal life, is reborn as something completely new and alive.

Formal, physical relationships in art mirror the formal, physical nature of our bodies and the relationships between our bodies and the physical world we live in, and they communicate with the non-verbal, non-rational parts of our brains. Art—an art of words, too, if the words are poetic and imagistic, rhythmic or otherwise trance-inducing rather than merely didactic or prosaic—is a sort of silent, mysterious singing that moves below or beyond the conscious intellectual level; it is more than the sum of its parts. It is revelatory and regenerating. It is much more than a one-liner or a direct transmission of an idea or conviction or a message. As Goethe tells us in *Faust*, "Grau, teurer Freund, ist alle Theorie, und Grün des Lebens goldner Baum" (Grey, dear friend, is all theory, and green life's golden tree). How to measure the impact of the sound of the repeated 'g's (luckily repeatable in this case through translation) or the tripping, warbling effect of the last three words (not fully reproducible since our word for life does not have a "b" in it)? How to add up the seeming senselessness of the tree being both golden and green, or to calculate the effect of the uncertainty of the lacking "is" between "green" and "life's," except through the senses, which seem to intuitively understand such contradictions and textures as higher truths?

The work of art, especially if it is an object, is the perfect marriage between idea and materiality, spirit and matter. Born of an idea and manifested in an object or some material organization, it has the power to translate that idea into a language of forms, shapes, rhythms and other irreducible elements that can communicate to another person. That person, then, being activated by the idea embodied in the formal arrangement, turns around and re-engages with reality, seeing it in new ways and changing it forever. So why should materiality be seen as something frivolous, seducing us away from "higher" spiritual concerns? I suspect it has something to do with the way we have come to conflate pejorative "materialism" with materiality.

Along with materialism and commodity, a purely conceptual art strains to discard or neglect materiality. When spirit is left alone without body or materiality, it is very hard to see or feel. It is precisely when physicality is abandoned by spirit that it becomes nothing but materialism: a sort of commodity fetish or form of pornography, which is very much where we stand as a culture today. We worship bodies that are beautiful and often fake, and shiny metal machines, but this worship is fatally far removed from a meaningful aesthetic experience engaged with ethical responsivity, an experience that changes or motivates us to live in a more humane way or impels us to make the world more beautiful. While de-materialization aims to overcome the problem of empty materialism, it may further aggravate the Cartesian split by giving up on the possibility that some matter (works of art especially) may be bearers of a particularly powerful kind of life-transforming spirit.

The slick Vermont curator's cynical definition of a paintbrush, as a stick with dead hairs on it, reveals, further, a mechanistic, positivist bent, which is cryptically fueled by Platonic rationalism and intellection; a tendency to reduce all sorts of meaningful beautiful things—objects inhered by spirit—to mere dead tools or objects of use. While art for art's sake thrived in the late nineteenth century as a rebellion against Victorian morality, realism, and the rise of industrialization—a slap in the face to the bourgeois marketplace and utilitarian commodification whereby, in Benjamin's words, things were "freed from the drudgery of being useful"—now, in an age of moral and rational industrial progress, where artists are being replaced by technological "makers" of useful gadgets, art for art's sake is seen as reactionary. This is a subtle switch, and demands closer attention. Somehow beauty and pleasure were appropriated by industry and advertising and thus became commodity fetishes. By denying ourselves the pleasures and perils of beauty, we have been robbed of at least half of what makes human life meaningful. In return we get only a simulated sense of ethical purity and a few laughs.

While I am fascinated with the really metaphysical question of whether ideas need to be manifested or just thought or uttered to be real (why do we need to make things at all, when it would be much simpler to just describe them?), and also sympathetic to de-materialism's aim to de-commodify the art object and rescue the artistic impulse from the mercenary clutches of art dealers and galleries, I am curious and concerned about the way de-materialization is paired by Lucy Lippard with de-mythologization. One might presume that these two terms are opposites, as materialism could be linked to positivism and science, while mythologization might seem rather to belong to the realm of the irrational and mystical. Their pairing reveals the complex and subtle origin of the metaphysical flight from the real, which in this case has banished both materiality and mystery at once by separating matter from spirit and robbing matter of its magic.

Confusions about the nature of the real and the metaphysical are as prevalent today as they were in Kant's day (if less carefully analyzed), when his readers were divided on the question of whether the great philosopher was writing as a materialist or an idealist when he posited that the mind is not a blank slate taking objective imprints of the external world. Instead, he argued, the objects of the physical world are processed as subjective phenomena by *a priori* categories and structures of the mind. Was Kant a materialist or an idealist, then? The answer to this question is that it is the wrong question. There can be no separation between matter and spirit, mind and sense experiences, only an interaction between structures in our brains and external phenomena. And Kant himself, in explaining the difference between his type of transcendental idealism and that of pure idealists, wrote—first of the pure idealists: "The theorem of all true idealists, from the Eleatic school to Bishop Berkeley, can be summed up in this formula: all knowledge through sensation and experience is nothing but mere appearance, and truth can only be found in the ideas of pure reason and rationality"—and then of his own sort: "The fundamental theorem that rules and establishes my idealism is, in contrast: all knowledge of things from mere pure reason or pure rationality is nothing but mere appearance, and truth is only to be found in experience." That Kant's materialism is at once a special kind of idealism—one that maintains that the conceptions or categories of the mind determine, arrange, and limit what our senses communicate to us—may be hard to grasp. But if we take the time to grapple with this seeming paradox, we may glimpse an inkling of the way de-materialism is an extreme and unnatural case of abstract intellection and metaphysical posing. When we remove the physical, we are building castles in the air, and even that arch-transcendentalist Thoreau reminded his readers that such castles needed foundations beneath them. Kant wanted to clarify what could and could not be talked about, measured, and known, but that did not mean that he wanted to reduce the world or human experience to what could be rationally explained: he defended ethics and religion, and was an early advocate of art for art's sake. Wittgenstein is another important and confusing marker of this paradox: his careful, philosophical examination of the limits of logical language and the limits of our ability to fully know the world of phenomena through rationality led him to poetry—images, formal arrangement, irreducible mystery—as the only possible medium to communicate what otherwise could not be spoken.

While de-materialization may seem spiritual, then, it is in truth more related to a pure Idealist tendency toward practicality, utility, and morality than to an impulse toward a thrilling coincidence of opposites, a *unio mystica* of matter and spirit. And this pure abstracted Idealism is a tendency that has persistently plagued our judgment and enjoyment of the art object by emphasizing its didactic purpose over its aesthetic qualities. As Susan Sontag famously noted in her *Against*

Interpretation, the tendency since Plato to judge art by how close a likeness it is to the Real and the True initiated a sort of moralistic instrumentalization of art for a single purpose (philosophical truth and goodness or social engineering in this direction), divesting art of its material pleasure potential. But art kept being beautiful and inexplicably moving no matter how many critics continued to judge it by how imitative it was. Materialism—as the means and end of utility—seems then to have something to do with this Platonic criterion... and seems to require a certain level of mimesis in order to be useful, recognizable, purpose-driven. And this is, to some extent, the thorny and important problem with which the de-materialists were grappling. But they missed the difference between materialism and materiality, and they let themselves be so demoralized by commodification and the reign of mimesis that they forgot that matter can be meaningful too. Materiality—as aesthetic, non-utilitarian, sensual—does not require mimesis (though it may avail itself of it) and can be a very good digression—when it comes in the form of devastating unexplainable beauty—from purpose, progress, social engineering, or utility; or a robust antidote to petty presumptuous moralizing and ideological dogma. It can remind us why we would even want to save the world in the first place.

We have seen theorists and artists struggling for centuries to free themselves from the instrumentalization of their art and from Plato's moral imperative to make art True and Good according to his *a priori* categories. By complaining, in the 1890s, about those who knew the price of everything and the value of nothing, Wilde was suggesting that there is a difference between materialism and materiality and that dandies could be spiritualists. In the 1930s and 1940s, we saw artists relinquishing their freedom for political ideologies (on the left and right), at great cost to art—and, ultimately, society as well. In the 1960s, we saw artists and theorists rebelling against object-hood and art as commodity in hopes of freeing themselves from corruption. But was their sacrifice worth it? And was it, after all, the right sacrifice? In

Lippard's "postface" to an updated edition of her book, she noted that "conceptual art 3 years later turned out to be commodifiable after all." Conceptual artists were not, she admitted, "freed from the tyranny of commodity status and market orientation." "On the other hand," she wrote, "the esthetic contributions of an 'idea art' have been considerable." But if the ideologically-driven purposes of conceptual dematerialization were not fulfilled by the relinquishment of beauty, why do we continue to ascribe to its "esthetic"—or more rightfully expressed: anti-aesthetic—contributions?

A hankering after a purely conceptual art smacks of what Nietzsche diagnosed as a sick tendency toward "otherworldliness" and condemned as a blasphemy against the flesh. It can be a beautiful fantasy, especially when one is suffering from physical pain, to leave the world behind and live, like Valéry's Monsieur Teste, as nothing but a brain, or to be able to fly, or to be able to construct physically impossible architecture; but part of the "particular pleasure"—to use the phrase Aristotle coined to describe our response to tragedy—of these fantasies is that they are precisely not possible; they press up against the bounds of the real and create the most delightful and excruciating friction; the painted still life plays with the reality of time and mortality, and it really hurts us while we admire it. Love for another human being is all the more meaningful because he has a body that will age and die. What happens when we try prudishly to separate these lovers, Matter and Spirit? To attempt to keep them apart artificially is to strain toward a false ideal, a disembodied flight toward dystopia.

The problem of materiality has been with us always, and sages and philosophers have often tried to deride matter, whether in the form of bodies or of art objects, not only because it could not be controlled or, in the case of beauty, could not be defined or delimited by logic alone, but because Beauty is beyond the purview of their discipline. In his book *After the End of Art*, Arthur Danto makes this tendency terribly clear. Although he often writes about art, Danto is at bottom a philosopher and he is deeply disturbed that, despite Plato's very influential attempt to make art a matter of Truth and Goodness, art has been judged by chiefly aesthetic criteria from 1400 to Modernism (or from the post-primitive period to the Greeks and Romans, with a brief unexplained hiatus for the Middle Ages and then onward until the 1990s). Why is he disturbed by this? What possible problem could an art critic have with an aesthetic evaluation of art? Could it be that the poor man doesn't have a sensual aesthetic bone in his body? Why yes, of course, he feels left out! Poor philosophers! Ideas and concepts are not enough for them, let us give them art as well! Let us let them make it philosophical. This was apparently Hegel's idea too. Art would be lifted up from its purely aesthetic purposelessness to something more lofty (more masculine perhaps?), something disembodied and eternal: philosophy. Benjamin thought art would need to become politics; while Danto, like Hegel, prophesies that it will become philosophy. These various metamorphoses amount to the same thing, however, which is that art is to be divested of a large part of that which makes it art: sensation and its ability to communicate an essentially animalistic and sublime vision through a non-rational physical language of form.

Paradoxically, though, de-materialized art often has more thematically to do with the so-called "real" world than a more traditionally aesthetic or object-based artistic practice. Conceptual art is often engaged in political and social commentary and concerns itself with art's use or social purpose, while object-based art has more usually explored the other kind of "real" (sensation, aesthetic experience, emotion, spiritual experience). But by banishing the senses and sensibilities, extreme conceptual activity creates a dualistic isolation which may not be easily reversed: once we take ideas out of their grounding in real experience, we might be hard-pressed to turn around and apply them or use them to change the reality which was their source (unless of course we believe with Descartes that thought and body are indeed distinct, in which case the outside world doesn't matter at all!). When we take ideas too far away from the context of the real, we are like people walking on air who want to reform the state of the roads below. With every aerial step, we lose touch with what it is like to walk on the surface of the world, and our solutions for ameliorating potholes or bumps and icy surfaces become less and less relevant if not altogether misleading. It may be nice while it lasts, but sooner or later we will fall and come crashing down into the reality of gravity; sooner or later we stride smack into the inevitabilities of the real. Idealism, in other words, though a necessary counter to dull acceptance of the *status quo*, must always come back down to earth to see, literally, how the new idea really feels. De-materialization, although by necessity availing itself of real physical spaces and bodies, is born of—and stays as close as possible to—abstraction, intellectual activity. In 'Paragraphs on Conceptual Art', a 1967 Sol LeWitt essay Lippard includes in her book, we learn that "[i]n conceptual art the idea or concept is the most important aspect of the work... all the planning and decisions are made beforehand and the execution is a perfunctory affair. The idea becomes a machine that makes art. What the work looks like isn't too important. It has to look like something if it has a physical form. No matter what form it may finally have it must begin with an idea."

Today, "social practices" take off where de-materialist conceptualism left off, but with the important distinction that the art of social practices seems to be more engaged in materiality, albeit the materiality of the real world rather than that of an art object removed from the real world. Both movements do have in common the impulse to break down the separation between art and life. Social practices has taken this further, featuring such art projects as a map locating all the overhanging fruit available in an urban environment, or a communal project where the artists "grew colors" with plants, and it is easy to trace the idealistic impulse to make life into art back to those six years in the late sixties. Duchamp's "readymades" were not idealistic in the same way, and aimed rather to knock down a culture of beauty, while the de-materialists may have had a more constructive desire: to increase something they called "art awareness" in the general public, which would encourage people, outside of a museum or gallery, to appreciate, notice, stop, and observe phenomena, relations, surprises, juxtapositions, which occur randomly in nature and civilization, and also, I suppose, to empower the general public—*everyone is an artist!* was the dubious rallying cry of the day—to participate in making art. And, of course, you may well realize by now that I do believe that we all make the world together; but that does not mean that I think everything is art or that everyone is an artist, because I persist in believing that art is precisely something that is ritually and artificially removed from everyday reality. In other words, those of Oscar Wilde, "Art is art because it is not nature." And in contrast to many of the other artists featured in Lippard's book, Yoko Ono, for one, knew this, and that is why she attempted to make events that were consciously differentiated from life experience. "All my events," she said in a lecture at Wesleyan University in 1966, "are mostly wonderment. ... We never experience things separately... but if that is so, it is all the more reason and challenge to create a sensory experience isolated from the various sensory experiences, which is something rare in daily life."

In contrast, another entry in Lippard's book tells us that to exclude anything from the work of art is "fundamentally a formal or structural point of view" (which, in case you didn't know, is a no-no). The de-materialist break depends upon "an acceptance or rejection of the multiplicity of non-art subject matter" and a resistance to "the imposition of a closed instead of an open system." In another entry on a 1968 exhibition by Arnold Rockman, entitled 'Random Sample, N-42', the artist (if one can even use that term in this context) describes his "methodology" as follows: "no attempt has been made to arrive at an aesthetic arrangement. We're interested in naturalism and natural history." The reference to naturalism hearkens back to an earlier moralistic movement, Naturalism with a big "N," which likewise downplayed aesthetic considerations in the interest of influencing social change, but which failed to attain the glorious inartistic flair of Mr. Rockman's "work." In a much more seductive example, Lippard mentions that Claes Oldenburg, when asked in 1967 to submit his proposal for an outdoor art show in the city, suggested simply "calling Manhattan a work of art."

Again, I am sympathetic to this impulse—and maybe it is because Oldenburg's idea is celebratory, love-filled, because it is a hymn to the magic of the city, rather than a de-constructing blasé nihilistic kick in the beautiful complex face of human life. There is probably nothing more noble than an attempt to inspire people to pay more attention to the beauty of the everyday; but I am afraid that the results of this experiment have not been entirely positive. To the extent that the intention to break down the barrier between art and life has succeeded, art has consciously divested itself of its artistic (conscious, care-filled, devoted, worshipful, technically masterful, in a word: artful) qualities to become more like life, more random, less art-ificial, while it remains rather dubious as to whether or not life has become more artistic, or people more aware of its beauties, dynamics, ironies, and messages. In truth, it seems more likely that the denigration of the art object to everyday readymade random detritus (from high art to lowbrow) has contributed to a pervasive care-lessness and dehumanization of society. What had been the benefit of art in the past for humanity—wonder, sacredness, imagination, harmony, aura, inspiration; uplift, divine inspiration, vision, an ideal toward which to strive; a lightning bolt of beauty to the heart, a reminder of one's highest, best self and that of one's fellows, of one's true calling—is now suspect, and dragged down to the level of a studied carelessness.

When we remove materiality from art and replace it with abstract ideas or with images that are merely signs and not symbols, we are bereft of the essential transubstantiation of a sensuous intellection. While signs, in Susanne Langer's eloquent analysis, are information-bearing and important for utilitarian purposes, symbols are untranslatable, irreducible, and an incitement to dreaming and utopia. When we remove the art object from its place in a ritualistic context, conflating life and art and art and life, we divest art of its power to shift our consciousness from real to ideal and back again. We give up on the journey through the muck of matter, the challenges we would have faced had we gotten down in it and found out whether our ideas would work "on the ground," as it were, and we skip blithely and obliviously to an unexamined conclusion. This is also, by the way, a danger of the convenience of technological virtuality and the false sense it gives us of having gotten somewhere or having learned something effortlessly, painlessly. It is as if we have given up the magic of materiality because of its association with commodity and commerce, its hardships and heaviness. Beauty we have given up because of an association with oppression, judgment, and aristocracy, and because it fades, alters, and eventually dies. Materiality is fearsome. It does present awesome challenges; it does create terrible problems; and it causes pain. And yet there is no escape from it but to not live at all. And, as art is an incitement to more, not less, aliveness, we must ask: what does art become when it dares not engage in contact with beautiful surfaces or even in passionate struggle with the material world? It becomes a polemical, lifeless project which, at best, hurls about tendentious notions: conceptual politics—abstract in the extreme—as well as social censure, shock, and irony. But often enough, if truth be told, the alleged ideas transmitted by the residue of the conceptual practices are tenuous, vague, or possibly were never even fully developed in the first place. As Lippard implies in her 'Postface', most artists are not quite philosophers after all. Whether this non-object art succeeds in redeeming the world where the object supposedly failed is doubtful. If, on the other hand, its intention is cynically anti-utopian, denying any impulse to improve the world, so much the worse.

Since we are all bodies and souls, we are deeply familiar, if we have ever stopped to consider it, with the confusion that ensues if we try to understand which part of us is mind and which body, or how it might even be possible that there is or is not a difference. Just in the way that fairytales repeat archetypal mythologems over and over (the forgetful bridegroom motif helps us process faithlessness; the wise old witch helps us understand wisdom; the magical object helps us understand agency), the work of art, as long as it truly engages with physicality, comprehensively images forth our confusion about body and spirit, constantly rehearsing the union of opposites inherent in human life. This fruitful oscillation requires what the German Romantic Novalis called "the magic wand of analogy." Without supplanting the actual, the specific, the concrete, or the real with some oblique shadow of itself (Dickinson's "Tell the truth, but tell it slant")—without some illusion or leap of faith—we miss the metaphorical magic of art. Consider the puppet theater, which, whether it be miniature or larger than life, is emphatically a world of images and figures. See how the change in scale and change in material signals to us that it is a metaphor, an allegory, a moving image, and not reality? Even in regular theater one is often called upon to make props instead of using objects from the real world. This is a question of maintaining a consistent level of illusion, but also of transporting the audience from out of real life into some other temporary experiential zone. The pedestal, the proscenium, the separation of the stage and the audience, the margins around a poem, the silence between songs, all serve to create a ritual preparedness, a beckoning to attendance and reverence. I know that Artaud and Brecht saw this transport as anti-revolutionary, as a soporific, and called for the constant interruption of the illusion of the work of art. But their critique of this illusion, though it proved that they believed art could be powerful enough to alter consciousness and lull to sleep or wake up to engagement, did not stop to look at all that was lost in the process of dis-enchantment. Plato, too, pays paradoxical homage to art's powers by considering banishing it from his moralistically rational Republic; Benjamin also weighed the dangers and pleasures of the rapture of art, and likewise chose righteousness over ritual. But in the meantime, there has been little honest assessment of how much we have lost.

Conceptual artists seem often to be a strange species of moralistic descendants of Plato's critique of artists as liars and seducers from Truth. As Nietzsche noted, the arch-rationalism of Plato's Socrates signaled the beginning of the end of Greece's artistic glory. Contemporary conceptual artists follow this skeptical tendency by seeming to agree that art is suspect and merely a copy of a copy of the "really real." For Plato, this meant that the artist copies the illusion of the physical world, which itself is just a bad and deluding copy of the real world of forms. While the Neo-Platonists redeemed art by insisting that the artist had a direct line to the divine (Blake's "fourfold vision" in an earlier form), Plato's definition of art as a bad copy of a copy and of the artist as an untrustworthy liar has had a far-reaching and deleterious effect. For conceptual de-materialists, this might take the form of an overscrupulous transparency about methods, materials, and intentions, or an avoidance of any association with seduction, love, or the "tricks" of beauty: a noble and brutal honesty. The artist's touch is not hidden, but foregrounded. In fact, the art often disappears almost entirely behind the artist's giant grubby hand.

The Modernist perspective was about being critical, self-critical, critical of art itself. We can trace an evolution from what Schiller called the naïve and the sentimental approaches to art to what I characterize as the *ironic*—a bleak, heartless, destructive force, without any of the regenerating energy of other artistic revolutions. The *naïve,* a term Schiller used as praise, and which he applied to Homer's objective descriptions, simply sees a tree and represents it. The *sentimental,* which was for Schiller just as little a term of abuse as the naïve, described the subjectivity of the Romantic artist, investing what he or she sees with self, emotions, spirit. The *ironic,* in contrast, is so caught up in criticism and self-analysis that it can no longer even see the tree (let alone the forest) at all. The Classicist (as naïve) thus saw the tree and nothing else. The Romantic or Modernist (as sentimental) saw the tree filtered through his own vision. The ironic Postmodernist—who arrogantly finds the Classicist and the Modernist equally unsophisticated and unaware—can't even see the tree, but just sees himself. And the Post-Postmodernist isn't even allowed to do that. The author or artist is dead. Long live the critic! Representation becomes a subjectivist lie or a hopelessly naïve primitivism. To try to express something through imagistic material is seen by many today as a denial of radical subjectivity and a dangerous affirmation of the author's or artist's perspective over some other perspective; an appropriation, an imposition, an affront, an opinion; an assertion of insidiously constructed and probably oppressive ideas. The artist today is stuck in a corner where she may not affirm anything but her confusion, skepticism, neutralization, and her powerlessness without being labelled as reactionary.

Still, outside of all this theoretical prohibition of pleasure and beauty, there persists a timeless urge to use our hands to make things that initiate a ritualistic intermingling between reality and dreams, body and spirit, material and idea, human life and the search for meaning. It will not all be cancelled, as long as naïve and sentimental sensualists dare to love the colors, shapes, textures, and dynamics of physicality and learn to read within them the lineaments of their own eternally resonating presentiments of meaning. Material beauty will not be veiled, as long as we continue to be brave enough to sometimes reveal our own appetites, delights, and despairs without the cover of cleverness and ironic carelessness, as long as we dare to love this material-spiritual world—and the material-spiritual beings who inhabit it—in all of its flawed and broken majesty.

IV.

Portals

> le souvenir de ces maisons s'est deposé dans mon sang
> et court aux points cardinaux de mon corps
> Il leva le bras. Une petite troupe de chevaliers errants
> et d'assassins encercla le bourg comme une barrique cerclée de fer
>
> Francine Y. Prevost
> from *Voyage à Cythères*

AT THE MAISON GAI SABER, where I am trying to collect my thoughts about *Schatzkammer*, reliquaries, ornament, crime, and civilization and its discontents, all the matter has history: all of the earth, all the rocks, going back to the Paleolithic age, and the land, worked and harvested for centuries, the grapevines, the fig trees, the old stone houses with cellars and attics. Yesterday I worked in the garden with Francine, my hostess at this artists' residency in the Loire Valley, removing ten years of ground cover and vines from an area outside the *pressoire*, a house built by Francine's father, a master carpenter, which is so called because of a beautiful old wooden cask-press for grapes sitting on its porch. While we worked, we uncovered wild garlic and snails and small new prodding flowers. Every material thing here is bound or connected to the past via bloodlines, via deep ruts in the fields, etchings on the surface of earth's memory that reach deep down under the soil to places we cannot see but surely feel. Francine herself was born here, in this house, and her family's tenure in this place goes back generations. The earth we were working was worked by her forefathers and foremothers, again and again and again, hands like her hands in the same moist, rich dirt.

In the Maison library, where other vines go back to other roots, bifurcating out over vast geographic areas and times to ancient Greece, medieval France, twentieth-century German history and philosophy, Japanese courtly poetry, Arabian-Andalusian melodies, I picked up *Civilization and Its Discontents*, wherein Freud writes about the way our childhood selves are carried within our grown bodies, just as the ancient foundations of old cities may still exist beneath the new structures. I also rediscovered Marcel Mauss' wonderful book *The Gift*, about ancient and primitive gift exchange, called the "potlatch" in some traditions, and about the "mana" of objects and a world where objects are not reduced to commodities bought and sold without any emotional, social, or spiritual bonds. The mana that lives in an object once owned by someone is passed on to the recipient. As it is farther passed on, its power and value both increase. This reminded me of the sense we have of powers inherent in old things and old places, and in the late offspring of old families, with their mingled lines of influence and geography, ethnicities and languages. The tragedy is that these braids of meaning can be cut off, diminished, when the objects, persons, and places in question are used and abused in merely mercenary ways. Cut off from the circulating energy of community, history, nature, and the lifeblood of heritage and exchange, they become sterile and lose their *mana*. Severed from the forces that made it, the craftsperson who formed it, the animal and natural materials of which it was constructed, a relic becomes a mere thing, with no meaning.

A person, too, can become an object when alienated from her history and her roots, although occasional spiritual and physical journeys away from home are instructive and refreshing; and there seem to be some people—travelers and expatriates—who find their homes or perhaps their anti-selves in constant transition or in far-off lands. But even these wanderers are tracing lines of contact, walking paths and touching artifacts which seem somehow to be calling to them. Even they are treasuring places and objects and people who have either originated there or arrived via surprising routes—routes that are stories and heritages in themselves. These considerations compel us to reconsider modern-day prejudices against materiality and to work to understand why many of us continue to love objects, no matter how implicated they may be in things we ostensibly don't love.

It is difficult to imagine a time when social interaction was not driven so much by economic considerations. The roots of such a time are still traceable, however, and we may uncover them and cultivate them today if we choose. But in another, more popular book on the gift, Lewis Hyde suggests that, since gift exchange is a complex and fraught relationship, often dangerous and messy, some modern people may actually prefer the commodification of objects and life because it gives them a sense of freedom from the group, the commonality, the family, the tribe. Thus a "free society" may be not so much about political freedoms as about the freedom of individual determination, the sense of anonymity and of not being beholden to anyone. This explains why one may prefer a sterile hotel to the awkwardness of staying in a warm home with strangers who may become friends. While cleaning up after dinner, Francine and I agree that anonymity does have its charms too, for a poet or artist who escapes from everyone she knows to live awhile in a foreign city. And of course, in our modern world, we often stray very far from our homes and our people, abandoning native languages and customs and the obligations of kinship that go along with them. There are often good reasons why a person would want to be cut off from his family or his national heritage and culture, but such a separation can probably only be achieved by a truncating and repression of parts of ourselves that it might be better to bring up to the surface in all their messy material complexity. At best we adopt new families, learn new languages, invent new customs, putting down new roots and creating and collecting new keepsakes; and at worst we float amid shallow connections without identity, without meaningful possessions or mementos to hold us down, without a place to call home.

Here at the Maison Gai Saber, then, I am thinking of all these things amid the warmth and awkwardness and delight of strangers who have quickly become friends, thinking about our culture's ambivalence toward materiality, trying to parse the differences between some objects and others, to understand how much matter is enough and how much is too much. It is not merely a question of the objects themselves but of our social and spiritual relationship to them. Is it possible to imagine and foster a process of transmission, exchange, and ritualization of objects different from the process that governs today's anonymous marketplace? Mauss tells us that in the primitive gift-exchange societies he studied, "[t]he large abalone shells, the shields covered with them, the decorated blankets with faces, eyes, and animal and human figures embroidered and woven into them, are all personalities. ... A copper talks and grunts, demanding to be given away or destroyed; it is covered with blankets to keep it warm." Of course, good bohemians, even within our commodified context, have always known how to celebrate the life of material objects, giving and receiving treasures from crowded junk shops, reanimating neglected and forgotten relics, dusting off old lanterns to find they contain genies who can grant wishes. And we make our own reliquaries around the remains of meaningful matter—locks of hair, love notes, train tickets, feathers, an acorn, a seed, a butterfly wing, a faded photograph, a fragment of a dress—connected with some experience or person sacred to us, carefully enclosing them in a box, a book, a special little chest, and placing them on an altar in our boudoir or study. I immediately discovered that Francine is a good bohemian aesthete, a spiritual lover of material objects, when she took me, on my second day here, to the *brocante*, the flea market in Chinon. Chinon: where that great lover of material pleasures Rabelais lived, where that great saint Joan of Arc came to visit a disbelieving king. And she showed me, nearby, the beautiful crumbling remains of Châtteleraut, the city where Descartes, that arch anti-materialist, lived as a boy. Rereading the *Discours de la méthode* the other morning, I found Descartes' assertion that he was "une substance dont toute l'essence ou la nature n'est que de penser, et qui, pour être, n'a besoin d'aucun lieu ni dépend d'aucune chose matérielle; en sorte que ce moi, c'est-a-dire l'âme, par laquelle je suis ce qui je suis, est entièrement distinct du corps"—which was all the more disturbing after having visited his childhood home, a pretty house with physical walls, halls, floors and archways. Without succumbing entirely to the worst kind of ahistorical psychologizing, I couldn't help but wonder if perhaps his house was too narrow for him, too crowded, impelling him to escape to Holland to reinvent himself, to develop his method and escape his bonds to place, people, material world.

Even though I had to temporarily uproot myself to come here, it strikes me that my visit to the Maison Gai Saber is an object lesson in an opposite tendency to value the visceral threshing and braiding of matter. This journey away from and back seems to be a process of de-commodified exchange similar to the ones Mauss points to, since there really is no purpose or product to speak of here except for a sort of ineffable, practically mystical mingling of material and spiritual substances. It could not have been achieved from afar, for the material environment is very present in my musings and experience here, from the churned and tilled fields of fertile soil to the fences woven from thin dark rushes to the winding wooden staircase in this sixteenth-century house to the warm figs to the yellow of a lemon in an earthenware bowl to the fragrant walnut oil from trees in Francine's mother's garden, which we watched men in their blue work coveralls make one day with an ancient grinding stone and crushing and liquefying machines, to the dry wood crackling in the old fireplace with its smoke-darkened grate, the old pan for roasting chestnuts, the heavy cast-iron foot warmer and the white-gray ashes that must be taken out back in a pail along with the redolent food scraps and the cheese rinds. But what—besides the fact that I visited the Vienna museum of art, the Louvre, and the medieval Musée de Cluny on my way here, looking at rooms filled with reliquaries and imperial collections of exotica, scientia, and artificia—does all this have to do with the problem of maximalization and minimalization, *Schatzkammer*, ornament and crime, the physicality of reliquaries, the violence of iconoclasm, and the pleasures and discomforts of civilization? Let me see if I can make the connections.

Marveling at the richness and variety of the goods transported by train through Concord, our defender of the wild, our minimalist Thoreau, almost sounds like the more metropolitan and paradoxically spiritual-materialist Walt Whitman as he intones noun after noun in an ecstatic encomium to the ingenuity of workers, voyagers, inventors, artisans, and the restless energy and activity of Western civilization. "What recommends commerce to me," he notes, in *Walden*, "is its enterprise and bravery." The train carries lumber, fabric scraps to turn into paper, Spanish hides, lime, and torn sails, things suggestive of the wide world and of our ability to transform nature into culture and civilization. "I am refreshed and expanded," writes this lover of nature,

> when the freight train rattles past me, and I smell the stores which go dispensing their odors all the way from Long Wharf to Lake Champlain, reminding me of foreign parts, of coral reefs, and Indian oceans, and tropical climes, and the extent of the globe. I feel more like a citizen of the world at the sight of the palm-leaf which will cover so many flaxen New England heads the next summer, the Manila hemp and cocoanut husks, the old junk, gunny bags, scrap iron, and rusty nails...

And yet he stops three times in this chapter to warn: "If all were as it seems, and men made the elements their servants for noble ends!" and "If the enterprise were as innocent as it is early!" and "If the enterprise were as heroic and commanding as it is protracted and unwearied!" How can we then calculate the real cost, to the soul, to the environment, to humanity, to other cultures, of the "enterprise": the production, possession, and transportation of objects? And how assess the gain to humankind from craftsmanship, ornamentation, design, art, manufacture, collecting, and trade? Finally, is it possible to delineate a less damaging, less damning means to celebrate, collect, and touch the spirit inhered within the material riches of the wide world?

Why have some people been mad to collect and accumulate, to capture the variety and vastness of the world in their drawing rooms, and *Schatzkammer*, while others have urgently preached against avarice, materialism, and clutter? Why has Christianity, a religion with such a complex relationship with the physical, spent so much time, money, and energy creating elaborately ornamented objects (reliquaries) to house the physical remains of saints who are often honored for their transcendence of physical needs? My friend, Kate Barush, the pilgrimage scholar, answers that this apparent contradiction is explained and figured forth in the dual nature of Christ, in the incarnation itself, as the divine becomes matter.

And of course, again, it is a question of what kind of matter, for some objects are empty and degrading while others are replete with spirit and elevating. Is it possible that the impulse to reject physicality and the impulse to celebrate it are both bound up with the fundamental problem of fleetingness and of our human inability to be in two places at once? On the one hand, we attempt to overcome death and space by surrounding ourselves with eternal symbols representing the past and distance. On the other, we refrain from attaching ourselves to anything that will not last.

Indeed, our relationship to objects is a matter of our relationship to relating itself, since material objects are in effect portals, connecting us over time and space. They are symbols, illustrating our messy and dangerous relations to the world, to the past, to each other—relations some might prefer to repress, negate or destroy. How are we to respond to such complexity? Can we find some cleaner, more sustainable way to truck with matter? A way that honors natural resources, the fragile ecosystems created by cultures and civilizations? A way that imagines the long-term cost as well as the immediate pleasures of possession?

And even if it proves impossible to completely remove the negative results of materiality, might we, in the end, nevertheless choose to celebrate matter? Indeed, if we are not to be hypocrites, there may be no other choice than to embrace it in all its fraught reality.

We have strong-armed and pillaged, looted and swiped, bargained and bartered; we have carried away treasures from cultures that on some occasions would have melted them down for utilitarian purposes or to forge sculptures of new gods. Thus we have actually preserved some treasures from oblivion by transporting them to Western museums; and others we have purloined from their true worshipers to consider in our drawing rooms and galleries, often without the proper feelings of sacredness—as conversation pieces or worse; we have transported human beings to enslave them and to put them on display at world's fairs. And we have collected and uprooted not only objects and people and their natural resources, but also rich and marvelous new words for the spices, animals, fruits, fabrics, colors, and customs brought back from the voyages of discovery: cinnabar, arabesque, damask, cannibal, canoe, hurricane, chocolate, armadillo, crocodile, pelican, bastinado, machete, parakeet... William James Bouwsma writes in *The Waning of the Renaissance, 1550-1640,* that such discoveries

> may have marked the beginning of European Imperialism, but they also expressed a dynamic apparent in other aspects of European culture. As a result, a wave of new products, new knowledge, and new words swept over Europe, stimulating openness, wonder, excitement, and imagination. ... Curiousity, both cause and consequence of the discoveries and previously considered dangerous to the soul, was increasingly seen as a virtue. [Richard] Hooker [an English priest] noted, 'the wonderful delight men have, some to visit forrein countries, to discover nations not heard of in former ages, we all to know affaires and dealings of other people, yea to be in a league of amitie with them.'

Our thirst for knowledge has led us to scour distant civilizations and previously unknown cultures, changing them and ourselves through contact. It has spurred us toward invention and "mastery" of Nature, tearing back the "veil of Isis," but also toward the invention of musical, astronomical, medical, nautical, and culinary instruments, the printing press, the microscope and telescope; toward increasing life expectancy, decreasing death in childbirth, thus instigating the unintended problem of overpopulation; toward the study of languages and folktales and musical scales around the world; toward the exploration of outer space, of the inner depths of the earth, of our own psyches and our genetic coding. The *Beagle* may have been sent out for baser purposes, but Charles Darwin was onboard.

Is it possible to separate the hunger for power from the hunger for knowledge, which in part has been motivated by a desire to make life better? To perhaps "be in league and amitie" with strangers? Can we separate these impulses from the concupiscence of short-sighted grasping and destruction? Freud suggests that the instinct to aggression and destruction is paired with our instinct to creation, with the proliferation of eros, the force that binds people together and creates families and communities. Is eros the force that drives exploration and collection? Or is it aggression? Or are both forces working together, or against each other, in fruitful and destructive friction? The devil, Freud notes, is opposed by Goethe not with goodness and holiness but with the power to create and generate. Yet to create is to destroy. To be perfectly harmless, to leave no trace, one had better not even live. Aggression might also be associated with what Robert Musil called the "appetitive" tendency of mankind, which is also the drive to destroy. Thus, while Freud states that the primary, originary instinct of aggression is a threat to civilization, it may also be true that aggression is a positive energy that makes civilization possible in the first place. Further, while what one person or culture deems "good" can often create unintended bad consequences, sometimes seemingly self-interested actions can result in benefits for many. Take egotism out, Emerson noted, and castrate the benefactors.

Freud describes the development of civilization as a process by which humanity strives to protect itself against nature and to master it. Civilization, he contends, also requires that its inhabitants direct "their care too to what has no practical value whatever, to what is useless. ... We soon observe that this useless thing which we expect civilization to value is beauty."

Beauty, of course, is counted by many as one of the redeeming elements of life. While beauty also exists in nature, it may be our love of this natural beauty that impels us to make objects and works of art. Can it be that this imitation necessarily leads to a destruction of what it intended to revere? "Man has," Freud continues, "become a kind of prosthetic God. When he puts on all his auxiliary organs he is truly magnificent; but," Freud reminds us, "his organs have not grown on to him and they still give him much trouble at times. ... [I]n the interests of our investigations, we will not forget that present-day man does not feel happy in his God-like character." Wherefrom this unhappiness? Is it all because of the ambivalence produced by guilt and the repression of instincts, as Freud suggests? At a certain point, too much civilization separates us from the pleasures of being a human animal, makes us too comfortable and numbs our senses. When I was forced to use an outhouse over the course of a cold Vermont winter, I found compensatory joys in hearing the howling of the coyotes late at night and seeing the stars, which I would have missed had I merely padded on carpeted floors down a heated hallway. We want our wild experiences along with our more genteel passions, and are lucky if we can maintain both at once. But can we?

A classical musician friend of mine declared one day that Western civilization has done nothing but damage. This statement is not far from the lips of many another liberal denizen of contemporary America. But would he really be willing to give up the piano, the musical scale, Bach, or the philosophy and psychology that have put him in a position to make such an extreme statement from the comfort of his well-heated apartment? He had, indeed, already chosen not to give these things up, not even in exchange for a world where no-one has ever enslaved or tortured or demeaned anyone else, where nature has not been abused and devastated for short-sighted human interest and greed. For that is the bargain implied by such wholesale negations of Western civilization. Or is it possible to proceed with more subtlety and admit that we want to keep some parts of civilization and reject other parts, but that we really cannot possibly calculate which parts of our culture we might be able to have without the allegedly bad ones? Ought we not ask more carefully how much the appetitive nature of human beings has contributed for the good before declaring that it would be better if we had no desires or curiosities at all? For no matter how much we may criticize civilization, it is unlikely that many of us would be willing to revert to a time before language or agriculture or private property supposedly ruined our simple, happy natures (and, of course, the myth of the golden age has never been proven).

One may, one must criticize the damage done by civilization—to nature, and to humans, to cultures and to our sick modern souls. One must question the practices of colonialist occupiers, who destroyed and took egregious advantage of the cultures they "discovered." But we must also admit that many of these cultures have their own gruesome histories of abuse, slavery, and cruelty that allowed them to be the victors over other peoples before we came along and made them our victims. The complex historical truth does not excuse the horrible things we have done and continue to do, but it does demonstrate that civilization and Western rationalism are not the sole purveyors of barbaric atrocities. Thus, barbarous acts committed by non-Western peoples are not solely the result of our own interventions in their cultures and do not under any circumstances justify what amounts to a masochistic relinquishment of what is good about Western culture. Freud, in a passage considering the Marxist idea of abolishing private property as a cure for aggression, notes that "[i]n abolishing private property we deprive the human love of aggression of one of its instruments, certainly a strong one, though certainly not the strongest; but we have in no way altered the differences in power and influence which are misused by aggressiveness, nor have we altered anything in its nature. Aggressiveness was not created by property. It reigned almost without limit in primitive times, when property was still very scanty, and it already shows itself in the nursery." While civilization has certainly enabled us to cause harm more efficiently through the use of technology, and more coldly and impersonally through the distancing enabled by technology, this does not mean that it is more inherently cruel, destructive, or brutal than primitivism. For civilization has also benefited the world, generally made people gentler, kinder, and more tolerant, and created more "amitie." Furthermore, even the colonialism associated with Western civilization included at least a portion of well-intentioned scientific, artistic, and anthropological interest in the cultures and artifacts of other people, not to mention humanitarian efforts in the otherwise victimized countries. It has been a very mixed history, and one not easily judged.

In fact, Western culture has, for reasons decidedly both good and bad, looked outside itself to learn about the lives of others much more than any other culture has, demonstrating a curiosity that has certainly been related to, if not impelled by, a drive to dominate the peoples and places it studied. Our history has landed us here, as we make new history in the present, and many scholars, explorers, and collectors have found it meaningful to collect and archive facts, fancy, words, artifacts, stories, exempla of all kinds from the rich past, preserving them for the enrichment of future generations. While there are encyclopedia and libraries and archives that mainly collect intellectual and spiritual content, there are also collections of material objects.

Kunstkammer, also called *Wunderkammer*, were according to Phillip Blom in his *To Have and To Hold: An Intimate History of Collectors and Collecting*, "rooms transformed into images of the riches and strangeness of the world." These cabinets were seen as microcosms. In one famous chamber of wonders, Blom tells us, "objects in drawers were arranged as an elaborate allegory to represent the animal, plant and mineral world, the four continents, and the range of human activities. A particular *Kunstschrank* was itself 'an encyclopedia in objects, a programme of the world in microcosm, a theatrum memoriae' illustrating their place in the great drama of God's mind..." In Amsterdam, there were purportedly nearly one hundred private collections recorded between 1600 and 1740. Objects from all over the world were encased in cabinets that reflected the reach of Dutch colonialism and trading practices, from Japan to South America to Egypt to the Middle East. Tulips were brought to Europe by Emperor Maximilian's "ambassador in Turkey, Ghislain de Busbecq, as well as other plants, which were planted in the Emperor's gardens in Vienna and Prague." Maximilian was a great collector, a patron of scholarship, and the father of Rudolf of Habsburg (1552-1612), soon to be Holy Roman Emperor. Rudolf gathered artisans and craftspeople and scientists: "The castle on the Hradčany Hill [in Prague] and the streets hugging the slopes around it were transformed into a colony of gold- and silversmiths, stone-cutters, watch- and instrument-makers, painters and engravers, astronomers and alchemists."

Can we take away some kinds of desire, some kinds of pleasure in beauty and materiality, and not others? Or is the answer to the horrors of colonialism a repudiation of exploration, curiosity, materiality, and the occasional ritual delight of squandering? Is the answer to hollow materialism a moralistic, minimalistic prudery, a turning away from the beauties and riches of the world, of the senses, of delight? Criticisms of civilization tend to suggest that less is more and that our great fault as a culture is that we have produced too much and have, in so doing, abused resources and strained capacities; but there ought to be a reckoning and a differentiation between sorts of products: those that feed and inspire us spiritually and physically and those others that may not even feed us physically but rather drain us of vital energies.

One may praise the stay-at-homes who minded their own business, left well enough alone and left no trace, but one could also wonder why they were not interested in their neighbors, in other languages, flora and fauna, religious rites, art and customs. Indeed, it is easiest to do no harm if one becomes a hermit and never dares to do anything, carrying home no souvenirs. But today's trend toward cleansing one's life of extraneous matter includes a rejection of history, memories, culture, art. And it ultimately extends to a rejection of personal relationships, relationships which may seem too complicated, too much trouble, or too much like "possession." And both rejections may be connected to what looks very much like egoism—the egoism of the "whatever" generation, which sometimes covers up its ignorance of the rich complexity of culture with a self-righteous and hypocritical rejection of its own materialistic accumulation and "empire." We may righteously empty our houses of objects and speak of simplifying our lives, but we tend to keep the hot water and the electricity while moralizing against the other, less useful, more beautiful and meaningful objects. In fact, while fulminating against contemporary Western culture, moralistic critics themselves generally will choose to keep all the worst parts of it—fossil fuel waste, consumerism, their cellphones and expensive computers, and a hypocritical enjoyment of the fruits of a society they are free to condemn while rejecting its best parts. Autonomous minimalists don't need to learn anything from history, from anyone else; nor do they want to clutter their minds with historical facts, details, images, or their bookshelves or houses with old books or artifacts, because they already know everything that matters, much better than their silly, misguided ancestors. Or, if not, they can look it up with the flick of a finger.

But collectors and explorers and scholars, however morally inferior they may seem to today's politically correct minimalists, were often driven, by curiosity and a love of life, to accumulate, archive, and display the many strange and wonderful things made by culture and nature.

Some of the first collections were small studiolos: chambers filled with antiquities, gemstones, and sculptures, which were popular in Italy among men of means and learning from the fourteenth century onward.

In the *Kunstkammer* in the Vienna museum of art, compiled in great part from the collections of the Habsburg emperors and empresses, I read that such collections were considered "evidences... of human craftsmanship... a picture of the cosmos," that they were thought of as a Theatrum mundi and an archive of wisdom, including exotica, scientia, naturalia, consisting of objects considered both "materially and ideally valuable." I looked at vitrines filled with measuring instruments like a gunner's quadrant and a table clock; astronomical instruments such as a ring-dial, an astrolabe; a hanging clock locket in the form of a gilded book; a sundial in the form of a lute, where the strings cast shadows. I found a rhinoceros horn with filigree ornamentation of gold, rubies, pearls; and Indian bezoars from the sixteenth century, ornamented with gold and enamel; seventeenth-century Indian seal stamps of crystal, gold, and rubies; a sixteenth-century ivory-and-horn fan in the form of a peacock from Sri Lanka; and the famous golden salt cellar of Cellini, with sculpted Neptune and Tellus for salt and pepper, symbols of sea and earth. There was a Ming Dynasty Chinese rhinoceros-horn drinking vessel, of a curiously beautiful amber color; a German powder flask made of a gilded silver shell adorned with rubies, turquoise, and glass stones; a hunting horn of gold and enamel with a golden bejeweled woven strap; a writing set with utensils, its lid sculpted with tiny realistic animals, insects, and shells. There were automata and clockworks; an enamel smelling-salts bottle in the shape of a fish; a sixteenth-century bronze oil lamp from Padua in the shape of a shell mounted on an eagle's talon; and a pendant with a monstrous pearl in the shape of a Madonna. This last was grotesque and ridiculous to my modern eye, with tiny grimacing or smiling faces around the edges, its pearl Madonna a natural miracle like the face of Christ appearing in some rock face or cloth—but she had been given a necklace, a tiny gold chain, to mark where her neck must be.

There is a sense of fantastical but fulsome excess as the centuries advance toward the baroque, in the elaborate table ornaments that depict, say, a golden elephant upon whose back there rises an air balloon, which sports a serpent, which sports a sailing ship whose crow's nest becomes a bouquet of gilded flowers studded with precious gems—a sense that there is perhaps too much ornamentation, too many schnorkels, nowhere for the eye to rest. And as I leave the Kunsthistorisches Museum and walk around the corner toward the Vienna Secession building on Friedrichstrasse, I see the fruitful marriage of old and new in the refreshing combination of its elaborately ornamental dome of gilded leaves crowning a foundation of almost minimalist classical lines. I think of Vienna's Adolf Loos, that cryptic minimalist decorator and architect who attacked ornament and was the inventor of the eyebrow-less window. Loos argues in his book *Ornament and Crime* that only savages and women like ornament; thoroughly modern, sophisticated (masculine) intelligences, he suggests, must prefer utility and industrial design. Although he was a champion of American hygiene and efficiency, his rather utilitarian-tainted positions were only an extreme version of what other artists and designers of the *Jahrhundertwende* also criticized—as countermovement to what they saw as an excessive, falsified historicism, and a falsifying ornamentation of buildings and objects. This aesthetic reaction resulted in the new *Jugendstil,* with its combination of intensely ornamented areas and bold open spaces, on paper and building surface.

It is important to realize, however, that when the Secessionists, who were ecstatic ornamentalists themselves, criticized ornamentation, they were criticizing what they deemed a stylistically indiscriminate treatment of surfaces that was not connected in any way with the interior, usage, or meaning of a building or an object. The Secessionists, in keeping with Ruskin's critique of simulated façades, may have been arguing for a more honest relationship between material and meaning. They may also have been merely gasping for a little bit of breath amid a proliferation of ornamentation that must have felt to them like choking vines, and thus hearkening, as their contemporary minimalist composers had done, for a little silence and margin against which the sounds and arabesques of their designs could be better appreciated. But any extreme reaction requires a compensating swing back in the other direction in time. We have become all too hygienic and prudish about our surfaces. We have cleared away too many weeds we now recognize as medicinal herbs or wildflowers. We must let the life-force of organic ornament spread once more over the blank, bleak surfaces of concrete and metal.

Thus, our assessment of the fitting proportion or kind of ornament may be compared with our judgment about possessions, or with the happiest proportion of daily busyness. We need margins and spaces in order to appreciate the teeming excitement of smaller islands of maximalization. Yet we also need to experience the crowdedness of the crammed *Kunstkammer* and the wildly overcrowded junk shop or library of ideas to feel the impressive effects of multiplicity, variety, sameness, and difference evident when many materials, shapes, and textures are contrasted together in one space. We may speak of bounty and scarcity, aestheticism and asceticism, we may speak of feasts and of crumbs, gluttony and fasting. Economy of expenditure focuses the mind and spirit to appreciation and patience, while profligacy scatters and dulls the senses over time. Yet maximalization must do battle with minimalism, as its teeming proliferations mimic life's own generative energies. Compare a field of spring wildflowers with a cement parking lot: which is more natural? Thus maximalization signals, enacts, participates in more and richer experience and more life, whereas minimalization often smells of defensiveness, naysaying, turning away, of closing down the senses and the self. We need to allow for cycles and dynamics on a personal and an historical level. We need margins around each rich experience or object or person or taste or sound, to best appreciate its own manifold essences; and then again we need momentary liftings of boundaries, when the names and distinctions among things have been dissolved. A good bohemian will suffer cold to own a beautiful book, walk ten miles to see a sculpture, and dream, amid the collections of princes and contemporary museum donors, of being "Land-lord & Water-lord" with Emerson's poet. Thus a certain kind of sacrifice merges with an aesthetic self-indulgence or a relinquishment of practicality, utility, purpose. And we poor dreamers may wander very freely amid the collections of more implicated emperors.

Leaving Vienna, I proceeded to Paris, where, as Balzac wrote in the nineteenth century, "[t]he great poem of display chants its stanzas of color from the Church of the Madeleine to the Porte Saint-Denis." I had read this quotation in Walter Benjamin's fantastic *Arcades Project*, itself a collection of maximalist proportions, a collection of words about the materiality of Paris. Benjamin was a collector and rhapsodist of collecting, who despite his Marxist fastidiousness declared in his essay 'Unpacking My Library' that private collections are more meaningful than public ones, even though public ones "may be less objectionable socially and more useful academically." In the same essay, Benjamin writes that "[t]he most profound enchantment for the collector is the locking of individual items within a magic circle in which they are fixed as the final thrill, the thrill of acquisition, passes over them."

In the unfinished *Arcades Project*, Benjamin struggles with his ambivalence about materiality. Like Thoreau with his train-rhapsodies, he is obsessed and thrilled by the "great poem of display," as evidenced by the voluminous manuscript cataloguing the facts and the sociological significance of material culture within the compromised context of "commodity fetishism." He writes that the collector's task is "divesting things of their commodity character by taking possession of them. ... The collector dreams his way not only into a distant or bygone world but also into a better one... in which things are freed from the drudgery of being useful." As an artist, as a writer, as a collector, as a mystic, he loves objects and their auras; as a Marxist, as a moralist, as a victim of the National Socialist tendency to emphasize externals and to create propaganda of aesthetic spectacles and myths, he feels himself compelled to critique the romanticization of material culture as tainted by fascist and capitalist injustice and empire. We may comprehend his confused embrace and rejection of matter, considering the difficult position he was in, poised between brownshirts on one side of the street and communists on the other. Separated in exile from his beloved library, and threatened in life and limb, he had hardly any other choice in that historical moment but immateriality—and a truly tragic self-disembodiment: suicide.

Medieval Christianity, an earlier epoch consumed in often dangerous and violent ambiguity regarding materiality, did not have to explain its paradoxes with such critically complex theorizing as the members of the Frankfurt School. This is what I thought, anyway, when I walked from the "great poem of display" of the shopping boulevards of Paris to visit the Musée de Cluny to look at reliquaries. Despite the official encouragement to favor internal eyes and divine sensations over external observation and physical pleasure, and amid a long, drawn-out conflict between iconoclasts and those who defended images, medieval artists reveled in colors and shapes and materials. While some theologians, like Abbé Suger, celebrated color as divine light, others, like Saint Bernard of Clairvaux, deemed color to be a species of matter and therefore "vile and abominable." Other theorists worked hard to justify the spiritual benefits of beauty, often beginning with a key text from Psalms 26:8: "Lord, I have loved the beauty of thy house." And when it came to reliquaries, there were more specific justifications. In the twelfth century, Thiofred of Echternach wrote: "As the soul itself in the body cannot be seen and yet works its wonders therein, so the precious treasures of dust [relics] work unseen. ... Who with fast faith touches the outside of the container whether in gold, silver, gems, or fabric, bronze, marble, or wood, he will be touched by that which is concealed inside."

For reliquaries, made of matter considered by some to be vile and abominable no matter how pretty, were still certainly physical objects which were believed to facilitate spiritual contact with non-physical or no-longer-physical beings. The things they contained were often *truly* vile and abominable: they were often merely a pinch of dust or fragment of cloth. Their tendency to be repulsive needed, writes Cynthia Hahn in *Strange Beauty: Issues in the Making and Meaning of Reliquaries*, the "compensatory beauty of the reliquary." In a strange twist, the external surface of the reliquary, the exterior casing, made of metals and gems, was more lasting than the ephemeral substance within, those almost no-longer-physical traces of a spiritual being disappearing from the physical world.

According to Hans Belting in *Likeness and Presence: A History of Image Veneration Before the Age of Art*, the Christian refusal to venerate the image of the emperor was the central cause of the persecution of the early church. Whereas today we may mistakenly associate the prohibition on images with Islam alone, Christianity has a long and complex history of violent iconoclasm. Images in religious practice were often considered an open violation against Mosaic Law, which proclaimed one invisible God. The eventual grudging acceptance of images, Belting explains, was "backed by a theory that in retrospect justified the worship of images within the context of the theological debate over Christ's nature." Since newcomers to Christianity wanted to use images to know their new God, and because the people persisted in worshipping images even after they had nominally converted to Christianity, theologians had to find ways of either stopping this worship or justifying it. In 726 AD there was an edict against images, accompanied by destruction of icons of Christ. Believers in the divine nature of Christ were in conflict with the imagistic stress on his human nature.

But the iconoclasm came to a temporary end, under a woman regent, after the ecumenical council in Nicaea in 787. At the council of Nicaea, image veneration was allowed on these grounds: "When the population rushes with candles and incense to meet the garlanded images and icons of the emperor, it does not do so to honor the panels with wax colors, but to honor the emperor himself." The idea takes precedence over the material, but the material is needed to instill the idea. Then fresh iconoclasm broke out in 813. In 842, when another woman was regent, the worship of images was reinstated with the justification that insofar as the invisible God is visible in Christ, Christ then is visible in images of him. The synod of 869 established that "God, as the archetype, was materialized in the Son of Man as an image." Ultimately, the image and the object could not be repressed; the reliquary represents the uneasy but powerful marriage of the spiritual and the material message of the Church.

Every feature on a medieval reliquary "represented" something: the hierarchy of the Church, the trinity, the resurrection. Thus, individual elements in an object are fundamentally determined by their relationship to a particularly narrative idea, suggesting that their central purpose was moral: to indoctrinate and elevate. But why then were they made to be beautiful also? Perhaps they were made with precious gems to celebrate the glory of God's creation, the wealth and power of the Church or, on the other hand, to paradoxically show the importance of spirit over matter, since these extremely valuable materials represented money spent not to feed or clothe or house people but to enrich objects of spiritual veneration. Hahn, in *Strange Beauty*, argues that the physical adornment was a technique for inspiring awe, a strategic use of beauty to seduce. And while this may be true, it seems to ignore the relationship between the beauty of the natural world and that of some divine idea, as if such a relationship had to be artificially constructed. Rather than see the decoration of reliquaries as a social construction used to manipulate worshipers, I would prefer to see it as a spontaneous eruption of joy and pleasure in the divine beauty of the world. Wonder, according to Hahn, is "the key transformative response," which allows the viewer to experience the "divine presence in mundane objects and allows them to possess a striking power." Elsewhere she refers to the term "reverentia," explaining that it was a response that needed to be taught to the uneducated viewer of reliquaries. Hahn suggests that beauty is used to create an awe of the spiritual which might not be there otherwise, a sort of trick. But is not the physical world in itself worthy of worship? Do not bodies, beauty, textures, sounds, colors inspire reverentia themselves without instruction?

We experience ourselves as made of two parts, mental and physical, and we see this two-part structure in everything around us, breaking each thing apart and consciously or not labeling one aspect spiritual and another material. Art marries these separated parts together again. Our contemporary distrust of beauty tries to see the natural connection as false and insists that external beauty is unconnected to internal or spiritual elements. We are, I submit, at least nowadays, actually educated to not revere the physical. But it powerfully attracts us no matter how well we are trained to respect the spiritual more. And the history of taboos and prohibitions surrounding the worship of relics by common, uneducated people suggests that the natural response toward beautiful things is to kiss and touch and kneel down before them.

Use of precious materials for the making of spiritual objects removes the stigma of monetary value from them, almost radically spurning financial and utilitarian cares in the interest of spiritual devotion, squandering precious gems like the chiefs of Mauss' potlatch. As artists have done always. And gazing at such objects may lift one away from worldly concerns. As Suger of St. Denis notes, "[t]he loveliness of the many-colored gems had called me away from external cares, and worthy meditation has induced me to reflect, transferring that which is material to that which is immaterial. ... Then it seems to me that I see myself dwelling, as it were, in some strange region of the universe... from the inferior to that higher world in an anagogic manner." But the encounter of pilgrim and relic may have been less abstract; and, despite injunctions to favor inner vision, symbolic ingestion, and divine embrace, the encounter often included touching, tasting, smelling, and kissing. A prohibition against touching at some pilgrimage sites seems to be a taboo necessitated by the pilgrim's desire for sensual contact. There are tales of pilgrims biting off chunks of relics as if in confusion with the Eucharist. Hahn tells us that the persistence of an "improper approach" to relics shown in legends and stories was thought to "cause serious injury or death." The exception was the "ritual humiliation of relics, in which they were 'exposed.' ... Such rituals would not have had an impact if they had not been profoundly shocking to sensibilities that had learned a certain reverentia toward relics."

In this age of reason, for the non-believer, a reliquary is just a box filled with dust, not a revered ritual object carrying the remains of a long-dead but still wonder-working saint. For the believer, conceptuality and de-materialization play a great part in the worship of that handful of dust alleged to have once been the bones of Saint Ignatius or the eyelashes of Agnes or the handful of nails from the crucifixion. There are enough splinters from the True Cross to reforest the wasted, paved-over gardens of all modern metropolises. All the Eucharistic wafers ever swallowed would embody a Christ large enough to embrace us all—I am imagining him like some impossibly gigantic Bread and Puppet Theater papier-mâché effigy come to life, his arms draped in pale colors, with the green fields of Vermont spreading out forever behind him. This coming-to-life, however, would be only one direction of the oscillating magic that circulates when objects are made part of a ritual exchange from real to imaginary to real to imaginary to real to imaginary and ever back and forth again—objects, by the way, that can only be representations or simulations, symbols or emblems of once-real things or real people whose spiritual qualities were often considered more significant than their material forms. The coming-to-life is followed by a dying, or an eerie emptying-out of the object of anima, significance, energy.

But to return to the reliquary, with its preposterous claims: that a pinch of dust is really the remains of Saint Agnes' eyelashes, or a sliver of wood a piece of the cross. It is not to make fun that I refer to these impossible promises, but to try to understand why a religion predicated on a complex relationship between spirit and matter so desperately needed material objects as portals to the allegedly separate and superior Spirit and to trace what this paradox has to do with our contemporary drive toward de-materialization. Embodiment as a basic means to spiritual understanding is, as mentioned, most blatantly illustrated by God's message of Christ: a body inhered with His essence which must have seemed the only way to transmit immaterial understanding to obtuse humans. Reflecting on reliquaries draws us into the unfathomable, alchemically fluid osmosis of matter and spirit activated by anagogic participation with art objects. The relic does not have to really be what it pretends to be; yet we must at least temporarily believe, despite all evidence, that it is. The art object, made of dreams and imagination, from observation, rejection, and celebration of the world as it is, enters the world in order to change it forever. We are all, as human beings, made up of both anima and physica, spirit and body, and if we are honest with ourselves, we will admit that despite the fact that we are always breathing, we can still always be more alive, more spirited, more inspired.

In the small Romanesque churches around Leigné-sur-Usseau, I find the physical traces of Paleolithic stones, the artifacts of Pagan worship and the ornamentation of the simple, graceful piety of early Christianity. There are zodiac signs painted in an archway above the apse and ancient baptismal basins, crude stone crosses with hearts carved in their cruxes, heavy wooden doors with cast iron handles, small stained-glass windows letting faint light into the dark recesses of these chilly, echoing sanctuaries. The gargoyles and paintings on the columns are older and more primitive than any I have ever seen, depicting Rabelaisian potbellied peasants, grotesque grimaces, two-headed beasts, a foolish-looking man bent over with his head between his legs. Francine's necklace suddenly breaks, and its heavy beads go rolling along the ancient stone floor, leading her to a nook where she finds two exotically colored dead butterflies at the feet of a statue of Joan of Arc, reminding us of the precarious but persistent threshold of matter and spirit.

On the nearby grounds of the park where Cardinal Richelieu had his immense castle and collection of art in the seventeenth century, there are only a few crumbling buildings left. His family fell on hard times and sold the stones, which his architects had once taken from neighboring towns to build his castle. They were sold back, one by one, so they are now scattered about the area, returned more or less whence they came. But these few ruins of buildings, like the wine cellar with Silenus-faces grinning over the doorway, surrounded by stone grapes, with its dark interior of wooden beams, are magical conduits. Standing under their roofs we can almost hear the grunts of the servants rolling out the wine casks and the nearby laughter of the elegant guests and the beat of the horses' hooves and the rattling of the carriages along the long promenades lined with old trees. Matter itself is a portal—a portal that we hold for a moment to peek through, a portal that we ourselves are—for a short lifetime only, before we let it slip, before it lets us slip into other worlds.

There is so much time in a day here at the Maison Gai Saber, and so little interruption and busyness, that one can—one must—experience the very character of the air, the changes in the weather, the changes in one's psyche. One palpably senses time and space when looking at an old sampler on Francine's bedroom door (the room where she was born), stitched by a foremother, Anne Prevost, in colorful threads that have bled over the years onto the background. And the time and space are suspended when drinking freshly brewed tea in a china cup possibly hundreds of years old, purchased from a flea market in the town where Joan of Arc came to visit the king. One feels the energies of the people who made, owned, enjoyed, lost, and loved these things. We can hear their voices in the halls and in the ancient woods.

Americans like myself can hardly understand this sense of connection to an old house, I suppose, beyond a certain point, even though many of us, like myself, come from families with roots in the Old World—some uprooted violently. My mother, a hidden child of the Holocaust, says that she herself has never felt a connection to a place or to materiality, and she wondered if my fascination with objects was in some way a compensation for her own displaced spirit. Perhaps it is, for even if we try to separate ourselves from our difficult histories, there will always remain traces, unfathomed, unintegrated, as shadows and repressed pathologies. Some of us still feel these old stirrings, hear these old songs, and sense these old ancestral longings in our bodies; second and third generations may have the requisite distance to face and to touch the remains of these dark ghosts, as well as the more friendly spirits of these traces passed down in genetic memories, in stories, instincts, atavistic echoes. Maybe that is one of the reasons we make the long journey to the Old World, and to other places where our ancestors have lived and loved and suffered and enjoyed, even if we didn't know it when we set off.

The sun is shining and the sky is very blue through the casement window in my lovely "resident room," where I sit at my cluttered desk. Laid across it is a huge piece of tracing paper which I purloined from the "ballroom," upon which I have hand-written all my notes on *Schatzkammer*, cabinets of curiosities, and reliquaries, in many-colored inks in non-linear waves. The large piece of paper is covered with open books, including the hand-bound one I made here and am filling with drawings; it is covered with leaves and flowers and feathers I have picked up in my walks; with ink bottles and ribbons; with small spools of thread and a large spool of golden cord bought at the flea market, and buttons and scissors and slips of paper with notes scribbled on them, and even a camellia from the garden—all physical-spiritual things that are valuable in very personal and symbolic ways, none of them worth money and few of them worth much to any but the rare person with a taste for such shreds and shards of a mind's processes. Portals they may be, hems we may cling to on the skirts of ancestors, conduits between earth and more disembodied memories, traces and entryways backward and forward, in and out of time and space.

V.

Making Meaning I

The Categorical Imp of the Perverse

It is a radical, a primitive impulse—elementary.

Edgar Allan Poe
'The Imp of the Perverse'

Act only in accordance with that maxim through which you can at the same time will that it become a universal law.

Immanuel Kant
Grounding for the Metaphysics of Morals

THE CATEGORICAL IMP OF THE PERVERSE is a hybrid of Poe's imp of the perverse and Kant's categorical imperative. This strange imp will leap about in the following pages amid all manner of philosophical confusion and try to sew together again the patches of thought that have been ripped apart, but in motley fashion; for she is but a poor seamstress for such complicated quilting and, besides, the seams will, in the best of circumstances, burst again and require some new arrangement. There are tried and true patterns she will revert to, and for good reasons. But like all artists, she will deviate from the patterns, too, beginning new traditions and conventions in place of the old. That however all the patches are made of the same fabric—a fabric woven of the mind's sympathy with the material world—we can be quite sure.

Two myths regarding the origin of language haunt our presentiments about the way we know reality and, thus, our conclusions about how and what the world means. One posits an absolute and legible world of meaning; the other an utterly meaningless world. The first tells the tale of a lost *Ur-Sprache,* wherein words were identical to the things they signified. Mixing Kabbalistic creation magic with esoteric Renaissance alchemy, this myth is one source of Romantic views of the world as whole, harmonious, and inherently logical ("worded" and in accordance with Reason). The assumption is that things mean, and that their meaning is at least partially legible—if not transparently through the dark glass of the fallen language of man, then at least through the visible language of nature, its patterns and repeating hieroglyphs. From ancient times through the mid-eighteenth century at least, scholars and mystics have searched for traces of a perfect language, supposedly lost after the collapse of the Tower of Babel or after that other fall in Eden, claiming sometimes that it was a form of Hebrew and, at others, inventing new symbol systems that promised to heal the rift between word and world, human mind and cosmos. Suspending for a moment belief in the myth's more esoteric tendencies, the idea that language could be intrinsically related to reality is somewhat supported by etymological evidence tracing the roots of words in the world of matter, binding thought to history, nature, and social practices. Most compelling of all is its occasional call—as in Dante's *De vulgari eloquentia* (1303-1305)—for the modern poet to bridge the chasm between both words and the essences of ideas and things with a creative regeneration of language.

The second myth denies any correspondence between words and world, and tends to insist that individual experience cannot be translated from one person to the next. It came more recently to prominence, though there were proto-believers, or shall I say skeptics—for it is a skeptical myth, though myth just the same—even in ancient times. It came to hold sway in the late nineteenth century, along with other skepticisms, gained considerable ground at the turn of the twentieth, and is currently one of the most pervasive articles of faith of the twenty-first century social theorist and even many writers who, in holding to it, undermine a belief in their own work. In this explanation of the origin of language, words have never been, and never could be, anything but arbitrary labels for things. This arbitrariness signals a kind of treacherous deceit. The way we think is, they warn, directed and controlled by these arbitrary signifiers—masters, which have no right to such guiding and limiting power over our thoughts and the world they pretend to describe. Words, in this story, coalesce into controlling concepts, cutting up the world into arbitrary categories and quickly shutting down thought and vision. As if that were not bad enough, this tyranny of words deceives in yet another fundamental way. By presenting an order that is invented, words give the lie to the actual disordered state of the world. Words cover up a chaotic, fluid abyss that cannot (or rather should not) be reduced, differentiated, or delimited. Words impose definitions where there should be none, separating, distinguishing, discriminating. Perhaps by the end of the twenty-first century, light itself will be decried as another separator of substances, an arbitrary surveyor of imperialistic boundary lines between brightness and shadow; but, for now, we may enjoy our chiaroscuro, virtually guiltlessly. Not so our words. Words in this myth fail to translate between thing and mind and between person and person and language and language. All is a jumble. This myth of untranslatability marks a kind of second Babel, inaugurating a dire suspicion about the ability of words to mean anything, and about meaning altogether.

A driving force of the myth of untranslatabilty is the myth of social construction, which, in its most extreme form, denies any relationship between our social attitudes and customs and our biology, instincts, or experiences, thus cutting the lifeline between materiality and ideas. Neither the myth of the perfect language nor that of non-translatability are true in their extreme forms, but both contain germs of truth, and both are analogies for the fears and hopes of human beings who are, naturally, quite concerned with whether or not the world has any meaning and how we might know what it is and then communicate it to others. But like all strict dualisms, their extreme polarity avoids the fruitful unification of opposites where the world meets word and both might be expanded through contact.

Over the course of the twentieth century, philosophers continued the exploration begun in ancient times of how we know the world, focusing more directly on how we know the world through language. In the twenty-first century, these queries have often been reduced to a set of conclusions about how we don't and can't know the world, neither through language nor otherwise. Although these philosophies have often been liberating, breaking down preconceived limits and questioning restrictive assumptions, when taken to their logical extremes they lead to silence and solipsism.

Social construction is, of course, grounded in the much older philosophical supposition that it is impossible to experience, see, or know "the thing in itself." We see only phenomena and not realities, and our seeing is determined by filters or structures in our brains that mediate the ways in which we see. Over centuries, this realization has been transformed to mean that what we see is necessarily either wrong or extremely different from what is, an assumption that was not present in Kant's *Critique of Pure Reason*. Although Kant conceived of the *a priori* mental structures that determined our perception as divinely given, we might secularize his exploration by accepting that there are basic biological constants in human brains through which we see, sense, and experience phenomena. While Kant might say that each person sees a different shade of red, he did not suggest that we each see entirely different colors, or that colors themselves did not exist.

The "categorical imp of the perverse" acknowledges that there are some *a priori* givens or essences in both our minds and the world and that, whether we can see the "thing in itself" perfectly or not, we still have some access to a reasonable sense of reality in its basic forms; that our individual perception, although subjective, is not so radically different from that of others as to prohibit correspondence and communication; that we can use words and images to approximate our meanings and expand our own perception and that of others; and, finally, that while we may follow the categorical imperative as a general law, we also will, like Poe's imp, perversely deviate from its strictures when an uncontrollable irrational impulse, a creative urge, an ethical scruple, or simple taste dictates.

This impish, un-categorical imperative is an unfashionable idea, to be sure, for it does not provide the satisfaction of either complete wholeness and harmony, on the one hand, or of complete nihilism and alienation, on the other. Instead, it hovers uncomfortably in a middle realm where some things are real and repeating and others open to interpretation and change. It leaves us neither completely omnipotent nor completely helpless.

Nietzsche, inaugurating the "linguistic turn," made us aware of the way language conceptualizes reality by creating names or descriptions of things that may leave out as much as they contain. Words are inexact figures and metaphors, inaccurate and incommensurate attempts to describe reality. We group similar things that nevertheless exhibit many differences into general categories; and this process induces a sort of simplification of seeing. We come to perceive dogs, trees, men, women, instead of each individual creature and entity. This eventually leads us to create abstractions and reifications, such as love, good, bad, noble, moral, money, which may become more and more removed from physical reality and experience. Yet while many theorists after Nietzsche came to see the use of language as a treacherous crime committed upon reality, he tended to see it in a more creatively joyous light. Just as long as we do not come to be the slaves of ossified constructs and concepts, just as long as the "creative subject" (to use Nietzsche's term for all humans who act upon the object of the world) continues to make new terms, new words, new metaphors, new figures to describe a changing reality from his own shifting perspective—just as long as individuals stoke the flame of a living language—language can be a prod and a stimulus to new seeing.

Social construction theory has tried to moralistically discredit this joyous aesthetic and existential world- and word-making activity, and has replaced it with an imperative to strip every word and every concept of its given meaning by calling all designations and conceptualizations into question. Berger and Luckmann, authors of *The Social Construction of Reality*, reduce all human culture to "an assemblage of maxims, morals, proverbial nuggets of wisdom, values and beliefs, myths, and so forth, the theoretical integration of which requires considerable intellectual fortitude in itself, as the long line of heroic integrators from Homer to the latest sociological system-builders testifies." Thus the enlightened skeptics discard all of literature, philosophy, and history in one fell swoop—excepting of course, their own myth and narrative, of a social system occurring randomly and *ex nihilo*, which just appears and dupes all subsequent humans into following new rules and belief systems which have nothing to do with human tendencies, desires, or human nature. The champions of the subsequent puritanical silence would discredit myth, historic narrative, fairy tales, religious legends, songs, poems, paintings, totems, and talismans as random and traitorous social constructions. They would have us scoff at any product of the human imagination as if it had been made by some abstract non-human author, as something necessarily imposed upon the passive human from some extraneous force that would have to be virtually extraterrestrial, not ourselves, not natural. They would insist that a human is not capable of experiencing his or her reality without being blindsided by the already constructed way of seeing determined by his or her society, as if construction only works in one negative, exclusive, terminal direction, when in fact new ideas, new conceptualizations, new abstractions exponentially proliferate over the ages, as new details, microcosmic particulars, and relative complexities are incorporated into our shared cultural, scientific, and artistic discourse.

Of course, our visions and perspectives are colored by our social context and these visions vary from one culture to another, often extremely. The variations between cultures must be the product of many different influences, from genetics to climate to landscape to the requirement for survival of a particular place and a particular people (gene culture co-evolution). Originary group social experiences are passed down from generation to generation, and are altered or not over time. Certainly, old customs can be kept longer than necessary and humans on the whole may act according to originary evolutionary necessities that are no longer useful, and even sometimes harmful in our current context. But these ways of seeing and ways of acting are not random. In other words, while there certainly are many social constructs, there is no such thing as "just" a social construct—a phrase that suggests that the construct appeared out of nowhere and has no validity whatsoever. Social constructs, including language, education, and art, are the positive product of human interaction with nature, the physical world, social groups, experience. They may always be questioned and often must be challenged, but they are fundamental and indispensable to human culture.

Over time, there is oscillation between repeated forms and invention, including the benefit of influence, interaction, discourse, criticism, the scientific method, testing of assumptions, positing of hypotheses and theories, gathering of facts and evidence to support the hypotheses and theories, foregrounding certain facts over others, selecting out and focusing on one or another aspect, evaluating based on differing values and differing relative needs of the moment.

Without the interventions of the foolish imp (pointing out naïvely that the emperor has no clothes, for example) an utterly de-materialized form of reader response theory might prevail in the social scene, regardless of the "text" that is being interpreted. The categorical imp wags its finger at an "anything goes" interpretation of the world, blurting out "foolish" truisms to make sophisticated social theorists blush, but also does not stay long within any constructed system that can be exploded or questioned. One can say that different people notice different things when they read a story; that their experiences color what they will remember and the emotions that different words or images inspire. But one can't say that the story itself is different. What is in it is what is in it. A test consists in the subjective reader pointing out something, making an observation. Is it really there? Or is it a wrong reading, a reading into, a hallucination? Do others see it too, now that it has been pointed out? Indeed, since people do largely see mainly what others have seen before them, it takes a particularly brave or odd reader to suddenly find something there that others have missed repeatedly. Different reading capabilities will see more nuances; simpler people will miss complexities or misread altogether. Someone may grasp the literal but not the allegorical or ironic level.

But here we are talking about a story, something made with some level of intention by a conscious being, something limited. What of the vast and contradictory text of the world? How do we read it collectively even though there is no author and no given purpose? Arrive at an interpretation of its infinite elements and relations? Not all readings are acceptable or right. Yet they persist. How do people live entire lives misunderstanding reality, or not understanding aspects of science, biology, history, anthropology? We still come to absurd conclusions about observed phenomena, like primitives inventing myths to explain the terrors of nature. What of these myths? They are readings and explanations. Technically, scientifically wrong, but often they are allegorically, humanly right. People lived, perhaps, more beautiful and richer lives believing in Zeus and the divinations of the Oracle than we do today with our scientific knowledge of cause and effect. But there have also been instances when superstitions and wrong-thinking have led to terrible misery and violence (as they still do today, alas). What we want would rather be myths that are "true" to the most healthful, life-affirming essence of Nature: myths to help us understand who we are and face up to the fearsomeness of the unknown, myths that help us to embrace change and mortality and reality. The myth of a perfect language and the myth of untranslatability can be classed in the larger philosophical categories on either side of hope and despair. Which myth is most true to our potential as a species and which do we want to dream on? Do we want skeptical solipsism or holistic idealism? Again, as in all such extreme polarizations, the sweet spot is in their synthesis, in the creation of a new myth: perhaps that of the categorical imp of the perverse.

How much then is our reading of the world, of events, of words, of symbols invented or constructed; and how much, on the other hand, is it inherent in our nature, our biology, our evolutionary coding? Words and symbols describe, denote, suggest, but they may also coerce and imprison; words calcify clichés, but they also can be rearranged and newly coined to make us see and be in new ways. The relationship of the material world with the world of words and ideas has, of course, significant bearing on the very question of meaning, not just the meaning of words, but of the meanings or values we attribute to the world and our ability to share, compare, and translate these meanings with others over time and space. Meaning in the sense of an intentional, predetermined purpose by some external agent is not credible. We are not here for something (short of evolutionary processes which cannot always be counted on our side or in our interest). And yet our biological sensory essences are replete in themselves with a life-force, a will to power, a will to pleasure and also, surprisingly, an evolved ethical and social sense. According to E.O. Wilson, in *The Meaning of Human Existence*, "[t]he origin of the human condition is best explained by the natural selection for social interaction—the inherited propensities to communicate, recognize, evaluate, bond, cooperate, compete..." If this is the case, what would it mean for the continuation of our species were we to turn our backs on these originary processes? We create and find meanings, valuations, scales of significance about things, acts, people, as a result of our shared experience. These conclusions are not random or arbitrary, but based on our own bodies, on nature, on what seems to work, on what brings pleasure, excitement; on instinct, on counter-instinct; and, yes, also by conditioning and resistance to conditioning. By denying the direct influence of material reality on our ideas, we undo the bonds between thought and action. By breaking the current from world to word and mind, we break the current back as well: a disembodied idea cannot touch an embodied world.

Modernism introduced both freedom and alienation through the recognition of perspectivism and relativity, expanding non-linear modes of communication such as symbols, metaphors, and novel arrangements of forms to express the newly significant internal states that could not as easily be expressed in didactic or expository language. Postmodernism robbed the individual of even the comfort of her own temporary, provisional, shifting view—relieved by moments of being as extratemporal, exceptional moments when all flux was set in a harmonious form before being dispersed once more—and then further denied the notion that these experiences might be translatable to others through poetic form. Declaring that everything cancelled out everything else, and that any interpretation was as good as any other (thus: none were any good), postmodernism simultaneously opened the airwaves to an inchoate cacophony and closed many mortal ears to the music of the spheres. Ostensibly taking away the privilege of the elite reader, any reader of the world was now equally entitled to affirm his own arbitrary reading over any other. Some contemporary theorists go a step further—lacking, however, the compensation of another world that may have softened the blow of Berkeley's eighteenth-century de-materialism—by suggesting that there isn't even a world or a reality to know in the first place.

But through materiality we are literally in touch with the textures, the colors, the approximate spaces and dynamics of iteration and difference in our shared physical world. Although our experiences of the real are necessarily colored, limited, or expanded by our personal experiences and subjective lenses, we need not give in to alienated despair and a rejection of the possibility of translation from person to person, language to language, culture to culture, or past to present to future. Although my perception of the world is filtered through my own mind, temperament, experience, and interests, it is possible that the words I use and the images I make in order to evoke that world will mean something to you. And the differences between how I see the world and the way you see it are in fact enriching and expansive variations of individual and collective worldviews, creating awareness of individual sentience and self-consciousness.

Schiller's distinction between naïve and sentimental approaches to poetry, the former exemplified by the simple objectivity of Homer, the latter by the subjectivity of Romanticism, is again instructive. We are all-too-aware, today, that all vision involves re-vision (even Homer's supposedly objective reportage) and that all expression comes from a particular perspective; but this need not mean that each representation is hopelessly inaccessible to other humans who share, at least to some extent, much the same cellular structure, much the same instinctive apparatus, and much the same social and natural experience. Thoreau, though labelled a transcendentalist and thus supposedly a proponent of innate knowledge rather than empiricism, was really committed to what he called "fronting the facts" of reality: "All perception of truth is the detection of an analogy," he wrote, "we reason from our hands to our head." Analogies would not mean anything to us if they did not correspond to something we recognized from a shared real world.

In an age when alienation is taken by some as a mark of sophistication, I would rather hearken back to a time when sentimentality—a mode of perception and expression that infuses some external entity with a subjectivity—was not a dirty word. For the cost of abandoning communication and correspondence between persons, and between persons and their world, is far too high to uncritically accept philosophies that insist on the absolute incommensurability of perception and phenomena, word and thing, individual and individual. The ultimate cost of abandoning an approximate translation of some shared meaning, is not only culture and community, as George Steiner and others have noted, but also any impetus for individual or group agency. For, if we cannot know the world well enough, and cannot know others more or less, and cannot know even ourselves, it would not only be impossible to function on a daily basis, but it would be impossible to dream about and to work to minimize the space between what is and what could be. The kind of knowing that helps us with practical functioning and the kind that helps us dream and engage with the world are both proximate, but they have different uses. The former is a pragmatism that accepts certain probabilities for the sake of efficiency and practicality. The kind of knowing that allows us to dream and act, however, is one that fathoms the difference between what is determined and what is yet determinable, keeping always a lifeline from the palpable facts of nature down to the subconscious, the watery depths of the imagination, a kind of knowing which must continually measure what in our life is necessity and what might yet be changed.

If constructs in the form of language and images have a tendency to direct thought, thereby potentially limiting how we see the world, then the "creative subject" has an ethical and aesthetic responsibility to rejuvenate where ideas have become ossified, and to invent new living language where vision has become merely conventional. Even evolutionary and genetic coding can be resisted to varying extents—according to Dawkins' concept of the meme—so that individual and group choice may deviate from long-repeated patterns and veer away from social and biological conformity. Environmental events also alter what is beneficial for survival, inducing adaptations which change the course of social behavior. But extreme forms of social construction deny the biological and evolutionary foundations of our thought and action. According to Stephen Pinker's *The Blank Slate: The Modern Denial of Human Nature,* the long-established model of social science made a religion out of the idea of the impressionable empty mind waiting to be imprinted by any external force whatsoever, denying any connection between one's physical characteristics, one's material surroundings, and one's behavior, shifting the entire cause of social systems to conditioning and social engineering. Pinker's radical stance is that

> [w]e have reason to believe that the mind is equipped with a battery of emotions, drives, and faculties for reasoning and communicating, and that they have a common logic across cultures, are difficult to erase or redesign from scratch, were shaped by natural selection acting over the course of human evolution, and owe some of their basic design (and some of their variation) to information in the genome.

Although, as Pinker notes in his introduction, most people acknowledge that everything is both nature and nurture, when it really comes down to it (in a liberal milieu, in any case), politically-correct assumptions veer sharply away from biological causation. In tracing the ideological shift from biology to historical materialism to social construction, Pinker first quotes Franz Boas—"We must assume that all complex activities are socially determined, not hereditary"—and then Durkheim: "Individual natures are merely the indeterminate material that the social factor molds and transforms." He notes also that B.F. Skinner's behaviorism was based on a belief in the complete malleability of individuals. The blank slate model has been used, of course, as political leverage to affirm the equal potential of all persons; but, as Pinker argues, it also works against the development of the kind of innate ethical behavior that can do battle against totalitarianism, the shadow that looms large over this discussion. Marxist historical materialism—which, certainly in its received form, oddly leaves the material of the body out when calculating what material forces shape the individual—is based on the blank slate model; whereas Nazism was, of course, grounded in an ideology of ethnic cleansing with direct links to biology. Rescuing the humane exploration of the extent of genetic causes of behavior from its associated calumny, Pinker reminds us that "[g]overnment sponsored mass murder can come from an anti-innate belief system as easily as from an innate one." The Stalinists, in pursuit of a political goal based on the blank slate, killed just as many people as the Nazis (or more). Noam Chomsky, whose research on universal grammars leans in the direction of the perfect language myth, echoes Pinker's reservations about the political benefits of the blank slate model:

> If, in fact, man is an indefinitely malleable, completely plastic being, with no innate structures of mind and no intrinsic needs of a cultural or social character, then he is a fit subject for the 'shaping of behavior' by the state authority, the corporate manager, the technocrat, or the central committee. Those with some confidence in the human species will hope this is not so and will try to determine the intrinsic characteristics that provide the framework for intellectual development, the growth of moral consciousness, cultural achievement, and participation in a free community.

Social construction theory, dependent upon the total malleability of the blank slate model—although ostensibly a radical attack on exploitative and oppressive essences, universals, and absolutes—has a paradoxical tendency to discourage rather than inspire radical activity. This is because it is cynical about the individual's participatory agency in creating and if necessary reconstructing our shared world, the essential ethical agency affirmed by existentialism. Adorno finally conceded that there could be some form of poetry after Auschwitz, but can we find our way back to a scientific and philosophical ideology that balances the influence of both biology and environment, an assessment of language that allows for some measure of conceptual correspondence with reality, a way to appreciate the significance of civilization amid its cruelties and kindnesses? And if we cannot, how shall we possibly proceed as a culture, as members of an extended and complex cultural and ecological system? Centuries after the *Kantkrise,* when people rightfully experienced the disequilibrium of a world from which, somewhat later, the horizon, in Nietzsche's image, had been wiped away with a sponge, a world wherein all established values were subject to re-evaluation, a mature attempt is called for: to do our best, despite subjectivity, perspectivism, and cultural differences. Because the real costs of abandoning the possibility of communication are nothing less than culture, community, and ethical agency.

Nietzsche characterized language as a "prison house," and Wittgenstein famously noted the challenge of struggling against the walls of language, but both concluded that there was no choice but to attempt to communicate despite the challenges. Nietzsche wrote: "We have to cease to think, if we refuse to do it in the prison house of language." I suggest that instead of a prison house, what we really have is a misprision house, a house where misunderstandings haunt our communications; a house, however, which we may readily transform with all manner of expansion, rearrangement, implosion and explosion. A house of our own making, subject to our own renovations. A house of any kind requires foundations. In language, these foundations are words and concepts; in society, the foundations are shared universals. Cultural relativity is one of the largely unexamined assumptions of contemporary society, but many anthropologists and sociologists have made the case for a wide number of behavioral constants across all cultures. Pinker includes a list compiled from Donald Brown's *Human Universals* as an appendix to *The Blank Slate*, featuring such commonalities as ambivalence, figurative language, rituals, gift-giving, in-group and out-group consciousness, nuclear family structures, incest taboos, art appreciation, attempts to predict the future, punishment for anti-social behavior, distinguishing self from others, sexual jealousy, synesthetic metaphors, taxonomy, language applied to misinform or mislead, synonyms, co-operation, selfishness, status-seeking, explaining events by causation, fear of death, proverbs, ethnocentrism, private inner life, redress of wrongs, risk-taking, hope, and others. Chomsky, as already noted, argues for an innate and universal grammatical structure for all languages. Despite manifest differences, he writes, "it seems that very heavy conditions in the form of grammar are universal. Deep structures seem to be very similar from language to language, and the rules that manipulate and interpret them also seem to be drawn from a very narrow class of conceivable formal operations." Although there are variations across cultures in terms of language and customs, "the deeper mechanisms of mental computation that generate them may be universal and innate."

There are more things in heaven and earth that are universal than the social constructionist will usually allow, and the tension between these universals and individual will and choice is the same tension present in the categorical imperative, put into new and equally paradoxical words by Emerson, who received his Kant filtered through the German Romantics. In his famous essay, 'Self-Reliance', Emerson writes: "To believe your own thought, to believe that what is true for you in your private heart is true for all men,—that is genius." In other words, if you follow your own conscience instead of blindly following conventions and social constructions, you probably will find yourself where the most conscious humans before you have found themselves; but it is not something an ethical person can take for granted. Thus, one must assess and experiment anew—while keeping the experiments of others always within reach.

A young male friend of mine told me of an experiment he conducted with a woman friend to try to "be together without preconceptions," without language, without definitions. It fell flat. What is left when we take away history, archetypes, essence? Some preconceived images and roles are still meaningful, though others have become empty shells, simulacra, and conventions. What still reverberates, and why? Consider Proust's Swann and his comparison of his beloved Odette to the women in old paintings. Her beauty in the present is enhanced by its comparison and relation with the already delineated forms of archetypal female beauty. When I was a young woman, I was attracted and repelled by de Beauvoir's encouragement in *The Second Sex* to simply live as one is, and let that define what a woman is. I understood the problem with any individual woman trying to fit into a pre-existing role of womanliness, and judging her success and failure as a person based on the extent to which she does so, especially in so far as the myths have often been written by men. Indeed, de Beauvoir's discussion constitutes one of the clearest illustrations of the existentialist motto: existence precedes essence.

But much is lost if we abandon the ancient archetypes altogether. Some essences do precede existence, and they cannot easily by altered by even the strongest will. A woman is whatever any particular woman is; but at the same time a woman is an echo and a continuance of what women have always been: in poetry, history, song, painting, myth. Today's blank slate theory is tantamount to a total blankness, a neutered neutrality, especially as it threatens to wipe away not only history and archetype, but even biology and instinct. If fantasies of roles and patterns do not excite the contemporary moralistic lover (who may try to be blank even in his or her perception of eroticism), then at least biology ought to do the trick. But even that is repressed or denied. Nothing is supposed to be determinative except social context, which is allegedly random and created by oppressive institutions. Shall we then sacrifice erotic imagination and sexual pleasure for a sterile—indeed blank—moralistic neutrality? Or is it possible to play affirmatively with the fruitful tension between innovation and an engagement with determined biology and past archetypes? Today we speak of fluidity and the social construct of gender, often without considering the implications of these ideas. Fluidity is consistent with a rejection of the "construct" of gender, but transformation of physical and stylistic trappings seems still to keep faith with the gender roles it claims to repudiate, only changing the individual's physicality to match a pre-created role. I certainly have nothing against each individual pursuing his or her or their own sense of sexuality. I sometimes feel like a thunderstorm, a mountainside, a young boy, an old book, a lioness, a flower, a lightning bolt, a field of moss. Yet I am concerned about the way in which this new mode of thought joins other current ideologies to deny the reality of the material world.

I suppose I am rather old-fashioned, though, believing even that words mean something that can be traced back to nature through their roots. Emerson, who nowadays is also old-fashioned but in his time was a proponent of the new thought, wrote that words were "fossil poetry"; and an archbishop of Dublin, Richard Chenevix Trench, D.D., elaborated on this suggestive phrase in a book much loved by Thoreau. Trench writes:

> [A] popular American author has somewhere characterized language as 'fossil poetry.' He evidently means that just as in some fossils, curious and beautiful shapes of vegetable or animal life, the graceful fern or the finely vertebrate lizard, such as now, it may be, have been extinct for thousands of years, are permanently bound up with the stone, and rescued from that perishing which would have been theirs—so in words are beautiful thoughts and images, the imagination and the feeling of past ages, of men long since in their graves. ... Language may be, and indeed is, this 'fossil poetry' [but it is also] fossil ethics, or fossil history.

How far from this belief in the significance of etymology we are today! Some contemporary people seem to really not believe that words have any meanings at all. They do not keep their words, and speak untruths easily, just as advertisers do, with rampant euphemism, ignoring the proper use of grammatical symbols like possessive apostrophes (perhaps a subconscious attempt to do away with private property and possession?), sprinkling them around haphazardly, in hopes that one might make some sense somewhere or sprout into a sentence.

Sounding much like Wittgenstein, who came to believe in the organic, communal development of language over time, Trench writes:

"Man makes his own language, but he makes it as the bee makes its cells, as the bird its nest, he cannot do otherwise." Indeed, why should human language-making (like the mind) be something outside of nature? Why an imposition upon nature? Trench compares the natural growth of the tree of language to a "house being built of dead timbers combined after his own fancy and caprice." "Language," he writes, prefiguring the coming Modernist crisis, "is as truly on one side the limit and restraint of thought." And he continues, landing on more solid ground than the later language philosophers, declaring language to be "on the other side that which feeds and unfolds thought," and that "there is... a reality about words." Words to Trench are not mere arbitrary signs, but "living powers... growing out of roots, clustering in families, connected and intertwining themselves with all that men have been doing and thinking and feeling from the beginning of the world till now." Tribulation: from tribulum-harrow, a threshing instrument; caprices—from capra, a goat; daisy—eye of day; laburnum—golden rain. Words are like artifacts in curiosity cabinets, except that they are living, evolving.

If originally words were arbitrary, they grew out of each other in accord with reality. But why do we worry so much about the distinction between what is and what is perceived or how named, when the perceiver-namer is made of the same nature as the observed? Why would the structure of the human mind and its brainchild, language, commit treachery on its own kith and kin, its own world? That sometimes false etymologies are attached to words whose real etymologies have been forgotten may only prove the connection of words to realities all the more, since the new explanation relates the old word to some existing reality. We are always binding words to what is, even if they do not strictly come from one particular is. Trench writes: "errors survive in words" and "disprove themselves": tempers, humors, saturnine, mercurial, jovial (descriptions of people born under these planets); to charm, bewitch, enchant, lunacy, panic, auguries, and auspices (from divination), initiating (from rites)—all mark the persistence of pagan words in Christian lands. The universe was named "cosmos," or beautiful order, probably by Pythagoras. Was this not an expression of natural human sentiment voiced by one man? It is surely one possible good name for the universe, though not the only or ultimate one. Someone else in a later era might choose rather to name it "chaos."

Words born of a specific culture attest to that culture's history and tendencies. Though sometimes it may be difficult to ascertain which is the stronger and dominant friend, language or reality, we cannot deny that a relationship obtains. Smith comes from smite; wrong from wring; haft from have. Shire, shore, shears, share, shred, shard are all connected to the idea of separation. The contemporary fear of mastery and dominance denies even this relatedness. Some people would rather have no meaning than a meaning that is possibly imposed. Rather not use language at all, they think, than use the language of the oppressors. Why not, instead, make new words? Become ourselves creators?

A belief in the meaningful relation between words and the world extended in Thoreau to a belief in man's ability to read the visible meanings in nature (*verba visibilia*) as lessons in human conduct. In his 1837 journal, he writes: "How indispensable to a correct study of nature is a perception of her true meaning. The fact will one day flower out into a truth." A few entries later, he observes ice crystals on the lake:

> When the ice was laid upon its smooth side [the crystal] resembles the roofs and steeples of a Gothic city, or the vessels of a crowded harem under a press of canvas. ... Wherever the water, or other causes, had formed a hole in the bank, its throat and outer edge, like the entrance to a citadel of the olden time, bristled with a glistening ice armor. In one place you might see minute ostrich feathers, which seemed the waving plumes of the warriors filing into the fortress, in another the glancing fan-shaped banners of the Lilliputian host, and in another the needle-shaped particles, collected into bundles resembling the plumes of the pine, might pass for the phalanx of spears.

Thoreau cannot help but draw meaning, make stories and connections between observed natural phenomena and human life and civilization. We all make meaning when we look at Nature. We say the moon is smiling on us lovers, or fancy that an overcast, stormy sky is melancholy and a bright one happy. These are merely natural phenomena with no intentional meaning. But spring blossoms make us think of newness and rebirth because they *are* new re-births; just as autumn's gloominess is death, a temporary going-under, a symbol system of the *Ur-Pflanze*'s recurrence. This surely is no invention, but the truth of their significance. We naturally tell ourselves stories of human life when observing nature (as we do when we listen to music, as sounds suggest landscapes and actions, crises, moods, narratives from human life). And Thoreau would have us learn from Nature how to be more noble, more hearty, more equanimical about changes and cycles: "So let it be with man," he writes, over and over, after describing a natural process.

But just as there are repeating natural laws we can reliably study to learn about the world, ourselves, and each other, there is the categorical imp of the perverse, which, again and again, proves that man can break the patterns of thought and behavior constructed by his forefathers and foremothers. Changing presentiments over centuries have been initiated by individual discoveries and inventions, by accidents and reactions, by experiences that prove old presentiments wrong, and in response to new physical realities: infinity, entropy, solar heat death, eternal recurrence, millennial apocalypse, chaos theory, robotics, creationism, evolution, and social construction itself.

Is evolution ("just") a social construct? No better than the one it replaced? Darwin's critics accused him of gathering data to support his hypothesis, as if such a process were a manipulative and dishonest method of forcing existence into a certain essence. The opposite was true. In the twenty years of gathering and testing evidence from the natural world leading up to his writing of *The Origin of Species*, Darwin worked from observation toward hypothesis in a remarkably innocent way, not expecting to find (to borrow Nietzsche's wonderful image) the truth he had himself (subconsciously) hidden behind a bush. But ironically, he actually discovered data that undermined Creationism—and his own religious beliefs—the socially-constructed truth of his society, thereby demonstrating that individuals are not all such dupes as social construction theory makes us out to be. Social construction theorists tend to reduce the rich history of human thought down to a few institutionalized oppressive ideas, ignoring the variety and ingenuity and complexity of any given society's presentiments, dreams, and beliefs.

In fact, not only are there repeating universals and also deviations from these universals over time and space, but differences among cultures and throughout history may in fact depend on a vital interplay between universality and deviating human agency. If everything is not entirely, externally, randomly constructed, or else entirely determined by biology, inheritance, and evolutionary urges, then we have some degree of agency to choose what we love and hate and favor and impugn. We have the agency to break out of established patterns and create new ones, which then create individuated modes and variations. Paradoxically, then, differentiation proves comprehensive universality, as the deviations of so many things that usually repeat (archetypes, life forms, ways of living, attitudes toward beauty, others, family, nature, ethics, deep structures in languages) can be attributed to choice rather than coercion or random conformity.

In *After Babel,* Steiner talks about translation (by which he means not just from language to language but from person to person) as a process including destructive aggression, appropriation, and expansion. We break the meaning of the other when we attempt to understand and re-present; we appropriate it into our own idiom, idiolect, understanding. And then we also add something to it. We expand it with interpretation, elucidation, interest, passion—thereby deforming it. This is analogous to all relations between individuals and countries (passionate love, colonialism, anthropological study) and I suspect that the current distrust of language has something to do with our sensitivity about appropriation and mastery. No-one dares speak for someone else or for another kind of person, assuming incomprehension and practicing silence. At the Vermont Studio Center where I was resident one winter, some of the other writers were sensitively discussing whether a white person could write a black character, or a male a female one. But is not at least one part of what a writer does imagining the "other" and delineating and dissolving, dissolving and delineating, the differences between everything? With such fastidious exclusions, most of literature would have to be banned. Today it seems that many people don't dare express themselves, or dare love or enter into relationships at all, for fear of overcoming or being overcome by another person's personality, power, desires.

What are the consequences of such paranoia in regard to appropriation? Steiner writes: "If a substantial part of all utterances were not public or, more precisely, could not be treated as if they were, chaos and autism would follow." Although language can limit the horizon of our consciousness, it is also one of the ways—or maybe the only way—to expand it. Poetic language, as Wittgenstein suggested, is the answer to a cliché-ridden, ossified thought. Living language, as Robert Musil practiced and preached it, is the active process of revivifying stale meanings through the magic of metaphor-making. Although the process is inaccurate, metaphors, writes Musil, "bring beauty and excitement into the world." Steiner concurs: "Vital acts of speech are those which seek to make a fresh and 'private' content more publicly available without weakening the uniqueness, the felt edge of individual intent." And continues:

> In significant measure, different languages are different, inherently creative counter proposals to the constraints, to the limiting universals of biological and ecological conditions. They are the instruments of storage and of transmission of legacies of experience and imaginative construction particular to a given community. We do not yet know if the 'deep structures' postulated by transformational-generative

> grammars are in fact substantive universals. But if they are, the immense diversity of languages as men have spoken and speak them can be interpreted as a direct rebellion against the undifferentiated constraints of biological universality.

Steiner suggests that we use language to hide, keep secrets, lie, imagine fictions; that groups use language to differentiate and leave others out, in ways that give us advantages evolutionarily. Of course, over time, the circle of insiders grows larger, as the unknown becomes more and more rare. Amid persistence of sameness, however, there exists persistent resistance to sameness and a constant generation of difference.

The existential requirement is that each person decide for herself, in all circumstances where there is choice, paying heed to the essences and facts that cannot be altered. The best way to make meaningful decisions is to choose based on the real characteristics of real life. This does not mean we must choose always the most practical, the most reasonable action for survival. We may choose to throw all our comfort and safety away because of the perverse beauty of an irrational gesture or passion, or an act of ethical bravery, or to act in direct contradiction to nature and society as an affirmation of our free will. The biological, evolutionary imperative would seem to favor survival or protection of self, but sometimes we do things that are certain to mean our downfall. Why? Out of a sense that there is sometimes something more important, more beautiful, more brave than personal safety, possibly to protect our genes living in the bodies of our relatives, possibly in consideration of the greatest good for the greatest number in the long run; mayhap for reasons we will never understand.

Consider these three gestures:

1. Sophie Scholl, the young German resistance fighter, who with her brother smuggled anti-Nazi propaganda into the university while classes were in session, stood at the top of the balcony

as the professors and students streamed from the classrooms, her work already safely done. Instead of sneaking home and avoiding arrest, she flung the rest of the fliers down over the heads of her fellow Germans. Papers flew freely in an atmosphere of terror. She and her brother were beheaded because of her action, but for one moment the word sang. For one moment, everyone was free.

2. Nastasya Filippovna, in Dostoevsky's novel *The Idiot,* is courted from all sides by scoundrels and maniacs. Her "virtue" has already been compromised due to her situation as a woman without means, yet she has a lofty soul. Beloved of Myshkin, the "idiot," she glimpses, then loses faith in, a possible redemption. When Rogozhin, one of the scoundrels, comes to a party with 100,000 rubles with which he effectively means to "buy" her, she agrees to go with him. But first she casts the bundle of bills into the fire with a last wild gesture of free will, daring another suitor to plunge his hands into the flames to take the money for himself. He does not, and Nastasya transcends for a moment the petty laws and priorities of her society.

3. In Orwell's *Nineteen Eighty-Four,* Winston Smith and his lover Julia risk torture and death to resist the stronghold of their totalitarian society. They do many useless things (Winston buys a cloudy glass paperweight and a creamy papered journal even though either of these acts, if discovered, would mean arrest). But the most powerful symbol of these many resistances is repeated twice in the book, once as a pre-vision in Winston's dream of the "golden country," and the second time in reality when he and Julia meet for the first time in a landscape strikingly similar to the dream: "She stood looking at him for an instant, then felt at the zipper of her overalls.

> And, yes! It was almost as in his dream. Almost as swiftly as he had imagined it, she had torn her clothes off, and when she flung them aside it was with that same magnificent gesture by which a whole civilization seemed to be annihilated."

Nineteen Eighty-Four, a picture of a totally constructed universe based on a brutally-enforced ideology of the blank slate, shows us how close and how far we are from being infinitely malleable today. A "magnificent gesture" is a great threat to such a system.

Consider a paved path in a city. Sometimes, even though the powers that be have paved a sidewalk and expected the citizens to conform to its guidelines, someone feels that there is a better way to get from here to there. And when enough people feel their feet drawn to this alternate way, they begin to tread a new path through an area that was intended to be grass. There are desire lines stronger than pre-established social constructs, and these desire lines insist on new arrangements of the world even though (or perhaps precisely because) the old ones have been established by asphalt. The new paths, which were once rebellious and eccentric, become in time established, sanctioned, and limiting; and new people may find that there are better (or worse) ways to get from here to there. If language has tendencies to close down against thought, language users also have tendencies to disrupt these patterns. If people in power attempt to coerce and control, less powerful people also have always subverted these attempts. No path is made without the desire of some person, without the choice of some person or for some reason (however good or bad). The path may be made in a certain place because of beauty or because of utility; for sentimental reasons; for access to a view; because it is private; because there are obstacles adjacent to it; because there are special features along the route; or because there are no other options left. Yet any path will revert to wildness in time if no-one walks upon it.

Herbert Marcuse's classic book, *One-Dimensional Man* (1964), is an indictment of what Marcuse characterized as the flattening-out of contemporary American consciousness into a closed system of self-reflexive rationality that resisted external (two-dimensional) critique. It begins by noting that the current social construct originated as a "project" chosen by people at one time out of a number of alternatives. In a footnote, Marcuse explains that his use of the word "project" alludes to Sartre's linkage of autonomy and contingency, and presupposes a freedom and responsibility, despite the fact that the choosers most likely were the most powerful people in the original society. His whole book is an explanation of how very difficult it is to see beyond the "rationality" of any given social construct, but also an imperative to create the conditions under which we might. Marcuse calls for a rediscovery of a lost dialectic, a two-dimensional space which keeps alive the friction between ideal and real, *status quo* and possibility, subjective and objective, calculable and incalculable, appearance and essence, universal and particular, concept and specific iteration, and, not least, spirit and matter. A hero of the New Left, Marcuse nevertheless criticized many of the basic assumptions of leftist ideology, including the democratic rejection of European intellectual and artistic culture, the increasing conflation of art and life, and the increasing de-materialization of sociology, linguistics and science in his time. Contemporary physics, he notes, does not entirely deny or question the existence of the physical world, but "in one way or another it suspends judgment on what reality itself may be, or considers the very question meaningless and unanswerable." This then shifts the emphasis from a metaphysical what to an operational how and "establishes a practical (though by no means absolute) certainty which, in its operations with matter, is with good conscience free from commitment to any substance outside the operational context." Materiality in this dystopian reality becomes assessed only in terms of its quantifiable use for humans, diminishing our relationship with the qualities of matter and weakening our ability to counter and critique the material *status quo*. The end itself, of one-dimensional consciousness, is a closed system of democratic totalitarianism, controlling every aspect of our lives.

While everything is filtered through our human interests, and thus somehow 'instrumental' towards our human 'use', some uses are more strictly utilitarian than others; some serve the continuation of a *status quo* more than others. Individually and collectively, we have an underdeveloped interest in the qualitative experience of materiality, in dreaming induced by matter, not merely efficiency, practicality, exploitation of resources. Critical yet utopian thinking occurs as we free ourselves from the condition of what and how much and begin to consider the why and how; two-dimensional discourse helps us to transcend the needs of the current system to consider not only alternate answers, but completely different questions.

Marcuse ended his book in a less than hopeful mood, but the revolutionary movements of the late sixties, encouraged in part by his ideas, surprised him and gave him cause to hope. But where are we now, over half a century later? We may, indeed, not be able to save the earth, or stem the rush of species loss, and we certainly cannot undo the lasting legacies of political and social havoc wrought by man's inhumanity to man in any simple way. Although *Candide* provided a picture of what Voltaire had deemed an inevitably cruel and destructive force rampant in what was already in his time far from "the best of all possible worlds," today climate change changes the equation to an extent that should prick the conscience of anyone who has retreated to his garden instead of trying to make sense of the world or make it better. We have arrived where we are because of who we are as a species. We are responsible for the good, the bad, and the ugly, for the beautiful and the damning, in compliance and resistance to genetic coding, evolutionary habits, environmental changes, and the social and cultural memes we have created together out of the deeply imbedded contradictions of our natures: competition and collaboration, love of nature and exploitation of nature, curiosity and will to ignorance, practicality and squandering, ethics, aesthetics, and hypocritical morality. Thus, it is up to us to try to reverse the damages we have wrought, and to preserve as much as possible of what is precious and essential about life and of our cultural history, both for ourselves and for all the other species with whom we must learn to empathize. But this can only happen if we begin to see again the meaningful connections between ourselves and the natural and created world, mediated through words, images, and our senses, and only if we learn to use whatever languages possible to communicate a fullness of feeling about what it means to be a deeply fraught, complex human being in a world in this state of crisis. We can, furthermore, only reverse the damage wrought if we deviate from the business-as-usual *status quo* of our society's current "rationality"—replacing quantifiable with qualitative, empty materialism with materiality imbued with spirit. To do so will inevitably seem foolish and perverse to those too entrenched to imagine other ways of living, to anyone too committed to the immediate profits of the current system to consider that they might, actually, be much happier without all of the possessions and processes they misconceive as necessary. If we do not, however, manage to succeed against what really are terrible odds, we must at least bear witness to the tragic fall and leave some traces of the aesthetic and ethical consciousness of humankind, even if no-one ever comes after us who can decipher the script.

We have often been capable of overturning the paradigms created by our predecessors, challenging, criticizing, or revising the constructs and narratives of other humans, following old errors to new truths or old truths to new errors, bungling sometimes, but doing our best. It has been a conversation and debate, a love song and a lamentation over the ages, among strangers and friends, enemies and kin, all of us trying to understand the world and our place in it; trying to balance the many voices within each of us with the many voices within others. We can continue to discourse in this polyphonic chorus of the past and the present, or we can decide, with the social constructionist theorists and their deconstructionist allies, that no way in which anyone has ever described the world, no poem, no theory, no evaluation or re-evaluation of values is reality-relevant (except of course the social constructionist theory itself); that language is a crime against nature; that the history of ideas and the idealistic pursuit of education is an Enlightenment plot to impose random ideas of good and bad on a benighted populace. We can just do away with our libraries and our picture galleries, our approximate meanings and our attempts to understand what can never be completely mastered, our mythologies and our delightful misprisions, and smugly, certainly, moralistically and accurately, resort to grunting and sneezing. No misleading words; no oppressive influences; no images to teach us that one thing or person is more beautiful or more valuable than another; no theories; no ideas at all. Only a purportedly honest, gaping, silent void.

VI.

Psyche's Stolen Pleasure

Women Who Like to Look, Objectification, and Animism

Beauty—be not caused—It is

Emily Dickinson

WHEN EROS, the god of Love, transported the mortal Psyche to their love nest, Apuleius tells us, he left her to enjoy the exceedingly pretty cottage, its well-stocked larder, the ministrations of invisible magical servants, and freedom from material care, while he flew about making other people fall in love—often through enchantment by the eye. He came back to her only in the dark, to bed, to make love, where she was warned never, ever to look at him. When she became pregnant, she was frightened by her envious sisters: "Perhaps he is a monster," she was told, "and you are carrying a monster-child in your womb. You had better take a look." But when she did, a glimpse of his lovely form as he slept ignited her passion and he awakened, either troubled by the light or by a drop of oil from the lamp. For this transgression, she was punished, banished to undergo countless difficult and painful trials before she and he could come together again, at which point their child was born—and was called *Pleasure*. Psyche means *spirit*, or *soul*, a soul supposedly purified from human passions—and freed from the pain (and the pleasure) that accompanies them. Eros, the male god of *fleshly* desire, infects humans with the dreaded and delightful disease of carnal and passionate love. Pleasure, the love child, is thus born of a well-punished crime, the subversive marriage of spiritual and sensual love, a transgression of a fundamental taboo. The punishment is a sacrifice of the soul's simple happiness and equilibrium.

Like Psyche, all women (and men, too) are endowed with mind, spirit, and imagination—but we are also primarily flesh. And some of us persist in looking, in igniting the flame of carnal love, despite its sometimes punishing dangers, in hopes of giving birth, now and again, to a little pleasure.

When I was thirteen, I began studying life drawing at the Art Students' League in New York City. Every Saturday my parents would drive me down from Westchester and drop me off on 57th Street, where I would spend all day drawing nude models with my best friend, Shireen. We left the building only to go to the pizzeria down the street, where we would have conversations with strangers, including one regular, a large black man who claimed he was Jimi Hendrix reincarnated. Safely back in the studio, it was understood that there was no erotic element in the drawing of nudes (supposedly different from "nakeds"). And yet, in the event, sometimes there *was* something thrilling, something subversive and, yes, even sexual, in the air. Some decades later, when I took to reading about evolutionary psychology and feminism, I read that women did not really like to look at bodies, and that most studies had shown that women in scientific tests were not aroused by images in the way that men were. Even though natural scientists would acknowledge that the mating rituals of non-human animals are marked by female mate choice—part of a selection process in which the male of the species preens and parades before the female—I read that, when it came to humans, it was only the "male gaze" that chose by the eye, and that this gaze was appropriative, predatory, and objectifying. But how did such unadulterated looking feel to us young girls, set free for a whole day from our parents, playing and practicing at being artists, grown-ups, attuned to the fleshly material—and to the spiritual that cannot help but course through all matter? Did the idea that we were drawing "nudes," not naked people, really mean that the experience was safely non-erotic? What then were we doing, sepia chalk in hand, electrified by the loveliness of a particular line or shadow, a mysterious curve or texture? Did it mean we did not see the models as objects, but as people, whose emotions we tried to express in our drawings? Or did we see them *so much* as objects that we might just as well have been drawing drapery or a still life? Were we guilty of the "crime" of objectification?

Martha Nussbaum's very helpful discussion of objectification enumerates seven categories, including fungibility (*i.e.*, exchangeability), violability (lacking appreciation for boundaries), denial of autonomy and agency, ownership, instrumentality, and the thing-like treatment of a person, analyzing the way in which we treat some objects (a work of art, a tree, a keepsake) differently than we treat others (a ballpoint pen, a rubber ball). Nussbaum notes that using her lover's stomach as a pillow may be instrumentalization, a form of objectification, but not, therefore, an abusive or dehumanizing act. In some special cases, she argues (citing a passage from D.H. Lawrence in which the lovers temporarily relinquish their individuated personhood in a mystical sexual union), a loss-of-self—a sense that one's body is a vessel through which extra-personal energies move, a temporary freedom from thought and mind, a sense of being just a body, *any* body—can be liberating and even enlightening. Defending a statement made by the legal scholar Cass Sunstein, she affirms that objectification can be "compatible with consent and equality and even [contribute to] 'wonderful parts of sexual life'." This does not, of course, mean that all is sunshine and roses in the world of seeing and being seen; like all sexy things, it has dark sides that will be more or less censured or enjoyed by different people. Yet objectification, like all concepts tailored to explain extremely complex interpersonal phenomena, is much more interesting and a lot less evil than one would think, were one to listen in on some of today's dogmatic gender war discourses.

All cases of objectification are classed by Nussbaum as cases of "treating one thing as another," which happens, I noticed, to be very close to the definition of *metaphor*—an act of *seeing* one thing as another or representing one thing by its likeness to another different thing.

I am reminded of the way in which Proust's narrator in *In Search of Lost Time* describes the magic of Elstir's paintings, wherein the texture and atmosphere of one element has miraculously taken on the feeling of another substance altogether, a curtain becoming sea-like, a rock resembling the coarseness of an old man's face. Of course, people in Proust's novel (consider the "young girls in flower") are also seen in reference to things and even paintings (as with Odette, who is beautiful to Swann *because* she reminds him of a certain painterly type). Searching for formal conceptualizations or universal archetypes for human experiences—of beauty, of pain, of jealousy, of time, of love—is, after all, one of the great quests of this novel, whose narrator notes that the experience of discovering a likeness between one thing (or person) and another thing (or person) is one of his greatest pleasures. As the boundaries between objects and objects, objects and persons, landscapes and fabrics, the alive and the dead temporarily melt away, poetry is born. The fluidity of spirit that runs in and out of matter, rendering matter itself less solid, less separate than it usually seems, is a central aspect of the artistic idiom. Thus, we not only sometimes seem to depersonalize and therefore dehumanize persons (by looking at their form *qua* form—as simply, stunningly lovely shapes and color, or by using their shoulders as a step-ladder, or their bodies for our sexual pleasure), but we also anthropomorphize or animate inanimate objects.

If we look closely at the looking we two girls were engaged in as aspiring artists, we will see that such absolute distinctions between object and person, animate and inanimate, are not always clear. Artists and mystics have always recognized a relationship between supposedly dead matter and the spirit they sometimes see coursing through it, and an equally fluid oscillation in live beings, who sometimes seem drained completely of spirit, and appear momentarily merely as form, as vessel. Consider the two paradoxical phrases *nature morte* and *still life,* and the fact that this genre of painting usually features symbols of the fleetingness of life, of freshly-killed game, of grapes and flowers that may yet be alive, but will soon rot, as well as solidly inanimate objects such as vases and bowls so vivid that they sometimes seem to be breathing. Consider Van Gogh's shoes, and Heidegger's famous discussion of the living "presencing" of painted objects, and consider the way in which mystics and mystical people of all times and places have recorded the experience of suddenly seeing inanimate objects come alive. Jakob Boehme, the seventeenth century German mystic, was impressed one day by vivid forces he perceived in a pewter jug, suddenly seemingly aglow. For me, it was a fence outside a Berlin café, as I sat within drinking some strong tea. The sun was shining on the cast iron ornamentation and the metal seemed infused with meaning; it was alive—more alive, it seemed in that moment, than the man reading his paper at another table. Animism, studied by anthropologists and theologians, is a mode of experiencing non-animate objects as if they were possessed of anima (spirit) and meaning. But it is not necessary to literally believe that inanimate objects have mind, spirit, will, or any other kind of consciousness to sometimes experience a sense of aliveness in dead objects, which may, by their participation in human culture and history and natural development, be possessed of all sorts of traces of meaning and spirit. Since we now know, moreover, that even inanimate objects are shot through with living molecules, which move in and out of their permeable surfaces, it would be unscientific to assert that any things were entirely inanimate. The two-way passage between Objectification and Animism speaks to the spirit that courses in and out of matter and our fascination with its quicksilver sliding.

Kenneth Clark, in his essay 'Moments of Vision', speaks of the magic of suddenly seeing an inanimate object come alive, those "moments when the object at which we have been gazing seems to detach itself from the habitual flux of impressions and becomes intensely clear and important to us." And he reminds us of a Yeats poem which sings: "I would find by the edge of that water/ The collar bone of a hare/ Worn thin by the lapping of water/ And pierce it through with a gimlet, and stare/ At the old bitter world where they marry in churches," and concludes that, "[t]he collar bone of the hare has made the poem; Yeats, given his myth-creating, or myth-hungry, turn of mind, has at once recognized that an object so vividly perceived must be a symbol; and he has even tried to use his moment of vision to create others, by the fairy-tale device of boring a hole in it and looking through." Yeats has infused the bone with meaning—has, Clark tells us, rendered the object a symbol, with endless reverberatory powers. And he tells us of a Greek conception of "urgent personal emotions inspired by certain natural objects," noting that the emotions are "supposed to be caused by their having once been human beings." The observers of such suddenly animate objects "recognized," Clark tells us, "that the moments in which these objects reveal themselves to us arouse a feeling of ecstasy, almost akin to physical passion; and it is for this reason that it is at the crises of amorous pursuit that almost all of the metamorphoses takes place."

This transformation—as in Ovid's *Metamorphoses*—in the act of escaping from an "amorous pursuit" (less euphemistically, an attempted rape) is relevant in our discussion of the dangers, if not the pleasures, of objectification. What if all objects came into being because some maiden had to run away from a pursuing god and some other god took pity on her and turned her into some object, a tree, say, as in the case of Daphne? Surely, however, most objects do not come of such drastic provenance, and our desire for a particularly intriguing object or a particularly lovely person need not (it usually does not) turn violently predatory or inconsiderate of its object's pleasure or sanctity. In fact, following the Kantian aesthetic of "disinterested appreciation," some people—Umberto Eco, for one, in his *History of Beauty*—would define the act of appreciation of beauty as an appreciation that explicitly *does not* want or need to take physical possession of the thing or person it admires. And yet most of us are quite capable of desiring things or people that or whom we admire, without overstepping the boundaries of civility and respect for their inviolability or personhood. That some people *do* lack such an ethical faculty is not a good enough reason to discredit desirous looking.

One looks at the world (if one is lucky, through the collarbone of a hare, or some other fairy key), and finds it filled sometimes with meaning, or else sometimes drained completely, empty, meaningless—but it is always the same world. Different modes of seeing will color or fade its tints variously, will intensify or blur contours, infusing what is seen with tenderness or dread; but this subjectivity does not change the nature of reality. It only seems to. Although we cannot help but imbue matter with such subjective coloration, matter does not necessarily need our editorializing to be impressive. Even without added significance, sensory experience is a pleasure or a pain, depending on its nature. One truth I know, even when I am at a loss for any other reason to love life: we are lucky to be able to experience the world sensually. When we see: the colors, dynamics of contrast, sizes and shapes, textures. When we can hear: the melodies of sound, its textures and rhythms, its syncopations, suspensions between chord changes, harmonies and dissonances. Taste and touch, too. The senses are great gifts, whether we attribute meaning to any of their messages or not. Indeed, the world may be justified, as Nietzsche would say, only as an aesthetic phenomenon. But we *do* find and we *do* attribute meaning, when abstraction moves us, when a piece of music seems to tell a story, when an object is suddenly animated and is rendered a symbol, or when we admire someone's mouth—the way its color after much kissing contrasts with the color of a curl of hair or the texture of a pillow—and when we call this admiration "love." Material, come alive, through our own vision of it, makes us feel alive too; things and parts of people seen as beautiful are portals to a world where everything is alive and filled with meaning. A world where everything is in love and sometimes—yes—also in hate—just as long as it is alive with some contrast or correspondence—in contact with everything else. Just as long as the world is not reduced by a pious morality to some casual, uncared-for, blasé, undifferentiated backdrop for a depressed and nihilistic existence, where nothing is favored over anything else, where everything is "whatever." For most of us, there is oscillation between differing moods of vision. Sometimes, in other words, the physical—whether object or person or tree or work of art—is filled with spirit for us; at other times, it is a dead object. Or merely useful, which in certain circumstances is just as uninspiring.

The desiring and aesthetic appreciating of physical bodies has often been wrongly equated with a certain kind of vulgar objectification, which reductively tends to rather remove the meaning and life from things altogether than imbue them with a more appropriate spirit. Such looking has been given a bad name by the behavior of people who may not even recognize beauty in anything—in the same way that material*ism* gives all *matter* a bad name. A lack of spirit in one's pleasure, however, is hardly worse than a complete lack of pleasure—or a lack of material in one's spirit. And yet the lack of spirit marks the difference between pornography, which may excite temporarily, but often leaves one feeling empty (as materialism makes one feel empty), and eroticism, which (as in the appreciation of beautiful objects, rather than empty materialism) includes the imagination and the spirit, thus making one feel enduringly alive.

In any case, let us not banish looking, not even solely aesthetic or sexual looking. While matter without spirit can be deeply depressing and often inhumane, spirit without matter cannot be seen, touched, embraced, or tasted at all. If you try to really imagine what it would be like... but of course, you can't. There is actually no such thing as one without the other, though different proportions of the two are likely. A hyper-propensity for either may be dangerous, to both seer and seen, male and female. But Nussbaum notes that certain feminist theorists, like Catherine Mackinnon and Andrea Dworkin, believe that due to the power relations that obtain between men and women, it is only women who are subject to objectification, as the victimized objects of male needs. This, I think, shows a fatal lack of imagination. These theorists choose an ideal of an absolute absence from fear over a more complex and meaningful freedom. To eliminate all modes of objectification, in other words, might serve utilitarian aims, as prisons do, but would rob us of subtle and rich aesthetic and human experiences.

For, in truth, my adolescent experience of drawing naked models, both male and female, was a mixture of many aspects, some certainly objectifying—a heady cocktail of eroticism, empathy, and abstraction, all depending on the model, the mood, the light in the room. It was all there for the taking. And we young girls took, and took. We were, of course, already reading Anaïs Nin's diaries at the time, as well as her erotic stories, which often featured suggestive vignettes about models and painters, voyeurs and exhibitionists—among a liberating panoply of other sensual possibilities, stories wherein women, too, looked and desired. But I think that even without these literary suggestions, we would certainly have found our way to enjoying the amoral pleasures of looking at bodies all on our own. It came naturally. Meanwhile, what combination of feelings, impulses, fantasies, dreary workaday duty, pain and pleasure, was in the minds and bodies of the models on the platform? Did we care to know? Should we have worried? Was our looking objectification? An act of erotic and aesthetic imagination? A perverse projection of our own fantasies onto the physical and emotional reality of other persons? A natural, healthy response to aesthetic and emotional phenomena? Probably all of the above.

I sometimes had the great fortune to go to the Metropolitan Museum of Art to look at the Greek and Roman statues. My adolescent eyes lingered unapologetically on the lovely lips, the jaws, the smooth necks, seductively framed in stray curls; my eyes would move down, shyly at first, to the rounded shoulders and hairless chests of the young athlete gods. In no time, my gaze would arrive at the most stunning feature of these Classical ideals of beauty—these ubiquitous, beloved *Kouroi* (young boys) of Greek art—namely, that subtle swoop from the area on either side of the belly, suggesting the inner hipbone and gesturing towards the loins. The lovely line culminated in a sweetly pointed penis, more caricature than pornography, and sent the eye back, around the loveliest boyish hips, toward the smooth marble buttocks and perfect thighs. I appreciated the sculptures of females as well, with their soft, small breasts and bellies, their slightly androgynous jawlines and runners' legs, their strong, consummate grace. But somehow the experience of visual contact with the lovely nude boys (or were they merely—or also—*naked?*) thrilled me in a different way.

Camille Paglia, in her brilliantly controversial *tour de force, Sexual Personae,* tells us that the nude Greek *Kouris,* born in the seventh century BC, initiated the "[f]irst cult of personality in western history... an icon of the worship of beauty, a hierarchism self-generated rather than dynastic." In contrast, the archaic *Kore* (maiden) was always clothed. In Paglia's complex but compelling narrative of the evolution of Western culture, the *male* enjoyment of the passive, cold, and sharply delineated form of the beautiful boy was an antidote to the chthonic, undifferentiated chaos of what she deems *female* nature, an Apollonian corrective to the Dionysian loss of self. Think of the difference between a cool, composed, sharply delineated painting by Ingres and a painterly storm of uncontained brush strokes by Delacroix. The conception of the objectified boy as desired, but not desiring, was a preview for the later construct of woman as passive object of male desire. Paglia goes on to explain the development of the female *sexual persona* as sex object as a continuation of the male attempt to escape the overwhelming power of his mother's (and nature's) undifferentiated fluidity: "By focusing on the shapely, by making women a sex-object, man has struggled to fix and stabilize nature's dreadful flux. Objectification is conceptualization, the highest human faculty. Turning people into sex objects is one of the specialties of our species. It will never disappear, since it is intertwined with the art-impulse and may be identical to it." I agree that without conceptualization, the differentiating between one thing and another, the naming and delineating of material shapes and forms, we would have no art, and no civilization. As Paglia writes: "Beauty is our weapon against nature; by it we make objects, giving them limit, symmetry, proportion. Beauty halts and freezes the melting flux of nature..." But I do not believe that women are more natural than men, nor that our experience of beauty—or our sexual response—is entirely constructed, and thus I believe that the way we see and the way that artists have abstracted forms from the real cannot be explained as *anti-natural*.

Nature itself is replete with delineated forms and patterns, and our naturally-born brains are equipped with mechanisms for separating out and conceptualizing these forms. As the human eye and brain grow out of infancy, we all—men *and* women—see by distinguishing forms within the swirling chaos of non-differentiated everything-ness. Our brains, as Frank Wilczek reminds us, are "naturally gifted geometers, adapted to organizing our visual perception." Seeing patterns is one of the things humans do best and, Wilczek continues, a "large fraction of our brain is devoted to visual processing." Does not form *naturally* bring a shock of pleasure, in nature and in art—or must we really be trained by the "aggressive male eye" to respond to it? I am certainly appreciative of the massive and brilliant contributions of the "male eye" over the centuries, and it is obvious to anyone who looks fairly at history (even the feminist art historian Linda Nochlin admits as much) that the lion's share of such contributions in the visual arts has thus far been created by men. Nevertheless, I certainly do not agree that women are *incapable* of seeing conceptually or creating art—thereby objectifying others themselves. All of us, men and women, are constantly in conflict with the undifferentiated mass of everything-ness, and all of us, sons and daughters, are caught in an ongoing process of individuation away from our mothers (and fathers) and others, learning from and also rejecting parts of what we are given, accepting or changing nature and culture, but always acknowledging all parts of the past as our complex beloved and bewailed heritage.

Indeed, as discussed earlier, the conceptualization inherent in seeing and in language naturally leaves out, cuts up the undifferentiated everything of reality (nature as it is) in order to help us make provisional meanings and sense, to help us to act, choose, interpret what otherwise would be a life of floating boundarylessness. Of course, Paglia, like all conceptualizers, necessarily leaves out things that do not fit in her concept, or tailors what does not fit, by special pleading. And, after her initial discussion, she rather immediately abandons her particular divisions of male-female, describing her exemplary artists—the *sexual personae* and makers of *sexual personae* in art—as a parade of men and women who are *all androgynous.* In fact, the voluminous evidence she accumulates seems to support another thesis altogether: that great art is made out of the struggle between conceptualization (abstraction, separation, naming, framing) and undifferentiated flux—a tension personified for her by male and female, or Apollo (as male) and Dionysus (as female). Although I grant that the relationship with son and mother is different from that of daughter and mother, I am certain that we all struggle, to different degrees, against the smothering, drowning world of motherly love, and against nature's devouring unlimitedness (which is not the same thing, insofar as nature can really be no more male than female). We all attempt, to varying degrees and in different ways, to keep chaos at bay, to escape the watery, murky realms of entropy through the clean, artificial lines of art, beauty, grace. We endeavor, despite all the odds. In the end, all of us will be, once more, mixed in with the World-All, rotted and at one with earth, worms, nature.

In the meantime, women may learn to enjoy looking, differentiating, and delineating too, if only our whole society did not seem bent on dissolving differences and discriminations, thereby abandoning art in the spurious interests of morality. If Paglia's traditional male artists cultivated what she saw as their "femininity" as an opening to the savagery, flux, and non-differentiation of nature (think Whitman's all-encompassing embrace, or visualize, again, a Delacroix painting in contrast to an Ingres), today we seem to go in the opposite direction and increasingly aim to eliminate what Paglia calls the Apollonian and masculine, by deconstructing and decrying language, concepts, categories, names, and any sort of conceptualized seeing at all. Such wholesale de-construction is dangerous, leading indeed to utter chaos and a mass of self-same nullity.

Linda Nochlin argues that the main reason there have or had been "no great women artists" is because of the lack of supportive social institutions for our education. Nowadays, we can no longer lean on this excuse. Perhaps one reason for the relatively lower numbers (besides the "distraction[s]" of childbirth and childcare) is that women have never been sufficiently encouraged to revel in and cultivate their ability to see, to objectify, to imitate and invent forms. This could explain why women *writers* have been richly represented throughout history, despite a lack of education and social support: the writer must see and conceptualize—of course—but she translates such seeing through her mind, through words, into internal abstractions, not into the flesh of paint, marble, or space. Many theorists, including Paglia, believe that the world of the Word is masculine, a replacement and usurpation of the goddess' realm of unity and oneness by division and category—see, for example, Leonard Shlain's *The Alphabet Versus the Goddess.* According to this theory, the world of the feminine is pre-verbal, visual, irreducible, complete, whole. But then why is it that women have excelled so much more in writing than in the visual arts? Can it be that we are caught in conflicting narratives, conflicting concepts, which fail to fully articulate the individual realities?

Overturning common narratives about women's desires, the poetess and *femme fatale* Edna St. Vincent Millay wrote:

> I, being born a woman and distressed
> By all the needs and notions of my kind,
> Am urged by your propinquity to find
> Your person fair, and feel a certain zest

> To bear your body's weight upon my breast:
> So subtly is the fume of life designed,
> To clarify the pulse and cloud the mind,
> And leave me once again undone, possessed.
> Think not, for this, however, the poor treason
> Of my stout blood against my staggering brain,
> I shall remember you with love, or season
> My scorn with pity,—let me make it plain:
> I find this frenzy insufficient reason
> For conversation when we meet again.

Millay's celebration of female lust and rejection of traditional female romantic tropes is proportionate to her brilliance as a poet—conscious of form, of shape, of the boundaries of the sensual and spiritual world. Hers is one voice, decrying the stereotype, but there are certainly more of us who hearken to her subversive vision. How many does it take to rewrite or question a category? If there are individual aberrations, do we need therefore to do away with all conceptualizations?

Today, many people seem to believe that certain individual deviations from theoretical conceptions are enough to overthrow and discredit conceptualization itself, as if the fact that individual entities do not perfectly fit into categories and names means that we would be better off without language altogether. But I, being born a woman, more or less, can only say that, despite theories to the contrary, I see and enjoy bodies, I make paintings, I draw pictures and I write books. Yet I do not feel compelled to throw away the categories or archetypes or even all of the stereotypes of male and female, or the subtle variations between them—for to do so would be to abandon communication and the worthy attempts to make meaning and temporary order of the world. Even so, we can certainly question the categories, stretch them, create new ones. Nietzsche, in his posthumously published essay 'On Truth and Lying in a Supra Moral Sense', delineated just this sort of relationship between concepts and reality: we all know that words and concepts only provisionally define individual realities, but that does not mean that we should abandon definitions or language or art. Instead, he argued, as discussed above, we must continue as "creative subjects," always participating in the joyous generation of ever-new concepts and arrangements, new words, new definitions, new ways of seeing that celebrate both the real—for there is a *real,* and a natural, despite deconstruction's attempts to deny it—and our shifting, curious, desirous vision of it. Studying the prior conceptualizations of other artists and writers—admiring the work and words of previous humans who loved to look—and testing them against my own new seeing was part of my education as a young woman drawing bodies at the Art Students' League.

In later life, I experienced immense pleasure in gazing at the curves and colors and contrasts of real, living lovers' faces, bodies, body parts. Sometimes I would draw their naked bodies while they slept. Such looking has been one of the most delicious parts of a richly emotional and spiritually deep romantic life. Why shouldn't it have been? And yet I continued to read that heterosexual women choose their mates based on the male's ability to provide financially or to help support their future children, or that women—unlike men—are drawn to the spiritual rather than the physical qualities of their potential lovers. Whether or not this may be true for most women, I for one certainly do not recognize my own desires in these sweeping statements of fact. I *always* look at beautiful men, strangers and friends, often men who are now, as I creep past middle age, much younger than myself. Love, wrote Yeats, "comes in at the eye": and I think he meant for women too. I have almost always chosen my lovers by the eye *first,* by the shock of their beauty and its effect upon my own body and mind (be that biological, aesthetic, chemical, evolutionary, constructed), and only secondarily based upon whether there happens to be any worthy or compatible substance beneath the primary physical surface. "Chosen" may, indeed, be the wrong word. It may be more correct to admit that an experience of beauty chooses *me,* leaves me no choice but to tremble, part my lips, sigh and stare. Beauty possesses me. Is it because I am missing the usual "androgen inhibitors" that most women have? Is my desiring eye male? Is it because I am an artist—and does that also imply that I am somehow androgynous?

Or is it, perhaps, that the desiring female gaze is more common than we are led to believe? I certainly was not the only adolescent girl who had a poster of a bare-chested Jim Morrison—arms spread wide, apparently crucified, like the scantily clad Jesus beloved by centuries of young women—on the wall above my bed. Exposed like Jim, Jesus is pinned down, nailed to a cross, at the mercy of some indulgent Mary Magdalene who might come and moisten his full, open lips with some vinegar. Apparently, he is even more victimized than the many supine female nudes that John Berger, in his anti-sensuous and influential classic *Ways of Seeing*, points to as evidence of the evil of masculine objectification of women.

I am assured by a friend who is an art historian that people no longer read Berger's book but certainly it has been read and misread—simplified, in other words—enough to have already framed and formed the *ways of seeing* of much subsequent pseudo-aesthetic theory. The little book preaches, from a Marxist pedestal, against the purely aesthetic evaluation of art, deconstructing the sinister hierarchy of masculine, capitalist power-mongering that its author sees glorified in Western art from the Renaissance up until the allegedly more enlightened age of Postmodernism. Like all polemics, it might be excused for seeming to take an extreme stance against what it opposes. Its author, I am assured, expresses much more nuanced views in later works; but in this book, Berger often seems to see nothing but oppression in the works he describes. Although it is undeniably true that Western culture has been strongly associated with the hierarchy that privileges the power of the rich European men who had the wherewithal and the vision to commission art—and we may thank Berger for making this truth widely apparent—this screed tends to present all art made between the Middle Ages and the twentieth century as *nothing but evidence of a shameful polit-*

ical and social ideology. This tendency to judge art according to a litmus test of moral correctness represented the beginning of a deleterious trend for subsequent art theorizing, justifying contemporary attempts to destructively malign the magic of some of the world's most meaningfully rich expressions of human complexity.

Furthermore, Berger's claim in *Ways of Seeing* that Western art exposes the evils of a privileged and oppressive capitalist ideology begs the question of what treacherous ideologies and practices might be revealed were one to look behind the iron curtain of, say, Soviet-style social realism. Since we know now that there was at least as much, *indeed much more,* suffering and cruelty under Stalin's reign of terror, despite the fact that much of the art of the period was proscribed (*on pain of death,* no less) by an anti-capitalist, equalist party dictate, we cannot really be blamed for preferring a Giorgione, painted under a monarchy, to a Communist propaganda poster. Great art, whether it seems to celebrate or criticize the *status quo,* helps us remember what is important about being human, particularly in times when such remembering is most needful. Although art is often affected to some extent by financial questions (sponsorship, commerce, the ability of artists to survive on very little compared to the wealth and comfort of possible patrons), and by the people in power, it is great, in part, *because* it manages to transcend such restraints. Even some Stalinist propaganda posters, glorifying a regime of terror and show trials, are strikingly beautiful works of graphic art. Great art, as Berger himself is known to argue in later works, insists on being a personal expression, even when it is a commission. It is alive, even if the drawing rooms or academy walls where it hangs are quite dead—or even deadly. But too many readers have ignored his more qualified subsequent discussions and have, instead, continued to regard art as a strictly moral or political affair.

Although art was previously more likely to be evaluated primarily on the basis of its form, after Berger's time it came to be judged more and more on its socio-political content, despite the work of Kenneth

Clark, whose more conservative vision was pitted against Berger's in their dueling television programs, *Civilization* and *Ways of Seeing*. Although there were many other critics—for example, the aforementioned Linda Nochlin, who complained along Berger's lines that "the imagery of the erotic is gender-specific and non-reversible"—Berger's early book, despite what may have been more complicated intentions, instigated the *popular* charge to re-educate our eye in a new and "better," more moral and less aesthetic, way of seeing. While he may have wanted to highlight the role played by economics in the production of art with a different aim in view—including highlighting artists' ability to transcend such oppressive strictures by aesthetic means—his *Ways of Seeing* nevertheless maligned something he deemed "mystification"—a force that had fooled humans in the past, a mystification now associated with the aesthetic, that was allegedly orchestrated by a "privileged minority" in order to "justify the role of the ruling classes," and to coerce us into "learnt assumptions" about beauty, truth, genius, civilization, form, status, taste. In a slightly less extreme register, Nochlin, in a condemnation of Delacroix's 'Death of Sardanapalus' in her essay 'Women, Art, and Power', admits that "Delacroix's painting cannot, of course, be reduced to a mere pictorial projection of the artist's sadistic fantasies under the guise of exoticism." Nochlin nevertheless claims that it is impossible to imagine a woman painting such a scene, wherein a ruler watched his slave women burn as possessions, along with himself and the rest of his kingdom, "a *Death of Cleopatra,* say." But she must have had a weak imagination, or not have heard the rumored tale claiming that Cleopatra had her male servants killed after having enjoyed with them a night of love, so that they would not have the chance to afterwards boast of having slept with the empress. Conceivably, a woman artist could very easily paint this scene. That she has not is hardly evidence that women are morally superior to men. In fact, there have been many paintings—usually by men, though occasionally by women—of violent and powerful women displaying the severed heads of men (*i.e.*, Judiths and Salomes) or of Medea killing her children. Delacroix painted a mighty Medea and, of course, the famous 'Liberty' leading the people in what would become a bloody revolution against monarchical authority. Liberty is personified as a woman, powerful despite—or perhaps by virtue of—her one exposed Amazonian breast. Those who are keeping count of depictions of male helplessness should also note the half-naked man in the foreground of Delacroix's *Liberty Leading the People,* who has unaccountably lost his pants, with his shirt seductively open, prostrate and helpless on his back. "Art," Berger nevertheless warns, "with its unique undiminished authority, justifies most other forms of authority... makes inequality seem noble and hierarchies seem thrilling." Berger is relieved to note, in echo of Walter Benjamin, that the age of reproduction has made inroads to remove and destroy the old, treacherous "aura"—what Berger calls the "authority of art." Nochlin, again more subtly, questions the wisdom of the attempted destruction by a violent suffragette named Mary Richardson (alias Polly Dick) of Velasquez's *Rokeby Venus* in 1914, suggesting that Richardson's act *may have been wrong,* not only because the iconoclastic gesture "did the suffrage cause little or no good," but also because "her gesture assumes that if the cause of women's rights is right, then Velasquez's *Venus* is wrong." We *may,* Nochlin reluctantly allows, respond to Velasquez's painting in a number of ways that are not primarily informed by feminist criticism and its awareness of the oppression of the male gaze, including responses to "qualities of shape, texture, and color... suggestions of human loveliness, physical tenderness, and the pleasure both sexes take in sensual discovery and self-discovery... [not to mention, reminders] of the swift passage of beauty and pleasure and the vanity of all such delights." But she concludes that "such readings" are only possible if we ignore the power relations obtaining between men and women inscribed in such visual representation. We may not, in short, *morally enjoy them*—not, at least, until we attain a utopian state of male and female equality. Such a tepid defense against iconoclasm is really not much better than that of the Protestant leaders who warned vehemently against the dangerous worship of idols, but told their parishioners that they therefore ought not go into Catholic churches to smash them. Velasquez's stunning painting of female sensuality is to be, if not slashed, then covered up by sheets and put away, or at least studied only as an example of the oppression (and the dangerous idealization and idolization) of women by men. What an infinite loss to humanity. Nevertheless, despite all the decades of proselytizing and re-education, the maligned works themselves (yes, even in reproduction) continue to attract and fascinate us, no matter how much we are taught to see something morally wrong with them. Likewise, the beauty of bodies (in reality and in art) still has an irresistible power, no matter how much we are told that to respond to the depiction of women's bodies with pleasure is to tacitly accept the unfortunate reality of unequal power relations inherent in such representations, no matter how much we are told that women, being ourselves powerless and merely passive, do not have any mutual consensual interest in the depiction of supine or passive male bodies. Nor will it be easy to finally and fatally re-educate us all, men and women alike, so that we love just the inside, not the outside, of people.

Perhaps Berger could simply not see the desirable naked or nude *men* in classical paintings and sculpture because he was blinded, like the poor capitalist misogynists before him, by *his own* way of seeing, a male, heterosexual, moralizing, Marxist view. (Nochlin likewise claims that male bodies are never exposed in art unless they are in action. Why she could not see them is another question.) Like a prudish priest, sneaking a look at the horror he is obsessed with, he thus seems to see nothing but passive, objectified women or celebrations of capitalist possession everywhere he looks. Berger ignores the history of the luxuriant depiction of the *boy* by the Greeks and Romans, although Jonathon Jones, in a 2013 article in *The Guardian*, asserts that "[l]ooking at naked men is what European art tradition is all about." But Berger can't see it. He can't see the repeated depiction of the crucified and otherwise supine (in *Pietas*) Christ, the exposed and wounded Saint Sebastian, the lovely sleeping Endymion, the drunken Bacchus, that mostly naked and utterly helpless (dead, or just asleep?) marmoreal Shelley in Oxford's University College, and other classic images of beautiful and passive male bodies. Berger insists that the history of Western depiction of humans prior to the nineteenth century is characterized by the objectification of women by male artists and male viewers, that males depicted in Western art are always standing and active, and that, despite the many empathic and emotionally complex paintings of unclothed women by men throughout the centuries, "[a] naked body has to be seen as an object in order to become a nude." This aesthetic theory leaves the realm of art to assert that *in reality* women (brainwashed by centuries of such painting) have so thoroughly internalized their submission to men as to really, finally, *be* nothing but objects, incapable of seeing themselves except through male eyes, incapable of seeing males, and incapable of action. Men, Berger tells us, "*are* and women *appear*. Men look at women. Women watch themselves being looked at" (emphasis mine). Looked at through today's moral prohibition against "cultural appropriation," Berger could be accused of speaking for women instead of letting us speak for ourselves. But I do not believe that cultural appropriation is a sin, and certainly some women would agree with him. Some of us, however, will not, which is why such wholesale generalizations can be dangerously reductive. "A man's presence," he continues, "is dependent upon the promise of power which he embodies." It "suggests what he is capable of doing to you or for you." Conversely, a "woman's presence" is reduced, by centuries of misogynist art, to "what can and cannot be done to her." Although he probably imagined he was defending damsels in distress from predatory, capitalist men who have made women into possessions, Berger radically underestimated female power, agency, and desire. Discussing the story of Adam and Eve, he rightly points to the original misogynist subjugation by God, the Father, who punished women for original sin by making them subordinate to the rule of their husbands, but he manages to forget (to *not see*) the part of the story that mythologizes female agency: Eve is the one whose transgressive desire dares to act. She dares to eat the forbidden fruit; Adam is just the passive accomplice, who had no overpowering desire to eat. Yes, Lilith, Adam's first wife, the legend tells us, was replaced because she wanted to be on top during the sex act, but her subversive hunger remains—in Eve's transgressive tasting of forbidden fruit and Psyche's criminal looking, in the insatiable desire of all women who like to look.

When we arrive at Berger's discussion of ideal sexuality, we damsels might be forgiven for crying out to be saved from his vision of demystified, moral, safe coupling—except that, of course, we have the agency to save ourselves, if only we can find a willing partner in crime. Nakedness, we learn again (different from nudity as objectification), confirms the *sameness* of all bodies. The moral lover is relieved to discover that his lover is "like any other," that "they are more like the rest of their sex than they are different." Before the lover removed her clothes, there was a problem: "the other was more or less mysterious"! Mysteriousness is like mystification, and, as we should have learned by now—from Lucy Lippard's conflation of commodification and mystification discussed above—both seduce us to believe in such politically suspect ideas as beauty, genius, individuality, and so on. We might make the mistake of preferring one lover over another, for purely aesthetic reasons, finding her or him more desirable than some other person, that is to say, unequal. But once the shrouded lover is defrocked, naked, Berger tells us, with relief, "an element of banality enters"—*banality*! So *this* is Marxist sex. And herewith we come to the ultimate anti-climax of Berger's celebrated way of seeing. If we have any aesthetic or romantic sense, any sense of the pleasure of dynamics, contrast, chiaroscuro, we might run, wildly lusting after raw, amoral beauty, out into the perilous world of natural human desire and difference. But sense—as in sensuality—is reviled nowadays, in small part as a result of the reverberations of Berger's book; in larger part because of the long history of moral denigration of the physical in favor of the supposedly separate, and higher, spiritual.

Despite the increasing secularization of culture, the surface—the 'superficial'—is still maligned in today's new, prudish Comstockery: maligned as, if not evil incarnate, then at least somehow arbitrary, not something we should judge someone on, not something for which a person is responsible or commendable. At the same time, so-called spiritual characteristics, like intelligence, kindness, humor, and emotional intensity are imagined to be something *truly* belonging to a person's worth, somehow truly *earned* through work and choice. Although I personally believe in ethical choice and free will, there are very good scientific arguments for believing that our choices and actions—or at least the possibilities for making them—are more or less pre-programmed by our genetic make-up, no less than our appearances. We are more or less passionate, curious, risk-taking, sensitive, have different sorts of intelligences, different tempers; and these in-born propensities are relatively fostered or stifled by our social and natural environments. We can alter the way we look, to a degree, by choices of health and fitness, hairstyle, make-up, mood, clothing, though probably (barring plastic surgery!) not as fully as we can make choices about the way we act. Nevertheless, the way we behave *and* the way we look are both related, to a greater or lesser degree, to our innate biology. The way we look is as much *who we are* as the way we think and act. That this even has to be said at all is a product of the successful brainwashing of centuries of anti-physical propaganda. Oscar Wilde, who did great service in battling the prejudices against materiality, wrote: "Beauty is a form of Genius—is higher, indeed, than Genius, as it needs no explanation. It is one of the great facts of the world, like sunlight or springtime, or the reflection in the dark waters of that silver shell we call the moon. It cannot be questioned. It has divine right of sovereignty. It makes princes of those who have it." Amen. But of course, nowadays, many people will tell you that beauty—and Genius and sovereignty and gender too—are socially constructed: by magazines, advertising, and movies, casually overlooking the fact that autonomous people both create and consume the media. Today's critics of socially constructed beauty may be hard-pressed to explain how the Greeks knew that Helen of Troy was beautiful enough to wage a war over—before the age of billboards. Paglia deliciously quips that beauty is "not a trick invented by nasty men in a room somewhere on Madison Avenue," but instead was, in her view, invented in ancient Egypt. In my view (and Emily Dickinson's!), Beauty was not *invented* at all, but just irrefutably *is*. But even if people cannot explain the source of ancient Egyptian beauty ideals, many will still affirm, with the dogmatic faith of all social constructions (for the idea that beauty is a social construction is itself a social construction), that they are the enlightened ones. But watch what they do, not what they say: they usually, if given the choice, will choose a physically beautiful lover (provided he or she also has at least some good character) over one endowed with *just* a beautiful soul. Some even just go for the beautiful body—though at some peril.

For, certainly, a spiritually ugly person can have a beautiful body, and a beautiful "soul" can be cursed with less-than-beautiful physical characteristics. But the assumption that *only* the invisible characteristics are real and valuable, and that we cannot also usually see with our eyes something of a person's inner character through a sparkle or a dullness in his or her gaze, smile, gait, expression, way of being in the world, and that these elements do not effect physical beauty, is a spiritualist fallacy. For to speak of physical beauty as if it were actually the antithesis of spiritual worth is a prejudicial vestige of that old Platonic and Christian dualism, as if the outside were decidedly not connected to the inside—as if the outside were nothing but a trick, a deceiving lure, which smart girls are supposed to easily see beyond (or rather not *see*, but somehow blindly know). Girls, whether smart or silly, are thought to be more virtuous than boys. It follows that they can virtuously keep their eyes down and concentrate on what is supposedly more important. Boys, being beasts who can't control themselves, must be policed and taught what we ladies are thought to know better.

In this common narrative (or construct, if you will), women are *all* spiritual, the "angels in the house" of Victorian lore. Having no desires to repress, we are expected to be sexless, selfless, and effortlessly generous. Men, by contrast, are thought to be all physical, bestial, aggressive, and hardly capable of controlling their lusts. Women are peaceable, communal, and kind, while men are warlike, competitive, and individualistic. Women are Spirit, men Matter.

This is the tradition carried on by nineteenth-century temperance ladies, preaching abstinence to keep the beastly men from drunkenly abusing their innocent wives. Men *can* be beasts—and this is a real problem—and alcohol has been shown to increase their beastliness, and this too is a real problem. But these ladies—the ancestors of what Naomi Wolf calls "victim feminism" in her book, *Fire with Fire: The New Female Power and How to Use it*—surely underestimated the animality and aggression of womankind. We are, most of us, no angels, and, *given the physical strength and accompanying freedom such strength would bring,* who knows how badly we ourselves might behave? Yet many feminists still paradoxically assume that women are somehow inherently good and men inherently bad—and that our alleged goodness is simply a measure of our relatively higher levels of spirituality.

There is, nevertheless, another, diametrically opposed narrative, wherein woman, synonymous with Nature, is *all* body, all matter, ruled by her womb and her menstrual cycles, her hormonally-induced emotions. She is ravenous, alternately filled with fury and smothering love, with appetites and whims so powerfully irrational that they surely can only have come from the most natural, hence abominable (see Baudelaire and Paglia) bowels of the earth. She is jealous and violent ("Hell hath no fury..."), sexually insatiable (nymphomaniacal or, as the teenagers still persist in saying, "a slut"), and incapable of thinking clearly or making decisions without the interference of her body. She is Medea, murdering her children, or a *femme fatale* man-eater, a siren, or even just a conniving minx, luring innocent men into the unwanted bonds of marriage and parenthood.

Men, in this narrative, are the spiritual ones, the only sex capable of abstract intellectual thought, objective and rational, whereas their female counterparts are all-too-physical and emotional. This narrative is promulgated in differing forms—some which celebrate the Mother Goddess and her power, others that denigrate the base and bloody bitch—by both feminists and misogynists, to varying degrees and purposes. And then there are others who adhere to parts of each myth, to varying degrees and with varying degrees of reason, who allow that women can be both animalistic and rational, spiritual and physical, beastly *and* reflectively ethical. And so can men. These latter are called "power feminists" by Wolff—they celebrate female sexuality, treat "women as adults and men as human beings," and expect women to be successful and significant contenders in the material and the intellectual world to whatever extent their desires and individual capabilities can impel them. While the "victim" feminist polices the desire, not only of men but of women as well, the "power" feminist acknowledges that looking and being looked at can often be a pleasurable part of life. I heartily agree that woman, part angel, part animal, is fully capable of looking with enjoyment at beautiful bodies, even of temporarily objectifying them. And if she, in general, is not as apt (due to biology or conditioning) to look at the bodies of her lovers with at least partially objectifying pleasure, perhaps such seeing is something that should be positively cultivated.

Instead we are, as a culture, currently on a crusade—understandable, considering the real nature of male sexual violence—to put out the eyes of predatory, objectifying men, but not, alas, thinking about what the crusade might mean for the future of sensual and romantic love or the possibility of our own visual and physical pleasure. When bad things happen, when people suffer, we often jump to extreme solutions in order to make sure that nothing bad ever happens again. We sterilize and lock up and lock out, we repress "dangerous ideas" and tendencies; we thus lean toward totalitarianism, without realizing that by so doing we are also destroying much that is good in nature and society; that we crush the human spirit in an attempt to make sure that everything is safe and that no-one's feelings, ever, ever get hurt. Paglia writes, rightly: "a pain-free world will be achieved only under totalitarianism. ... There is no such thing as risk-free anything. In fact, all valuable human things come to us from risk and loss." To banish all danger is the classic danger of dystopia, which tries to banish pain, difference, old age, ugliness, conflict, and criticism. Such censorship of real human complexity is notoriously treacherous.

If the danger that is being banished is important to you—say free speech or diving in unguarded waters, or taking hallucinogens or drinking raw milk, or reading subversive books—you might protest against such radical prohibition and plead for the reinstatement of the dangerous but valuable thing. The free enjoyment of beauty (in all its varying forms) is to me this sort of desirable dangerous thing.

At what cost do we purchase absolute safety and the unalienable freedom to never be offended? Yes, we must work harder to protect against rape and sexual violence—I personally have been a public defender of the abused and harassed, and will continue to be—but we must be careful about *how* we respond in order to ensure that the cure does not cause as much harm as the disease. To eliminate all danger, one would have to have never been born; to eliminate most danger would require staying home and taking no risks at all, never getting lost, never making mistakes, never learning. Some extremists would advocate for castration, or perhaps the murder of all men, others more moderately for *a gradual de-sexualization and de-materialization of life*, an ideological change of culture, amounting in some cases to a sort of spiritual or ideological castration. Do we really want to put out our eyes so we never see anything painful? Do we want to put out the eyes of all others—others whose gaze we might otherwise welcome—in order to protect ourselves absolutely from being ogled by the wrong person?

Today many women insist that they do not want to be seen as bodies, not "objectified," neither praised nor condemned for their physical characteristics. Children are taught not only to not insult others' physical attributes, but also to not even compliment each other on their hair, clothes, eye color. The inevitable consequence is to train them to *not see beauty at all*—for to recognize it causes pain to some and elevates others. Women complain that men comment on their appearance, and this harassment is said to be especially egregious in the workplace where, supposedly, romance and sex should not be countenanced. Certainly, unwanted advances can be unpleasant (it is a little different, isn't it, when they are wanted?); and, yes, when they come from bosses or other people who must be pleased to maintain one's job or to get promoted, such advances are too often further aggravated by unethical and oppressive consequences. But do we really want to become exclusively utilitarian when we are at work, utterly banishing our sexual and sensual natures? There are all kinds of ways in which we all (men too) sacrifice our dignity, comfort, and safety to please the boss, and this is a real problem. As Baudelaire suggested, there are many, many ways to prostitute oneself. But Americans, perhaps due to our Puritan heritage, are much more likely to see sin when sex is involved. Being forced to lie to cover up the company's dirty secrets, or to neglect one's family to work overtime on that special account, or to ignominiously lick the boss' shoes in so many small ways, is hardly considered abuse at all—just part of the practical game of capitalism. But are physical abuses—or verbal ones relating to physical attributes—really so much more damaging than spiritual ones? Rather than heedlessly sacrificing our sensual natures for so many hours of our lives, I believe we should rather question the shameful requirements of work (wage-slavery for many—a dire form of objectification) which have indeed often coerced women and men to put up with all manner of abuses just to keep their jobs. Strive to revise work, try to correct the dynamic that subjects people to the often unethical and reckless whims of corrupt superiors, but let us not banish sexuality and the daily pleasures of beauty!

There is an education that comes, if one is lucky, from sexuality, which teaches complexity of impulses and desires; which teaches us that things we might deem bad in "waking" life, in social and moral life, are really good and desirable as fantasies. The sharp distinction between good and evil is blurred in the arms of a person one loves and desires. Pain and pleasure, power and submission, fear and delight, role reversals of all kinds, are enjoyed within an environment of general trust. This is similar to what one experiences while being immersed in a work of art, where one can enjoy all sorts of things that might be disturbing or painful in "real" life. Sexuality, as an aesthetic experience, teaches us about what we value in art, as art teaches us what we value in sexuality and romance: difference, dynamics, contrast, *duende*. We often submit to dramas and catastrophes in our romantic lives, pretending that we are naïve enough not to have understood the risk, or else out of an obtuse lack of self-knowledge, or in the grip of that which we call passion. We may lament these events, these things that "happen to" us, as if we were the victims of some mysterious external force. But isn't it also at least sometimes true that we orchestrate them ourselves, whether consciously or not—out of an innate desire for some aesthetic action and satisfaction—some need for dramatic climax? There are very good psychological explanations for such complexes: we repeat pathological relations from our childhood in an attempt to heal them with some other player; we continue to hold on to coping mechanisms from a dysfunctional past when they are no longer helpful, or even harmful. But isn't it also true that we sometimes create chaos out of an irresistible aesthetic desire for cataclysm, challenge, change? We all know—

either from our own experience, or from being the *confidante* to a friend who continues to act out predictably tragic romantic dramas—how quickly such patterns can become deathly boring in themselves. Just the same, it would be a mistake to abandon all passionate dynamics, all complicated peripeteias as if one had already achieved perfect fulfilment and wisdom. Life is learning. And learning requires making mistakes and taking risks. The wholesome "drama-free" life may be healthy—but not particularly interesting or personally enriching.

Many who promote trigger warnings and the policing of sexual looking insist that no harm is done by the constraints, that men and women may still enjoy the same or even more pleasure, despite such limitations on human interaction and expression. But it has become clear that radical changes are currently taking place in the way we see each other and ourselves, changes that tend toward an essential denigration of physicality and desire and that involve the sanctification of the supposedly higher values of the spiritual and the non-erotic. Do we want such safety if it only comes at the expense of sensuality and beauty? Is there no other way for women to be powerful? Must we all relinquish our complex aesthetic, romantic, and sexual experience of each other and of the multivalent, immensely beautiful world? Perhaps the most foolproof precaution is for all of us to simply wear protective clothing, like the workers at some factories do, which exposes only the eyes (not even the mouth, which can be covered by a piece of netting) to the dangerous predatory gaze of fellow workers or higher-ups? To be sure, it would be more secure, and no-one would be distinguished from anyone else. No interruptions or distractions from *work* at all! Women, just as free as men to labor like machines for the good of the company! We would be neutered, neutral, automata almost. But do not fret, those of you who decry the dangers of seeing and being seen at the workplace: the experts in artificial intelligence tell us that full-scale automation is arriving soon enough. In almost no time, we may all be replaced by purely or primarily bionic entities, our bodies efficiently done away with.

Meanwhile, we are compelled to consider why it should be more dangerous for women than for men to see and conceptualize. Why should Psyche not be allowed to look? Paglia suggestively writes that Emily Dickinson, a notorious recluse, did not want to be seen because her own eye was so all-seeing and all-penetrating. She knew what looking could see. But if we can agree that the general taboo was not invented by women as a protest against being seen, we might consider that a taboo against women seeing is a taboo against women daring to conceptualize, daring to desire, daring to want things and people that we sometimes (or maybe even mostly) cannot or should not have. Could it possibly have been a taboo created to spare women the pain of heartache and disappointment? Or because overmuch romantic or sexually-impassioned love distracts us from the domestic duties at hand? Consider the words Sappho puts into the mouth of a young girl who did not properly heed Psyche's bad example, who hearkened to the goddess of fleshly, not spiritual, love: "It is no use, Mother, I cannot finish my weaving. Aphrodite, soft as she is, has almost killed me with love for that boy." But, indeed, suppose we now dare to hunger. Suppose we risk being distracted from our work for a moment...

No wonder, really, that there are so many taboos about seeing and being seen. Many cultures throughout history have believed in a variation of what we call "the evil eye": *oculus fascinus* (ancient Rome), *baskania* (ancient Greece), *aynhara* (the Hebrews), *arnabisa* (Syria). *Mal occhio, mauvais oeil, mal ojo, böser Blick.* And, for all cultures, this evil eye seems to have been thought of as a sort of "fascination"—a power which could capture and hypnotize, bewitch, harm, lead astray, and even kill outright. Men could wield their eyes in evil ways—but contrary to today's mythology, it was women whose eyes were once thought most dangerous. Possibly, if we entertain the notions of scholars like Jane Harrison, which delineate a pre-Olympian Greek religion where female goddesses are possessed of powers simultaneously beneficial and lethal, we may imagine that there was a time when female looking was powerful, active, and creative—and that it was maligned as merely evil and thus rendered taboo—by first the masculinizing Olympian pantheon and later, more forcefully still, by the Christian church and its precepts. The mythologist Barbara Walker tells us that

> the All-Seeing Eye of ancient Egypt once belonged to the Goddess of truth and judgment, Maat. The mother-syllable *Maa* meant 'to see'; in hieroglyphics it was an eye. A late text transferred the All-Seeing Eye to a male god, Horus, and the common symbol came to be known as the Eye of Horus, also representing the phallus as the 'one-eyed God'. Yet the same Eye was incongruously described as a female judge... 'Lady of Slaughter, Mighty One'.

One particularly moving story in this vein, narrated by Harrison, tells of Apollo, the "woman hater," and his takeover of the shrines and oracles of Kassandra. Kassandra's frenzy against Apollo, Harrison writes, "is more than the bitterness of maiden betrayed; it is the wrath of the prophetess of the old order discredited, despoiled by the new; she breaks her wand and rends her fillets and cries: 'Lo, now the seer the seeress hath undone'." Note that the power is all in the seeing, whether mystical or physical.

Andrew Lang, in *Custom and Myth*, devotes a chapter to the Cupid and Psyche myth, tracing versions of tales in various cultures that narrate the pervasive taboos against seeing and being seen. An ancient story in the Rig Veda, for example, tells of a fairy or sylph named Urvasi, who falls in love with a mortal man named Pururavas, whom she takes as her lover with the proviso: "Embrace me three times a day, but never against my will, and let me never see you without your royal garments, for this is the manner of women." The covenant with her Lord required that if this "compact were broken she would be compelled to leave him." Her kinsmen, who did not favor the liaison, tricked them by stealing a lamb from beside Urvasi's bed, impelling Pururavas to leap out in his nakedness, allowing his immortal lover to see him—and so she disappeared. Lang enumerates multiple other tales—sometimes where men may not see women's faces or bodies, and sometimes where women may not see men—and finally suggests that the tales evolved out of ancient taboos and marital practices, "to give sanction to the law" when its reason was no longer understood. The custom among the African people of Futa, he writes, required that "wives never permit their husbands to see them unveiled for three years after marriage." Lang refers us to the Bible for corroboration of the commonness of this practice: "Though Job had a daughter by his last wife, yet he never saw her without her veil, as having been married to her only two years." "Among the Australians," he tells us, quoting an Aboriginal legend, "the chief deity... Pundjel... 'has a wife whose face he has never seen', probably in compliance with some primaeval etiquette or taboo." And, finally, Lang refers to Caillié's *Travels to Timbuctoo*, wherein we learn that the bridegroom "is not allowed to see his intended during the day" (this is obviously related to our taboo against the bridegroom seeing the bride before the ceremony on the wedding day). He has, we learn further, "a tabooed hut apart," even after the ceremony, "and if he is obliged to come out, he covers his face. ... He 'remains with his wife only till daybreak'—like Cupid—and flees, like Cupid, before the light." The groom may not see the bride, the story tells us; but she, also, may not see him.

Sylvan Tomkins' studies on 'Affect Imagery Consciousness' tell us that brides were thought to be particularly powerful on their wedding nights; therefore, it was believed that the veil not only protected "the bride from harm, but also protect[ed] anyone she might see before arriving at her new home." "Menstruating women and women in childbirth have been generally regarded as dangerous," Tomkins continues, "and they have frequently been isolated so that, as with the Kolosh women of Siberia, they 'may not defile heaven with a look'." Witches were thought to have evil or "strange eyes." "Juno had an evil eye, and so did her bird, the peacock," while the "Egyptian goddess, Osiris, was reputed, by Plutarch, to have killed a small boy by looking at him in anger." Tomkins believes that most cultures teach children from an early age not to "look with sexual intent," since such looking is "sufficiently inflammatory to motivate society and parents to inhibit any sign of it in children, if and when it does appear.... In a culture which taboos sex, any connection between looking and sexual excitement would lead to a taboo on looking, and indeed the connection between the eyes and sexuality is close." And, as might be expected, Tomkins' analysis explains Psyche's prohibition: "There is reason to believe that in many, if not all, societies there is a more severe training of the female than the male with respect to sexual looking." In addition, touching on the widespread belief that female sexual response to images is less powerful than it is for males, Tomkins adds: "The female learns to be visually more shy, we think. Kinsey found that only 12 percent of his female subjects felt any sexual response to portrayals of nude figures of the opposite sex, whereas 54 percent of the males responded." We do not know, of course, what accounts for this discrepancy, though Tomkins suggests it is a matter of training, not necessarily biology. Other studies have suggested that women are actually aroused, but that the message does not get through to their brains; men, by contrast, seem to have immediate and powerful connections between the eye, the brain, and sexual excitation.

But what about romantic or aesthetic stimulation? Has anyone ever thought to measure which sex is more inspired by *beauty*? Or to research connections or disparities between sexual and other kinds of pleasurable looking? In any case, what about that 12% of women who do report a connection in the old Kinsey report? What about the women who both like to look and also do not feel offended or harassed by the male gaze? Those women who do feel aroused by images (sexually, aesthetically, romantically) may well be too afraid to admit it or to speak up, out of fear that such an admission of pleasure might do harm to their more sensitive sisters. I am very sensitive to the very real pain suffered by women (and men) who have been sexually (and emotionally) abused—and feel that many of them deserve and may well require more tender protection. But I do not think that even this very real pain should mean that we turn all of society into a blindfolded sanctuary for the traumatized. To do so would be, once again, to revert to some dystopian land of sterile safety and surveillance. We do not know whether such a widespread censorship on looking would help the victims or reduce the number of outrages; but it certainly cannot be right for some people to have to give up on a natural and healthy pleasure because others, more squeamish or more prudish, are made uncomfortable by it, either because of previous bad experience or out of some anti-sexual, anti-physical, anti-aesthetic bias. Are we to measure everything in this modern age by the standards of a neo-puritanical morality? As Shakespeare's Sir Toby Belch says to Malvolio in *Twelfth Night*, "Dost thou think, because thou art virtuous, there shall be no more cakes and ale?"

Tomkins notes the problem that the ancient Church had with female sexual looking, reminding us that, "Even the Old Testament attributes sexual looking to females (Genesis 39: 6-7), 'Joseph was a goodly person, and well favoured. And it came to pass... that his master's wife cast her eyes upon Joseph; and she said, Lie with me'." The Renaissance Church, too: "Early in the sixteenth century the Florentine artist Fra Bartolommeo painted a nude St. Sebastian which, according to Vasari, was praised for its beauty and especially its flesh coloring. But the picture had to be removed. The friars discovered through the confessional that some women sinned in their thoughts when they looked at it." Taboos on seeing and being seen indeed seem to bear traces of a fear of the undeniable power of beauty—especially of the beauty of nakedness—which inflames and intoxicates and sometimes makes people feel and do things that fray the seams of social morality. This power is all the more terrifying, it would seem, when it is unleashed in women. To some, it has seemed wiser to keep all of that passion and desire locked up, pent up, extinguished, pacified, covered. As if it really ever could be. Instead, we can all see the results of such repression, in today's scandals surrounding the exposure of decades of abuses by "celibate" Catholic priests. Natural sexuality is turned into perversity by unnatural prohibitions.

Some people today still argue that women wearing hijabs or nuns in habits are more free than women who may reveal their flesh, hair, ankles, thighs, or arms—free at least from the unwanted stares and intrusions of predatory men. But the masculine control of female sexuality that often accompanies such covering, along with the pervasive judgement and double standard, even in our permissive society, which regards girls and women who are sexually active as sluts or nymphomaniacs (while men who indulge in similar behaviors are seen as studs or, at worst, players), seems to tell another story—a story related to centuries of policing and denial of female pleasure. Unless one believes that being free of sexual desire and sexual fulfilment is freedom—and surely there are people who believe this—such taboos on seeing and being seen tend rather toward inhibition than liberation. From moral judgments on hem lengths and the shaming of "fast women," to the attempt to keep the good wife from experiencing orgasm in the marriage bed (for fear of what demons it might unleash), to the blaming and punishment of rape victims who were "asking for it," to female genital mutilation, the powerful union of women and pleasure has long been discouraged—often brutally. Today, the censorious word comes from elsewhere—from allegedly liberal realms—but it has the same chilling effect. We women have allowed our eyes to be more or less put out—and, with our eyes, a direct and thrilling conduit to our naturally pleasure-loving bodies and minds. Let us break the taboos and give ourselves the permission to learn to see and be seen anew. Let us dare to look beauty in the face, and to be astonished.

Up until now I have largely skirted the central question of *what* beauty is and whether or not a culture that celebrates looking would necessarily have narrow or exclusively punitive beauty ideals. I have suggested that there may be—contrary to one very entrenched line of social construction—some meaningful connection between outside and inside, that beauty might well *mean* something about a person who possesses it, something beyond or outside of reproductive fitness or good genes. I have felt it necessary to try to counter the prevailing prejudice against the "merely" superficial surface, without irrationally insisting that external beauty cannot, sometimes, be a mask for internal ugliness. But whether or not there is spiritual beauty under a physically beautiful surface, that surface itself at least ought not be maligned. It can be appreciated, with all due respect to its loveliness. And, likewise, wise old age—beautiful in its own way, possessed of fascinating wrinkles and the loveliness of all fading things—should not stoop to disparage the fresh promise of youthful beauty. We hear much about how American culture fetishizes youth, and certainly the ethos is different in Europe. On the streets of France or Italy, older women are appreciated and admired, whereas in the United States, everyone knows they are largely ignored—invisible. Again, perhaps this has something to do with our Puritan past—for older women in America, if they are not desperately trying to pretend that they are still young, have too often relinquished their sexuality, covered it and hidden it away, thinking it no longer seemly. If sex is for making babies, why would women past the age of reproduction be considered sexual beings? While the current Western culture of exhibitionism proliferates as a sort of despiritualized pornography, young would-be awoken people seem nowadays to not want to be admired for their physical characteristics at all. A merely functionalist materialism, once again, is pitted dualistically against an allegedly higher spirituality, as if there were no such thing as materiality infused with spirit.

There are many ways to be beautiful, and many types of beauty, and to celebrate the beautiful is not to suggest that ugliness should be banished, for that would only be another form of dystopia. And yet, beauty is not necessarily the opposite of ugly, at least not precisely. It should certainly not be confused with anodyne prettiness or saccharine deceit, which attempts to hide the real nature of the world—twisted and contorted as it sometimes can be, though also graceful and harmonious. A vision of beauty often includes pain, dissonance, darkness, strangeness. And one might argue, as Frederick Turner does in his magisterial *Beauty: The Value of Values*—a volume I read only in the editing stages of this book, which reiterates much of what I have written in these pages—that "the appearance of life itself might be interpreted as a response to apparently irreconcilable contradictions inherent in matter." In turn, he explicates, human creative acts may be seen as affirmative confrontations with the pain and shame of tragedy, and as "spurs to the emergence of new and more exquisite forms." Beauty, Turner writes, "is our word for that emergence." Only one who believes that the world as it is is ugly would think that the word beauty referred only to detached parts of life. To see beauty simply in what is real (Keats' "Truth")—be it youth or old age or sickness or health—is to capture and conceptualize what is otherwise difficult to grasp. It is a way of finding meaning, giving form to what is sometimes hard to bear. Proust's narrator, when he returns to Paris after being a long time away, thinks that everyone at the party he enters is wearing white wigs—but then he realizes that they have all gone grey. And he is moved intensely, because he knows what this physical reality *means.* The physical has become a symbol. And though it is a symbol of the approach of death, something difficult and painful, it is not a stretch to suggest that the encapsulation of the ungainly truth within this physical image—for *metaphors are mainly physical,* images drawn from the world to help us understand the abstract—is itself beautiful. Faded in soft colors, autumnal bursts of brightness, deep laugh-lines, scars from falls and accidents, the look of experience, sad or joyful eyes—remembering many winds, kissed by much sun, well-loved, having loved much—all might be admired in the complex beauty of an older face. Although there is beauty in the complex and painful, particularly in artistic expressions, which help us to bear the unbearable through some comprehensive, all-embracing way of seeing, there is also beauty in those rare moments of fleeting natural perfection—beauty as a relief and graceful pause, a heart-stopping, astonished gasp—something that must be seen.

VII.

Making Meaning II

Italian Journeys

> My real delight is in the fruit, in figs, also pears, which must surely be choice in a place where even lemons grow.
>
> Goethe
> *Italian Journey*

> My formula for greatness in a human being is *amor fati*: that one wants nothing to be different, not forward, not backward, not in all eternity. Not merely bear what is necessary, still less conceal it—all idealism is mendacity in the face of what is necessary—but love it.
>
> Nietzsche
> *Ecce Homo*

IN TORINO, ITALY, once called Augusta Taurinorum in honor of the bull sacred to Isis, goddess of fertility, where Nietzsche went mad, embracing a beaten horse and weeping, dancing naked in his room, and practicing Dionysian rites of auto-eroticism; where, before his collapse, he enjoyed the air, the piazzas, the cobblestones, and the gelato; where the ladies chose the sweetest grapes for this reluctantly German philosopher, it is easy to feel the sensual, life-affirming, pagan roots of myth-making, to understand those humanistic allegories that sing of life, love, pleasure, and appetite. At the opera, I heard Tosca sing,

"Vissi d'arte, vissi d'amore" (I lived for art, I lived for love). I indulged in long, wine-drenched lunches on unseasonably sunny piazzas, and gazed at gleaming artifacts from ancient times in dark museums. There was a secret restaurant where a small fierce woman named Brunilde roughly took my order, displayed magical cakes with her wide toothy smile, briskly removed the empty plates that once held the most delicious food I'd ever eaten, brought me a shot glass containing grapes soaked in absinthe with dessert, if I pleased her by ordering it, but growled me out the door if I was too full or too stupid to partake of her pride and joy. I was in residence at the Fusion Art Gallery on Piazza Amedeo Peyron, presided over by the wise and warm painter, Barbara Fragnogna, who told me about the market across the way which sold beautiful mushrooms, wild strawberries, and breadsticks studded with huge, juicy olives. When I wasn't eating, or wandering in museums, I was building an elaborate book which folds and unfolds, and is painted and glued and stitched, and "gold-leafed" with foil wrappers from the many *gianduji* chocolates I enjoyed. I threw off the layers of the Vermont winter to feel the wind and sun on my body, and was reminded of how much our conclusions about what life means are influenced by the relationship between our own physicality and the material world which surrounds us.

Meaning is not something that we need to artificially superimpose on the objects and events of the world through some transcendental narrative or morality. It is not something we need to be taught or coerced into seeing by external social constructions or manipulative indoctrination. If one is healthy, has an appetite, and senses for seeing, hearing, tasting, and touching, beautiful things or people everywhere will bear meaning, as "the promise of happiness" or, indeed, in the knowledge of the fleetingness or absence of happiness. We are given the gifts of colors and sounds, of textures and temperatures. And if all else fails, this should be enough reason to be grateful for life. In addition to this inherent meaning, this meaning without thought and evaluation, our intellectual response to the physical facts of the world makes us dream, imagine, and invent ever new celebrations and laments. These expressions will survive and proliferate insofar as other humans resonate with them. And what resonates will be made manifest in real, made things, in built places, in enacted experiments. This is a discourse and manifestation over millennia, from the ancient cave paintings to today: humans trying to make sense of the terror and tenderness of the world. We do not despair, we artists and "creative subjects." Nor do we invent meanings that attempt to twist the facts of nature: gravity and mortality are real. Instead, we work with what there is, and endeavor to embrace it in all its fractured glory. Thus, also, the things we make with our hands, out of paper, pigments, wax, string, fire, earth, water, and air, will fade, crumble, dissolve in good time. They are already fragile, already very imperfect, already mostly forgotten. And yet their ephemeral presence is of the utmost importance.

I am sitting on a bench in a church entranceway. A gray, cool, dreamy late morning. Some high school students, girls and boys, gather at the other end of the stone courtyard, gossiping, talking, laughing. Old people, alone, walk in and out of the church. It is a Monday, and most shops here are closed, their metal gratings pulled down. Dirty pigeons coo. In the back streets, a gentle squalor; clothing hangs from lines and abandoned bicycles rest against elaborate gates. On the walls are scraps of political agitation, left and right, shreds of old posters, graffiti scrawls. People talk, but I don't understand them. Markets everywhere, with abundance: artichokes and more artichokes, wheels of cheese, sausages, chickens, lamb shanks, lemons. People smoke and joke, are grim or warm. On my walk here I passed a waitress carrying a tray of espresso down the street from a café out of sight, and a silver piece of paper blew to the ground. I picked it up and handed it to her. *Grazie, signora*. An elegant lady walks up the church steps now, in perfectly matching brown and gold: a soft-brimmed hat with gold trim, a brown cane, a brown coat with fur collar, a purse of gold and brown plaid, little brown shoes, dark sunglasses—all her belongings and all her faith perfectly intact from another era. Trucks rumble by, but otherwise it is quiet, peaceful. Balconies preserve foliage from the summer, not quite dead, not quite blooming; vines dangle and a single bruised yellow rose lilts; while back in Vermont everything is covered in snow and ice. This is a life. Anywhere is a life. How different, how similar is this one to and from mine, from or to yours? And how does it happen that it evolved to be like this here and some other way somewhere else?

As Goethe noted in his famous *Italian Journey*, an experience of difference both enunciates one's individuated self and dissolves it. Visiting another world, you imagine that you might have been, could have been, still might be, sort of someone else, leading a different life in a different country, in a different language, with a different family, lover, children, vocation. Your certainties, the things you took for granted, are called into question. You would be more comfortable not examining them, not questioning: why do you and your fellows do what you do? Are these differences a result of customs, habits, social constructions, error, accident, nature? Are they the result of our upbringing, something atavistic in our blood, or determined by the atmosphere, the landscape, or the history that surrounds us? The external differences—are they petty? Do they alter from the outside who we are inside? Or are they representative of who we are, from the inside out? Ask a novelist or a method actor how much each gesture, each phrase, each seemingly minor choice reveals about identity. The way we eat, how much beauty we need, or how much labor, leisure, love, rigor, sleep, poetry, space, air, skyline, horizon, practicality, recklessness.

And now I am experiencing the differences, the strangeness here in Torino, among people for whom all of this is natural, normal. I enjoy this sense of difference, to a point, as most of us do. We seek it out, we are sometimes sick to death of our own lives and want to gaze at, play at others' lives; but only for a spell. It can be tiring; one feels alien; sometimes one wants to cry out of frustration because everything is so confusing and the simplest things seem impossible; and the people look at you like you are an idiot—and, in a way, you are. You are an adult who does not know things that a child knows.

I get lost often. Sometimes a piazza will have four different entryways with a statue in the middle. Who can remember which way one entered from? Since I am not usually in a hurry, I wonder why this should matter to me. Maybe because we want always to seem like we know where we are going and we already have everything we want. And this has something to do with desire and the desire for love, which is sometimes shameful. As a stranger one wants something. Is looking for something. Has left home to find something that one does not already have. Desire is the need to become one with what is foreign, to take it into oneself and to be embraced by it as well. As Anne Carson tells us in *Eros the Bittersweet*, we long to be one with the other, but when we have assimilated what was once strange, it is no longer the other and so it no longer serves its purpose. Knowledge comes only at the cost of desire fulfilled; we can only seek out more and more things, people, places, books, mysteries we do not yet know, have not yet seen or solved or read, so that we may experience that supreme thrill of coming to know again and again. We crave difference, but we also cannot keep from looking for likenesses. We seek both everywhere. And the new experiences we have are continually threaded back into what we already know.

In the Egizio Museum in Torino, I am astonished by the way the ancient Egyptians had the same instinct for symmetry as ours; for placing each depicted object or vignette centrally within a frame; for aligning each hieroglyph in a uniform square of space; for leaving the most graceful and harmonious negative space between the hand of the man holding a slaughtered bird by its neck and the fronds of the plant in a vase by his side. A sense of what is beautiful, evidently, is at least somewhat natural and universal. And the works of art or ritual made with this sense of what is beautiful still resonate with a mysterious significance, even if we today cannot fully understand or believe in the things that were sacred to the people who made them. Translation across time and cultures is needed for a more thorough comprehension of these artifacts, but something very powerful, something powerfully familiar is present even without a struggle. What we want is to maintain the strangeness, while approaching a comprehension. What we must avoid is to diminish difference in the interest of a complete and total homogeneity.

I am operating in a language I barely know, but I do make myself understood, more or less, with the few Italian words I mispronounce and the few I manage to understand. A good part of the pleasure of communication is in the *frisson* of partial misunderstanding, in the incommensurable distance between one mind and another, struggling to approximate a shared vision (as in the erotic desire to become one with the unknown). Translation is necessary even without a language barrier, and we all do our best to reveal and also conceal our meanings from each other. It is a dance. Sometimes clumsy, but sometimes surprisingly beautiful. The differences between language, as Steiner suggests, may be a result of a human need to differentiate one group from another, to keep secrets, to individuate from what may be a basically universal commonality. There are twin drives to compare and contrast, to find analogies, metaphors, likenesses; and to delineate differences, incompatibilities, untranslatables.

Today our basic assumptions about correspondence and difference are paradoxical. On the one hand, there are those who insist that everyone is equal, the same, indistinguishable (or that they should be, were we to look beyond external, physical differences). On the other hand, these same people tend to insist that it is impossible to understand the other; that there are no universals; that there is no shared sense of value; and that language barely helps us to communicate with each other at all, since it is so very distant from the things it claims to signify as to be more deceptive than descriptive. Both of these assumptions depend on a denial of the importance of the physical world; on a denial of any meaningful relationship between nature and cultural norms, between the physical world and the language that describes it; between the human brain and its sensory apparatus; and, finally, between one human brain and another. In reality, things and people are self-similar *and* they deviate from sameness; but even the deviations do not prohibit some approximation of understanding.

Those who deny difference and simultaneously insist on incommensurability are trying to do two contradictory things at once: to strip away differences that might cause conflict or justify hierarchies or discriminations, resulting in a neutering and neutralizing homogeneity, and to still deny that these newly neutralized beings will be able to understand each other despite the pervasive removal of the characteristics that seem to have caused all the trouble in the first place. Perhaps the unspoken hope is that the neutralization and leveling, the moral rejection of the physical world (beauty, ugliness, pain, pleasure, difference) will eventually really result in a homogeneity so complete that, even if we no longer have anything interesting to say or any unique artistic expressions to make, we will at least make no more war, at least harbor no more resentment or hate against the "other"—because there will be no more other. And no differential qualities whatever to get in the way of perfect, passive niceness. On the one hand, we are ignoring the inevitable consequences of our neutralizations, neglecting to weigh how much difference makes life rich and strange and fascinating. And, on the other hand, by critiquing conceptualization, deconstructing symbolic archetypes, and undermining the significance of language, we are denying the natural, affirmative instinct for finding likenesses and correspondences.

On one level, seeing shapes and patterns where they are not "really" present may be called *pareidolia*, most often ridiculed as a psychosis that finds the faces of Jesus and the Madonna in rock formations and baked goods, endeavoring to prove through argument and scientific study that the piece of fabric housed in a crypt in Torino once was wrapped around none other than Christ himself. The Shroud Museum has rooms filled with "evidence" of why we should believe that the shroud belonged to Him: there are blood stains from where His crown of thorns would have been; stains in the shapes of wounds suffered when He was tortured, an exemplar of the instrument with which He would have been scourged. The fact that there is just one wound mark where his feet would have been is explained by arguing that both feet were punctured, one atop the other, with but one nail. There is no mention in the museum of the carbon dating done on the fabric, which dated it to a time much later than Jesus' supposed death; but there is an example of the loom upon which the cloth might have been woven and an example of a crown of thorns, which is arched like a dome and not open like a wreath. Image after image is presented to convince the skeptic that the shroud belonged to Jesus. At first it is hard even to see the shapes that would suggest any face or body, but, as if one were gazing at one of those magical illusion pictures, if one looks long enough, the desired shapes begin to come into focus—and fade just as quickly into indistinguishable marks again. Desired shapes: the shapes one wants to see.

Fresh lovers often insist that they are "exactly alike," noting that they both amazingly enjoy chocolate or were born on a Friday as signs that they are made for each other. And even someone as wise and experienced as myself may choose to be deluded into reading into signs that may not be there at all, thinking that the intern at the artists' residency is making eyes at me, when really he probably just looks at everyone like that. He had told me tales of rituals in his home town where someone would dress up as Dionysus in animal skins and horns, a bag of blood hidden under the pelts, and someone else would chase after him and "kill" him, spilling blood all over the streets. But what did that *mean*?

Of course, as already discussed, all of our seeing is a process of selecting out, which to some extent overlooks the fact that reality is a mass of non-delineated color and light, a mass of shifting molecules temporarily huddled into seemingly distinct shapes and entities. We can question whether the things we see are rightly to be delineated as separate or whether our particular arrangements of what belongs with what, or who belongs with whom, are comprehensive contextualizations or merely constructed biases, wishful thinking, or limitations. We can say the same thing about words and the concepts they form—that words are a crime against the multifarious differentiation of reality, that they name and delimit what is really irreducible and unnamable. Names and words and categories pull some things together with other things, leaving yet other things out, and ignore the qualities of the named and categorized things that do not fit in with the given names—qualities that might render these things more fitting to be named and arranged in different categories altogether. Is the creation of a concept a form of psychosis, hallucination, wishful thinking, pareidolia?

When we note a pattern, say, of bird or insect movement, of repeating forms in nature or fairytales, or of habitual actions in our own lives, are we ignoring all the elements that would render the categorized thing, action, or thought unfitting to be classed within the desired arrangement? Or is there really a way to establish that something is enough like something else to conclude that it is a pattern and thereby attempt to draw meaning from it? Of course, this is essentially the scientific method, but we use it indiscriminately every day, without the necessary "controls" to make our experiments scientifically viable. And science itself is subject to the same kind of criticism: even if its trials are well-documented and avail themselves of responsible criteria for investigation, the scientists have, as we well know, already decided to ask some questions over others, thereby determining what kinds of answers might be found.

But here is the crux: we do all this because we want, we need to draw meaning. And we draw meaning most readily from things that repeat or seem to repeat, from something that seems to be universal or at least not merely an exceptional, random aberration. It might be absolutely accurate to say that, at least on a molecular level, everything is everything and thereby all patterns and all names and all conceptualizations are inaccurate and limiting, that the only accurate vision of reality is of a moving mass of colors and light without delineation or individuation. Babies start by seeing that way, but over time begin to recognize (or is it imagine?) shapes, distances, faces. Carl Sagan writes that pareidolia itself might be an evolutionary adaptation, since those babies who were first able to recognize faces responded to expressions, inducing them to smile and make eye contact, so that they were cared for and thus survived. This is rather suggestive, because if we were to consciously try as a culture to repress conceptualization, arrangement, and the meaning-making that rests on this patterning process, we would end up being unable to communicate with each other, and we would simply not survive as either individuals or cultures. Autistic children have a hard time making the kind of eye contact that Sagan suggests was good for survival. And many say that we are now becoming a culture of autism, one in which people do not communicate and are trapped in their own worlds without the ability to share experiences, emotions, ideas. Thus, although the process of making arrangements and making concepts does perforce leave things out, although it may sometimes be inaccurate, although it may sometimes look like psychosis or pareidolia, it is far better to make provisional arrangements and to use language and concepts (always acknowledging that they can change and rearrange) than to exist perpetually in an undifferentiated sea of colors, sounds, and non-shapes, unable to communicate.

But after visiting the Shroud Museum in Torino (the actual cloth is carefully hidden inside its box, only to be taken out on rare jubilee days), I do not believe that the shroud of Turin belonged to Jesus. The form of the body suggested by it is simply not sinuous and beautiful enough to satisfy our mythic desire for him. The image that the experts draw from the bloodstains is of a bulky, square-shouldered man, not at all the sweet beloved of the visionary mystics as depicted in paintings over centuries. Just as the scientists who discovered the shape of the DNA molecule knew that they had found it because the double helix was the most beautiful configuration, so we can see that the shroud did not belong to the Son of God because of the gracelessness of its traces.

There has to be a difference. Difference is thrilling, is *frisson*, is friction. If there were no difference, no distinction, no discrimination, no delineation, we would see nothing. Everything would be one blended morass, one moving, shifting mélange of everythingness. No shadows, no lights, no textures, no patterns or deviations. So we like to go away, discover new things, challenge ourselves, compare and contrast the familiar against the strange in order to understand, again, our expanded selves. And yet we find ourselves in a constant emotional oscillation, a cycle swinging between comfort, tedium, restlessness, curiosity, desire, risk-taking, danger, exposure, discomfort, exhaustion, homesickness, comfort, tedium—*ad infinitum*.

Thus we come to the necessity of maintaining some borders at a basic level: first personally, then globally. We need secrets, mysteries, in order to remain where we are, among our fellows in our homes, in our romantic relationships; or else it is as if we were running rampant around the neighborhood, around the world, continually searching for newness, making so many things the same as we unite with them, making everything homogeneous and known all-too-quickly. A promiscuous lover is someone who has not learned how to mine the depths of himself and his beloved, is quickly bored, doesn't have enough inner resources to discern the depths hidden in the one he is with: thus, he moves on quickly in order to stimulate his poor imagination. Curiosity, desire, conquest of new ideas and intellectual territory, all have their value: but they should not be gluttonous. If we are to feast, let us leave time for regeneration of resources; let us make sure we properly savor what we are sacrificing and devouring. The communion of the self with the other cannot be celebrated so swiftly that all differences are leveled out, sanded away, consumed by the Moloch of desire for newness. This touches on the problem and pleasure of materiality. The basic limitation of resources; that they are not infinite. You can melt down idols to make new ones, but then the old idols no longer exist. How can we contrive to keep the old ones and erect new ones, too? Of love, we can barely speak in this regard: the old lovers are replaced by new ones, yet they remain, one hopes, still within us, and we within them, in traces, some very potent, as we continue to consume and appropriate and expand, becoming new ourselves and shedding strangeness as we go, exploring our anti-selves, the characteristics we harbor that are anathema to our primary identities and the identities of our native lands and cultures.

After writing *The Sorrows of Young Werther*, and serving many years as advisor to the Duke of Weimar, Carl August, Goethe "stole" away at three in the morning, from his friends, his duties, and his romantic (but non-sensuous) relationship with Charlotte von Stein, to sojourn in Italy for two years. There he found himself, in contrast to the differences he experienced: he searched out the ancient remains of classical Rome, learned about architecture at the foot of buildings designed by Palladio, learned how to see by looking at Italian paintings, developed his concept of the universal *Ur-Pflanze* from which all plants metamorphose (*Alles ist Blatt*), and enjoyed, above all, the weather and the fruit. His wonderful account of his adventures includes detailed descriptions of the geology, flora, and fauna of the countries he passed through, along with evaluations of artifacts, architecture, painting, and peoples (he burdened his pack with rock specimens as well as heavy books). Referring to the Greek god, who could not be conquered in wrestling matches as long as he remained in contact with Gaia, Goethe writes, "I see myself as Antaeus, who always feels newly strengthened, the more forcefully he is brought into contact with his mother, the earth."

The Germans have always harbored a romantic longing for the

physicality of Italy, "the land where the lemons bloom," as Goethe writes, as the mythic antithesis of everything Germanic (stoical, cold, disciplined, abstract). Nietzsche sojourned to Torino, a Dionysus on the River Po, in conscious ex-patriot spirit. What meanings did he find there, that philosopher with a hammer who famously denied the existence of "Das Ding an sich," and called on us to bravely consider the abysmal probability that there is no meaning or purpose to life whatsoever? He certainly meant that there was no *predetermined* meaning or *God-given* purpose, no purpose ordained by a God. But he did not mean to repudiate the ways in which the world can be meaningful (affirmed, celebrated, enjoyed). For his rejection of the "thing in itself" was decidedly not a transcendental call to celebrate merely the disembodied life of the alienated mind out of touch with the physical world (a thing in itself, surely, despite Berkeley's skepticism, and despite the inability to know it absolutely or objectively beyond phenomena). Here in Torino, this city so beloved by Nietzsche, while I am struggling with the question of meaning, I feel compelled to come to terms with him on this question. We are in agreement on the central importance of the sensuous goodness of the world and a deep suspicion of any ideologies which aim to affirm something in contradiction to the facts of this real.

Ecce Homo, which Nietzsche wrote while in this city, begins with a serious discussion of the vital importance of digestion, weather, and music, all experienced by him (and by Goethe as well) as fundamental physical requirements for living the right life. The theological-metaphysical questions are deemed unimportant at best, treacherous deviations at worst. Thoreau, whose first chapter in *Walden* is called 'Economy', planted beanstalks as the most efficacious conduits to a realm where one might best consider "higher laws." It makes one wonder what would have happened to Thoreau had he visited Italy (he traveled a great deal, he noted, in Concord). Would he have abandoned his dietary restrictions against drinking coffee? Might he have succumbed to the animal spirits and fallen in love? Margaret Fuller, who translated that comprehensive man of spirit and sense, Goethe, and who complained about the disembodied tendency of her friend Emerson (and Thoreau was even less sensual than his mentor), did travel to Italy and fall in love, gave birth to a probably illegitimate child, and participated in the Italian Revolution. If she had not tragically drowned on her return home, she might have infected all of Concord with a new European sensuality! Just imagine. Nietzsche, who admired Emerson greatly, who was just about as abstemious and celibate as Thoreau, still knew how to reason from the hands to the head, as the bard of Concord counseled—and from the stomach, too, though it would have to be a strong one.

Love of Fate meant for Nietzsche an acceptance of one's life exactly as it is, without nay-saying or the bite of conscience (which he said was indecent), expanding to include a love of the world exactly as it is. Such a process seems to suggest a belief in a thing-in-itself after all: the world in itself, as it is—mediated by our senses, our tastes, our interests, our desires, yes, but not subject to utter transformation of its basic realities: mortality, gravity, pain, beauty, brilliance, energy, stupidity, music, pleasure, illness, cold, sunshine. Darwin explained all of this in his own way. We don't live in a friendly universe. The world cares not a fig for our personal happiness, though our genes may well fight mightily for their own generation. And the connection to Spinoza, greatly admired by Nietzsche, may be helpful: the world was not made for us humans, and thus should not be judged according to how well it does or does not serve our aims and desires. The world is good in itself—is, in fact, tantamount to god, is divine in itself, whether we are experiencing petty miseries or committing atrocities. The world is beautiful, even without the concept of beauty invented by humans. We are to look at the world from the "perspective of eternity," which is not a transcendental perspective but rather one which provides an angle beyond our own immediate interests. Objectivity? Well, not quite. With Nietzsche, we can speak of a perspective from the mountaintop, as far away from the flatland as possible, but with a knowledge of the subjective world of taste and senses. Nietzsche writes, in *The Twilight of the Idols*: "One would have to be situated outside life, and on the other hand to know it as thoroughly as any, as many, as all who have experienced it, to be permitted to touch on the problem of the value of life." For, if our reflections seem mercurial, shifting, and arbitrary from the perspective of eternity, closer up they are instinctive and healthy, responses to and engagement with the world.

As subjects, creative subjects, we make what we can of this world as it is. We cannot help but make meanings from it. But let these meanings be in metaphoric harmony with the real facts of nature. Let us make and preserve myths which help us to understand, to celebrate, and to weep over the true facts of human existence, its true pleasures and pains. Gilgamesh is struggling with the death of his friend. He searches for a way to be immortal, to conquer death. But when he thinks he has found it, a snake eats the magic herb he has foolishly left on the shore while he swims. Thus, although humans must be mortal, a snake can continually shed its skin. A true myth. The kind of fiction that Nietzsche railed against was of another kind: a false fiction, one that repressed the reality of death, repressed natural instinct and pleasure, repressed sexuality and the will to power, repressed beauty and energies and great health and desire in the interests of a transcendental idealism offering an afterlife, and some sense of pious righteousness, in exchange for all that makes life meaningful. The myth of Christianity he would battle with the myth of the beautiful drunken god: Dionysus versus the Crucified One. Thus he aimed not to do away with all myths (that, in fact, was Socrates' great sin, according to Nietzsche), but to celebrate the myths that are in accord with the true facts of life. Steiner quotes a cryptic passage from Nietzsche's notebooks: "God Affirms; Job Affirms." And glosses that Nietzsche was referring to his idea of the aesthetic justification of the world. The world of wonder and beauty. Look at what I made, says God to Job. I made the Leviathan. I am an artist. Don't talk to me about your petty troubles.

And here in Torino, Nietzsche, enjoying a rare respite from his chronic pain, in withdrawal from Wagner, the Wagnerites, the Germans and their obtuse idealism and morality, enjoyed the sunshine and the air and the food and the gelato (but not the wine); enjoyed the graciousness of the people and the lightness of *Carmen* (Torino was "tutti Carmenizzatto"). The world that Nietzsche celebrated was not so much a world of the future, a world of higher men, but a revival of Renaissance and pagan values—not at all the insipid, postmodern relativity of values with its snide rejection of beauty, nobility, genius, aristocratic individualism.

Meaning has been attacked from two sides. On the one hand, it has been attacked by the commercialization and commodification of life, by the simulacrum covering up an abyss of shallowness and the emptiness that is left over after the orgy of sensationalism, as humans become more and more bereft of any real connection to nature, relationships, history, culture, beauty, pleasure, divinity, sacredness. On the other hand, it has been attacked by the cold stewards of theory, who feel nothing themselves but only touch us with their clammy hands so that we too feel a chill and cannot sense the heat in what naturally should move us. These theorists even dare to claim Nietzsche as their own. Because he questioned the idea of a transcendent meaning, aiming with his iconoclastic hammer at the ideology that denied the real meanings of the world, they use his words as an attack on meaning altogether. Because he called for a transvaluation of values, they use his words as an attack on values altogether, missing his joyous celebration of the values of nobility, of the Renaissance, of ancient Greece, of great art and great men, of genius and beauty and rapture. Indeed, he had a hammer (though sometimes it was a tuning hammer for a piano, not a bludgeon) and there was smashing to be done. He was a great destroyer who called himself "Dynamite." But he destroyed only as a preliminary to creation. The epigones took up his hammer and began smashing even the idols Nietzsche himself had venerated. They smashed veneration altogether. And in their adolescent giddiness, in the din of their mob fury against what was once great, in their *ressentiment*, they did not hear the most important part of his message: the axes must be turned into chisels, to carve new idols, new values, new words, new forms, new metaphors, ones that honor what is vivid and beautiful in life, that affirm the instincts and the senses.

In a museum in Torino, I saw a painting of Santa Lucia, her bloody eyes on a plate. She was a pious girl, promised in marriage to a pagan. She cared for an ill mother and was called by an angel to devote herself to Christ instead of her pagan fiancé, and in exchange her mother would be cured. She willingly did so, refusing to bow down to the Emperor, and giving her dowry to the Church instead of to her future husband. For this, some say, her eyes were gouged out. Or else she cut them out herself so as not to be attractive to her husband-to-be. She is lovely and fierce in the paintings, and probably the man they had chosen for her was a brute and not to her taste; and her devotion to Christ healed her mother; but can we not think of a better story for her? Is this really a model worthy of *imitatio*? So many of these maiden saints (great aunts to our little match girl), who refused arranged marriages and instead gave themselves to the disembodied fantasy of the beautiful and scantily clad Christ, were exercising the only power they had, and for this they are admirable. They found, by religious subterfuges, one way of protecting themselves from drunken, brutish masters in the forms of husbands, pimps, and fathers. But their virginity was no great prize. Can we not imagine stories for them with better endings? Lovers to their tastes, freedom to choose, to adventure beyond the convent or housewifely walls? Rather than continuing to venerate the lives of these girls, we would do well to imagine new *vitae* for them, lives lived in rebellion, not against pagan emperors and sexuality, but against the control of their bodies and souls by male authority figures, lives lived in the full flowering of their sexuality and pleasure-loving instincts, in celebration of female desire. We must make new saints, and also revive old models worthy of veneration from the archives of history, woman and girls who knew light and dark, pleasure and pain, flesh, the devil, and the divine sweetness of the embrace of a beautiful, beloved, *living* body. Poor Santa Lucia. We pity her and regret the loss of her eyes. And then, in her honor, we go looking for traces of other myths, or at least a few fallen figs from some controversial historic feasts, to savor them from the safe distance of a relatively tame and unromantic time.

I am on my way to Gardone Riviera, on a pilgrimage to visit Il Vittoriale, the monumental house, shrine, and garden of Gabriele D'Annunzio, the Italian novelist, poet, patriot, lover, and aesthete. When I mention him here, some people seem uncomfortable: because he was wild enough to disregard the Treaty of Versailles and take over the island of Fiume so as to turn it into an artistic utopia; because of his relationship with Mussolini; because he represents or seems to represent many things that are nowadays in bad odor. To get to Gardone Riviera, I have to take a train to Milan and one to Brescia and then a long bus ride.

It is a misty, cool, warm morning in February, and confusions proliferate: about trains, ticket machines, banks, language, customs. They seem to do everything differently here, but for them that is how it is done. Then I realize that even in my own *milieu* I am strange. I am strange, wherever I go. An artist is outside of society, but also very inside it. Inside of life. Observing, but also feeling through and for everyone and everything. After writing that down I wonder if it is arrogant, as if I were suggesting that regular people don't feel, are not conscious. No, it is not that, but rather that their attention is mostly elsewhere, whereas ours is so often concentrated on reflection, on the symbolization of everything—watching gestures and configurations, listening to emphases and choices of words, noticing formal variations and repetitions. As Suzanne Langer notes, to use symbols (rather than just signs) is to talk *about* the world—not just to denote it, not just to deliver information, but to consider *how* things are, and *why*. And, as artists, our lives are consumed by symbols and their interpretations. The entire phenomenal world is to us a sort of symbol-picture of something else. No, not of another world, as Plato would have it, not a bad copy of some perfect original, but actually a symbol-complex of itself.

The phenomenal nature of the physical world *means* to us. We don't make of it what isn't there, but see in it all that there is to be seen in it. Not everything at once—that would be too much, that would be a jumble. But we see many things, one after the other, from different perspectives, in correspondence; we have many ways of seeing meaning in what is. We are curious about how things are made; where they come from; how they were invented; what human needs they answer; what history they contain; what natural materials; what miracles are evident in their existence; what they tell us about human and animal life, past and present, about desires, fears, curiosities, mistakes, kindnesses and cruelties, despairs and foolish hopes. Thoreau, allegedly an arch-anti-materialist, collected and used objects to trace history—as artifacts of material culture—looking, always, for the law and the deviation. Goethe, a naturalist and collector of botanical, geological, and artistic specimens, traced the variety of the plant world back to one original *Ur-Pflanze*, and then envisioned the entire world of objects and behavior as an allegory for this constant development, this constant Becoming (*Werden*) from out of the essence of Being (*Sein*).

All artists mine objects, physical acts, stories, events, speech utterances, places, buildings, man-made and natural, for their significance, for traces of how and what we have dreamt of and done battle for; for their own qualities and also for the ways in which they are allegories for other things, feelings, events, experiences; for the ways they seem to echo and repeat. When we see repeating patterns, we sometimes think, quite naturally, that we have learned something about life, identified some tendencies or natural laws; and, despite the doubts shed upon such instinctive correspondence nowadays, often we have done exactly that. But it would be foolish to take only one or two experiences and construct a final story about life. The largest, broadest field of vision (from Nietzsche's mountaintop) would be necessary to oversee all the conflicting narratives before drawing any conclusions from them. Life is brutal, life is tender. Humans are brave, are craven; are polygamous, monogamous; creatures of habit, craving change; we like to deviate and to stay close. So, whenever we try to maintain just one thing, we discover another side or possibility, but not to the extent that everything cancels everything else out. We may still come to provisional conclusions about the nature of the world, society, our lives, about what works and what does not; in fact, we must. But let these not be rigid or polarized, let us not base hasty conclusions solely on either the sum of the good or the sum of the bad experiences. A little hope is healthy, as is a touch of denial, since sometimes things turn out better than one expects, even in the worst of circumstances. As much horror as there is, there is also always good. Neither can be nullified by the other. We must see it all. Read it all into what we find before us. Find a way to embrace it all. *Amor fati*—love of fate.

I arrived at Gardone Riviera too late in the afternoon for a tour of the house, so I began my visit to D'Annunzio's Il Vittoriale degli Italiani with a sunset stroll around the "most beautiful garden in Italy." From my neoclassical hotel, with its palm trees, pillars, and reproductions of Roman sculptures, I walked up the steep winding paths and stairways to the grounds, past little houses perched amid orange trees and covered in vines, until I found the gate and entered D'Annunzio's strange dream: grottos with idols; walkways beneath portentous archways; a sudden St. Francis of Assisi; a fountain of spouting gorgon heads; a mausoleum for the heroes of Fiume; a giant boat docked on land; pedestals topped with statuesque nudes. A sign before a sun-dappled little garden made up of rocks, small columns, and upright missiles, informs the visitor that this is the most sacred spot of all. At the bottom of a steep ravine, the "little lake for dancing" awaits, reached only by winding down hundreds of small stone steps. The large amphitheater is encircled from behind by tall cedars and the snow-capped Alps, and its stage has a gleaming Lake Garda as its backdrop. I imagined Isadora Duncan, one of D'Annunzio's many lovers, walking there—as if on the water—in consummate Classical grace.

That night I wandered around the out-of-season resort town, looking for somewhere to dine, lighting upon Caffe D'Annunzio itself, one of the only places open, where three or four locals crowded around a counter to drink wine. I nursed a negroni on the closed-down patio while wondering what Il Vittoriale *means*. Why, I wondered, should it make us uncomfortable? D'Annunzio had a sense of the heroic about him that is out of fashion today. A sense of superiority and sacredness, a will to power, a contempt for sickliness, vulgarity, cowardice. D'Annunzio might well be censured or ridiculed for his celebration of militarism and his (uneasy) association with Mussolini, for his many lovers (whom he adored, but also treated atrociously), for his many dogs and his race cars, for the consciously elaborated mythology of himself as a demigod, for a combination of wounded pride and delusions of grandeur—except that he *was* a great writer, and his grand lifestyle enriches our collective imagination.

Compared to the lukewarm morality of today, our smug conformity and communal piety, D'Annunzio's mythic theatricality exercises a certain force of attraction. Considering all this, I found myself laughing out loud at the mad, mad world, strolling along the closed-down boardwalk. I was dwarfed by a nineteenth-century edifice crowned with a bright yellow Renaissance-style tower with the words GRAND HOTEL emblazoned in sparkling golden mosaic. It was a huge sprawling place where Churchill and Mussolini and many other mortally flawed heroes and villains stayed. Like most everything else here, this historic hotel was closed until May, and the boardwalk was surreal, empty, but for a lone palm tree swaying on the promenade. In my drunkenness, with the help of a kind stranger, I managed to work the cigarette machine I found on the way back to my hotel, and smoked a rare cigarette—which, in its rareness, got me even higher—and wondered about the difference between aesthetic individualism and fascism. The cigarette, in its naughtiness, helping me to flirt with the decadent charms of immorality.

Aesthetic individualism is associated with culture, beauty, delicate sensibilities, the collection and preservation of fragile artifacts, and an internationalism that revels in the multiplicity of the creative imagination; fascism is nationalistic, collectivist, brutally destructive, anti-intellectual, a danger not only to human beings and their ethical freedom, but also to the buildings and the artistic and historical artifacts so admired by the aesthetic individualist. So why would they ever, why do they sometimes, keep common cause? In the case of D'Annunzio, we have a man of letters whose only real political affiliation was with the Party of Beauty, yet who did in fact collaborate with a man who would subsequently become a fascist dictator. But even before Mussolini came to be *Il Duce* and to be called by D'Annunzio "an evil clown," their relationship was strained. They found one another at the start of World War I, united by a shared vision of a new Roman Empire, a romantic ideal that called for the re-annexation of Trieste, Fiume, and other territories that had once belonged to Italy and, they both agreed, should belong to Italy once again. D'Annunzio roused his countrymen to enter the war, to defend the French culture under siege; he issued his call with speeches and street theater, and he himself fought on the front. But after the Treaty of Versailles failed to reward the Italians for their wartime sacrifices, D'Annunzio took history into his own hands and, with a ragtag militia, easily stole Fiume back for the Italians, to the cheers of the mostly Italian populace, and tried to found an artistic utopia with a democratic constitution there. Mussolini kept himself scarce and watched from afar as the dream foundered over the course of a little more than a year, only later to seize Fiume from the Austrians himself—this time, much to D'Annunzio's displeasure, to make it part of a Fascist state. The Fascists were frequently embarrassed by D'Annunzio's eccentric, sybaritic antics, his poetry and his displays of what they considered "feminine" voluptuousness, principally his nude sunbathing and his worship of art. Matters were further complicated by his association with workers' collectives agitating for unions and civil rights. When D'Annunzio was not being swayed by the Communists, or being lured into shady dealings by the Fascists, he was doing whatever he fancied, collaborating with composers on operas, writing plays for his lovers, writing sumptuous novels and books of poems *about* his lovers, spending money he did not have on *objets d'art* and fine editions, and making love. He felt that Mussolini had abandoned him at Fiume and that he did not give him the credit he deserved for bringing Italy into World War I; but Mussolini the dictator saw to it that a national edition of D'Annunzio's complete works was published and that the extensive quixotic renovations of Il Vittoriale be funded in part by the Italian Government. D'Annunzio, in turn, dedicated his house and grounds to the Italian people as a monument to the soldiers who dared to take Fiume with him. It was also a retreat. Although he had dabbled sensationally in politics and war, he was, by nature, an aesthete who enjoyed comfort and sensuality. Luxury, he wrote, was as essential to him as breathing. He liked to sit at the feet of lovely women, and shower them with flowers, leaf through ancient leatherbound books, and recite poetry in the dark. Over the course of a five-year period, he once wrote over one thousand letters to one woman alone. They don't make men like D'Annunzio anymore. In the mostly empty dining room of my hotel, there were none to be seen, so I gave myself to a large piece of Black Forest cake with whipped cream, and the conversation of the owner and his friends, who tried to get me to drink more and more champagne and spoke to me in a mixture of broken English and mostly incomprehensible Italian. Somehow I stumbled upstairs alone, somewhat nauseous, and had a nightmare about D'Annunzio. Or was it a dream?

The following day I made it into the sanctum sanctorum, D'Annunzio's house. In the entryway to what he called "the Priory" stands a column to divide the guests into welcome and unwelcome. The many creditors would have to wait on the right, the women, mostly artists and poets and actresses, would be ushered in on the left to a room filled with incense burners and a helicopter blade hanging from the ceiling. The lucky ones would be brought to the music room, cocooned in dark tapestries. D'Annunzio had lost an eye in the war and was sensitive to light. Besides, music requires concentration of the mind. The floors are covered in carpets and pillows, for lounging or making love; busts of Michelangelo and Dante, his "brothers," stand like witnesses. Books and music folios line the walls, surrounding life masks, sculptures, lamps of blown glass fruit, leaded windows, an organ, lyres, lutes, bells. The predominant tones are red, gold, and black. From the music room, we proceed to a writing alcove, with a large desk, where D'Annunzio died, and a medicine cabinet filled with drugs. Over the doorway into the bedroom, we read: *genio et voluptati*—genius and voluptuousness. The bedroom is called The Room of Leda and overflows with chinoiserie and silken fabrics and cushions. But genius is not all pleasure and happiness. Consider the Leper Room, for meditation on the death of his mother and his beloved, Eleanore Duse, which features a bed in the shape of both a cradle and a coffin, "the bed of two ages." Two leopard skins are draped over the steps leading down from the bed. A painting of Saint Francis embracing the leper hangs nearby. We are to understand that D'Annunzio considered himself a leper in the eyes of society, in exile here after his failed attempt to raise life to its rightful gloriousness despite the philistine, lukewarm good behavior of his fellows. In his *Italian Journey*, written back when words like lofty, harmonize, exalt, true, and noble could be read without embarrassment, Goethe commented on the poor reception granted to a number of Palladio buildings:

> How poorly these choice monuments to a lofty spirit harmonize with the life of the rest of mankind. ... It occurs to me that this after all is the way of the world. For one gets little thanks from people when one tries to exalt their inner urges, to give them a lofty concept of themselves, to make them feel the magnificence of a true, noble existence.

Alas, Goethe saw the tendency of things, already at the end of the eighteenth century. Though I wonder what he would have thought of D'Annunzio's taste. The relics room is a syncretic temple to all religions, mixing sacred objects with profane military paraphernalia. There are elephants, bronze Buddhas, medieval crosses, rows and rows of Catholic statuary, and a Fiume flag on the ceiling. Over the doorway is written: "Five Fingers, Five Sins." Out of the original seven deadly ones, D'Annunzio had excluded lust and greed—virtues in his creed. A broken steering wheel on the altar, which had once belonged to an English racing car driver—a friend of D'Annunzio's—symbolizes the religion of risk. His workshop, the sole room in the house to let in natural light, can only be entered by prostrating oneself beneath a low ceiling and walking up a few small steps. The writer had to humble himself before his muse, his great love, the actress, Eleanore Duse, whose bust sits upon his desk, covered with a silken scarf so that her beauty would not distract him from his work. *La Duse,* as she was called, earned the full adulation that *Il Duce* was denied.

D'Annunzio called his house "the book of stones," and like all good books it is filled with symbols. Everything *means* something. And the many mottos written on ceilings and round the rims of rooms and over doorways help us should we falter in our interpretation. And yet, I probably will be trying to understand it all for a long time to come. What would D'Annunzio have thought, had he known that the souvenir shop outside the grounds would feature not only snowglobes with miniature Il Vittoriales inside, and coffee mugs emblazoned with his face, but also brass knuckles and ominous riding crops in a section devoted to his special "connection" and nemesis, Mussolini? Would he have approved? I would like to think he would have considered it an impudent intrusion, actuated by purely capitalist vulgarity, a treacherous rewriting of his more nuanced story, rather like the posthumous revision of Nietzsche's biography by his Wagnerite sister. (Elisabeth-Förster Nietzsche, as is well known, attempted to present her brother posthumously as a proto-Nazi—he who in reality despised the Germans and called in his last days for the death of all anti-Semites.) The Mussolini display made me feel queasy, so I quickly exited the little shop and walked down the hill to beautiful Lake Garda, which Goethe, on his visit, had called "magnificent," trying to separate the marvelous and admirable Italian writer from his unsavory companion. I caught the afternoon bus out of town, and made it back to Torino late the same evening.

Certainly, although it would be simpler to reject grandeur and beauty outright, because of their sometimes questionable provenance and bedfellows, I cannot moralistically deny myself the intellectual and sensual pleasure they bring. The provenance and history of objects is significant and fraught with tangled skeins of so much seeming good and so much seeming bad. Sometimes it is impossible to separate out which is which. I will continue to be curious about all the life and history that can be gleaned from material remains—portals to other worlds and times—and to embrace the wild, contradictory nature of humanity with an *amor fati*—a love of fate—rubbing shoulders with all kinds of complicated ghosts, neither forgiving nor simplistically censoring the transgressions of delightful and haunted spirits.

I spent my last week in Augusta Taurinorum wandering around gazing at everything, saying goodbye with my eyes, entering dark churches on rainy afternoons and returning to museums I had already visited. I abandoned my foolish infatuation with the intern from Sardinia. It had been a case of pareidolia after all, or a matter of witchcraft. I visited Brunilde one more time, who had been angry at me after the last lunch for refusing dessert, a strawberry delicacy which the blackboard claimed was "the cake of love." Probably she had cursed me, and my refusal to eat the cake was the cause of my romantic failure. This time I was all alone with her in the little restaurant. We talked despite my faulty Italian and her non-existent English, and she even gave me the name of another restaurant, scribbling it on a little piece of paper, which I did not lose and used the following day. I knew better now:

I would do whatever she said and eat whatever she suggested. Lunch was orecchietti with spinach pesto and a mouthwatering cutlet swamped in delicious artichoke sauce, a glass of red wine, sparkling water, and for dessert a divinely magical zabaione with roasted almonds, the traditional shot glass of absinthe-soaked grapes, and something extra this time, to mark my initiation: a little jar of sugar cubes soaked in liquor and spices, which I did not know really how to eat or drink. She became frustrated with me and took it away, "Only the sugar, only the sugar," but she had accepted me just the same, this woman whose gruffness was a legend but whose favor I had longed for. I was sure she was a witch, and that she could help me or hurt me. After the espresso, I paid the bill, but was short some sixty cents. She waved me away; it was a mere trifle between such good friends. I wished her a beautiful life, *una vita bella,* and Brunilde the fierce blew me a kiss! I was blessed.

On the way to the airport, the Alps, covered in snow, were visible behind the utilitarian architecture at the edge of the city. All along the street, shutters opened and green curtains were extended from inside to out and draped over the little balconies. From a tall building a white sheet, like a small cloud, was shaken out in the fresh morning air, in the wind and the sun. Church spires rose up, shopkeepers brought out boxes of fruit for display, and old men in gray caps trundled along the sidewalk, newspapers tucked in the pockets of their old tweed jackets, ready to be unfurled along with the far-off world at the nearest caffe. The time had come to leave, and I was shoring up the beauty of so much in-spirited matter to shield me from the barrage of empty American materialism. And this was my apotropaic spell:

> Whosoever today does not respond, does not resonate to the stirrings of beauty and the energetic life force of the world as it is, who is not filled with wonder at its teeming, multifarious richness, who mocks those in the past who have made objects and symphonies and written poems to celebrate the intricate, elaborate, strange, cruel, and tender rhythms of life, must be dead of spirit.

In the Palazzo Madama museum, after bathing in sunlight streaming from a grand window into a room of baroque golden splendor, I entered the tiny tower housing a collection of small treasures, and any lingering doubts about meaning were immediately purged from me. I knew that the doubters were blind, deaf, and dumb. These intricate treasures were immediate, palpable evidence of the perennial human need to celebrate the real delights and dangers of nature and civilization. Carved ivories, etched gems, blown glass, cast bronze. Fancy—made out of the real substance of the physical world, its colors and textures and qualities. I was thus armed to do battle against the skeptical intellectuals and their social construction blasphemy. I knew: whosoever does not love Nature and the artifacts of humankind's love of matter (colors, curves, sounds, textures, words, flavors, rhythms, light, light, light!) may as well be dead. Such a one is bereft of heat, of senses, of love, of lust, is a lizard of theoretical idiocy, is just as much a repressor of the instincts and the body and nature as any Inquisitor or poison-spider priest. Philistine sophisticates, parading as the new intellectuals and new anti-artists, may you choke on the dust of your own dreary scoffing. We others, we naïve ones, have been filled with wonder by the beauty of the world.

Prior Publications

'Apologia: Why Do We Write?', 'Spirit and Matter in Conversation', 'Making Meaning I: The Categorical Imp of the Perverse', and 'Making Meaning II: Italian Journeys' all appeared previously in *Numéro Cinq*.

'Almandal Grimoire: The Book as Magical Object', 'Rematerializations, Remoteness, and Reverence', and 'Psyche's Stolen Pleasure: Women Who Like to Look, Objectification, and Animism' all appeared previously in *The Georgia Review*. 'Almandal Grimoire' also appeared in *Rupture*. 'Rematerializations, Remoteness, and Reverence' also appeared in *Caesura*.

'Portals' won the Jeffrey E. Smith Editor's Prize for *The Missouri Review*.

About the Author

GENESE GRILL is an essayist, translator, and painter based in Plainfield, Vermont. She is also the author of a scholarly study, *The World as Metaphor in Robert Musil's 'The Man Without Qualities'*, and the translator of two volumes of Musil's short prose—*Thought Flights* and *Unions*—as well as *Theater Symptoms,* a collection of his work for and about the stage.

Lightning Source UK Ltd.
Milton Keynes UK
UKHW042114061122
411729UK00018B/104

9 781919 639871